Freedom of Expression

*La grandeur du génie ne consisteroit-elle pas mieux
à savoir dans quel cas il faut l'uniformité, et dans
quel cas il faut des différences?*
Montesquieu, *L'esprit des lois*, xxix, 18

Studies in Statesmanship
Harry V. Jaffa, Winston S. Churchill Association,
General Editor

Harold W. Rood, *Kingdoms of the Blind: How the Great
Democracies Have Resumed the Follies that so Nearly
Cost Them Their Life*

Jeffrey D. Wallin, *By Ships Alone: Churchill and the
Dardanelles*

Harry V. Jaffa, ed., *Statesmanship: Essays in Honor of Sir
Winston S. Churchill*

Thomas B. Silver, *Coolidge and the Historians*

Francis Canavan, *Freedom of Expression: Purpose as Limit*

Glen E. Thurow and Jeffrey D. Wallin, eds., *Rhetoric and
American Statesmanship*

Freedom of Expression
Purpose as Limit

Francis Canavan

Carolina Academic Press
and
The Claremont Institute for the Study of
Statesmanship and Political Philosophy

International Standard Book Number: 0-89089-269-5 (cloth)
0-89089-270-9 (paper)
Library of Congress Catalogue Card Number: 83-71826

Carolina Academic Press
Post Office Box 8795, Forest Hills Station
Durham, North Carolina 27707

Printed in the United States of America

The publication of this volume was made
possible by a grant from the Earhart Foundation.

690693

To my mentor,
John H. Hallowell

Table of Contents

FOREWORD

It is an honor and a privilege to add *Freedom of Expression: Purpose as Limit* to Studies in Statesmanship. Some months ago, I was engaged in conversation with a younger scholar who has published many articles and monographs in constitutional law and is already widely recognized as a luminary in the field. He mentioned, almost in passing, that of course the best thing ever written on the jurisprudence of the First Amendment was Professor Canavan's essay, published in *American Journal of Jurisprudence* in 1971, entitled "Freedom of Speech and of the Press: For What Purpose?" That essay, revised and enlarged, now forms the first part of the present volume.

I myself have over the last decade repeatedly expressed the same opinion as my younger friend. But I am, and must remain, a biased witness. Professor Canavan and I have been friends for half a century, having graduated together from the same high school in 1935. In the course of that time, we have also become unashamed Aristotelians and, in somewhat different ways and for somewhat different reasons, unstinting admirers of Thomas Aquinas. We both believe that there is a nature of man and that this nature defines and circumscribes the nature of human freedom. Many of the perplexities that jurists—and citizens —have had with the question of freedom of speech (and related freedoms) are attenuated, if they do not vanish, once one admits that there is a difference in the ends served by speech and that the degree and kind of protection that speech merits from the law may differ according to the differences in these ends. Nor is it as difficult, as some pretend, to judge justly the difference in importance of many of the ends that may be served by speech. Whether or not obscene or blasphemous speech ought to be protected by law may be a question. But it is not a question that political advocacy ranks higher among the purposes served by speech than does the relief or gratification that someone may feel in expressing himself obscenely or blasphemously. Abraham Lincoln once repelled a charge, made against him during a political campaign, that he had spoken with intentional disrepect of the Christian religion. He denied that he had done any such thing, and he added that he did not think that he himself could support for office anyone he knew to be "an open enemy of, and scoffer at, religion." "Leaving the higher matter of eternal consequences between him and his Maker," Lincoln continued, "I still do not think any man has the right thus to insult the feelings, and injure the morals, of the community in which he may live." That men may "injure the morals" of the community by speech seems to me, as it does to Professor Canavan and as it did to Abraham Lincoln, to be only the common sense of the subject. This may not, in any given case, constitute an argument for the suppression of injurious speech. Perhaps speech which elevates and instructs in good morals may be the proper antidote for speech which injures. Nevertheless, if the protection of the morals of the community is among the police powers of government, so must it be among those powers to set boundaries to speech which is injurious of such morals. For there are circumstances in which the prevention of a moral injury, like the prevention of a physical injury, may take precedence over finding a remedy after the fact.

Professor Canavan shows that the courts—like all the great writers in the traditions of freedom—have always, in fact, recognized these elemental realities. But the recognition by the courts, at least, has been of an unwitting and incoherent kind. When Justice Black, for example, finds speech too dangerous and intolerable, he simply labels it "action." When Justice Frankfurter finds speech in conflict with other constitutionally protected ends, he "balances" one constitutional right against another. But one cannot balance one thing with another without assigning relative weights to the things balanced. How much better it would have been for both Black and Frankfurter to have candidly admitted that the degree of constitutional protection merited by speech derived, in some measure at least, from the dignity and rationality of the ends that it served. I cannot but think that they might have done so, had they read Professor Canavan's book when they were still young enough to learn. Let us hope that our judges—and citizens of this republic—will now be better educated than they have been in the past, in this most vital matter.

General Editor   HARRY V. JAFFA
Studies in Statesmanship

Introduction

Our Liberal Shepherds

One of the more curious developments in recent intellectual history is the metamorphosis of freedom of speech and press into freedom of expression *tout court*. A bizarre but by no means unique example of this new conception of freedom appeared in the July 12, 1976 number of *Time* (p. 16), where it was reported that Mike Nichols, Colleen Dewhurst, Ben Gazzara, Gay Talese and Ramsey Clark had attended a meeting to raise funds for the legal aid of one Harry Reems. The magazine described Mr. Reems as "the actor convicted on obscenity charges in Tennessee for his singular stint with Linda Lovelace in *Deep Throat*." Why were these celebrities so concerned to have this conviction appealed and, if possible, reversed? Mike Nichols explained: "It's not about taste. It's about freedom of expression. People should be free to explore anything they are moved to."[1]

It no longer matters, it would seem, what is expressed, how it is expressed, or for what purpose it is expressed. All that matters is that someone wants to express it. The freedom of the press, under which films are now subsumed, has become freedom of expression, and freedom of expression is an absolute.

This view is now held not only by writers, actors and other artists, from whose well-known bohemianism one might expect it, and by publishers, who have powerful motives for holding it, but by men learned in the law. Thus Charles Rembar, a senior partner in the law firm of Hellerstein, Rosier & Rembar, has written: "The First Amendment does not exist to protect expression that is beneficial. It exists to protect expression."[2] Thomas I. Emerson, professor of law at Yale University and, in the opinion of the late Justice William O. Douglas, "our leading First Amendment scholar,"[3] states in his *Toward a General Theory of the First Amendment*:[4] "The fundamental purpose of the First Amendment was to guarantee the maintenance of an effective system of free expression." He explains that "the essence of a system of freedom of expression lies in the distinction between expression and action. The whole theory rests upon the general proposition that expression must be free and unrestrained, that the state must not seek to achieve other social objectives through control of expression, and that the attainment of such objectives can and must be secured through regulation of action."[5] In a later book he elaborates this theory under the title, *The System of Freedom of Expression.*[6] In this work Professor Emerson lays it down that "it is not a general measure of the individual's right to freedom of expression that any particular exercise of that right may be thought to promote or retard other goals of the society ... freedom of expression, while not the sole or sufficient end of society, is a good in itself, or at least an essential element in a good society."[7]

Emerson goes so far as to identify "the key elements in the First amendment" as "expression," "abridge," and "law,"[8] although the Amendment in fact forbids Congress to make any "law ... abridging the freedom of speech, or of the press." The phrase, "freedom of expression," as a shorthand rendering of "the freedom of speech, or of the press," turned up in a U.S. Supreme Court opinion, for the first time that this writer has noticed, in *Bridges v. California*[9] in 1941; not surprisingly, the opinion of the Court was written by the late Mr. Justice Black. Use of the phrase became more common in opinions of the Court of its individual members during the 1950s, and in the 1960s was stretched to cover broader and broader areas of "expression." Usage in this matter has never been uniform; justices of the Supreme Court speak as often of freedom of speech, or of speech and press, as they do of expression. Furthermore, they often state that the "expression" to which they refer is the communication of thought, opinions or ideas. So, too, for that matter, does Professor Emerson.[10] Nonetheless, the glide from "the freedom of speech, or of the press" to "freedom of expression" has been a significant one.

"Expression" tends to generate a dynamism of its own, because of which the substantive content of expression is progressively absorbed into its form. The freedom we defend is the freedom to express "ideas," but everything that is expressed qualifies as an "idea" by the mere fact that it is expressed, and all expressions are equal under the Constitution. The only legal question then is whether something has been "expressed" rather than "done." We need not ask, nay we may not ask, whether what is expressed can be taken seriously as thought at all.

A classic example of this assimilation of content by form in "expression" is Justice Douglas's dissenting opinion in *Ginzburg v. U.S.*[11] Here the "longing" of masochists "to be whipped and lashed, bound and gagged, and cruelly treated," and the urge of fetishists to translate "mundane articles into sexual symbols," become "needs." Catering to these needs through books and magazines is an exercise of expression as entitled to constitutional protection as any other, because it leaves us "not in the realm of criminal conduct," but of "ideas and tastes." One notices, however, that ideas have been collapsed into tastes: what satisfies an urge is *ipso facto* an "idea." For an even more *outré* example of what freedom of expression can be taken to mean, one may consult Justice Thurgood Marshall's dissenting opinion in *California v. LaRue*.[12]

Expression, in this understanding of it, becomes detached from rational purpose. As an end in itself, it needs no justification from a purpose beyond itself. Or conversely, it is assumed that expression, simply as such, always serves "the search for truth," that great purpose in the name of which freedom of speech and press historically has been advocated and defended. The effect is the same either way. In a freedom of speech or press controversy, we need only determine whether we are dealing with expression or conduct. All further questions about the content and purpose of the expression are barred. The vocabulary of freedom of thought and its communication continues to be used but is recognized as really irrelevant, since anything that can be expressed is by definition thought.

Now, freedom of expression so understood may be the logical term toward which the theory of freedom of speech has inexorably tended from the beginning. At any rate, enough people, particularly among intellectuals and journalists, now hold this view that one may call it the conventional wisdom of contemporary liberal society. As a conventional wisdom, it is seldom questioned but rather is taken as the unquestioned major premise of argument. The standard of criticism, as someone has remarked, is not itself criticized. The liberal shepherds of public opinion have succeeded in forming in the minds of multitudes an unthinking conviction that freedom of expression without limits was fought for at Bunker Hill and enshrined in the First Amendment.

This book is written to give reasons for thinking that this conventional wisdom is wrong or, at least, that it is permissible to entertain doubts about it. The book's primary object is not to engage in controversy with Professor Emerson or the ghost of Justice Douglas but to disturb an insufficiently reflective public opinion. That we have and ought to have a constitutionally guaranteed freedom of speech and press is not in question here. But the public—that is to say, all of us—needs to ask why we have it and what we are trying to accomplish by it as a people.

The first chapter of this book therefore raises these questions and presents an alternative way of conceptualizing freedom of speech and press in the light of the purposes it is intended to serve. In this chapter numerous statements of the U.S. Supreme Court or of individual justices have been used to show that the thesis here argued is a tenable one. The chapter also, though incidentally, demonstrates that the Court has not accepted the absolutist theory of freedom of expression, however many Americans may assume that it has done so.

The following chapters go behind the Supreme Court to examine some of the major writers who argued the case for freedom of speech and press, and shaped the tradition of freedom of thought and expression that has prevailed in the English-speaking world. I make no attempt to analyze the thought of these writers in its entirety or even to present in detail their views on the limits of freedom of speech and press. I have tried instead to answer these questions: On what grounds did they argue for this freedom? What purposes did they see it as achieving? The analysis of their arguments leads to the conclusion that there is little reason for thinking that they proposed an unqualified freedom of expression.

Which writers in this tradition should be considered major and therefore be included in this book is, of course, a debatable question. I have let myself be guided largely by Professor Emerson, who states in a footnote:

> Major sources in the development of the theory [of freedom of expression] include: John Milton, *Areopagitica* (1644); John Locke, *Two Treatises of Government* (1690); *Essay Concerning Human Understanding* (1690); and *Letters on Toleration* (1690); the writings of Thomas Jefferson and James Madison; John Stuart Mill, *On Liberty* (1859); Walter Bagehot, *The Metaphysical Basis of Toleration* (1874); the decisions of Holmes, Brandeis and many other Supreme Court justices; Zechariah Chafee, Jr., *Free Speech in the United States* (1941) and *The Blessings of Liberty* (1956); Harold Joseph Laski, *Authority in the Modern State* (1919) and *Liberty in the Modern State* (1948); Alexander Meiklejohn, *Political Freedom* (1960). The best reference to the English and American material of the seventeenth and eighteenth centuries is Leonard W. Levy, *Legacy of Suppression* (1960).[13]

Plato's *Apology* and *Crito,* and Spinoza's *Tractatus Theologico-Politicus* and *Tractatus Politicus* are also often mentioned as classic works in the tradition of freedom of thought and speech. I have omitted Plato from consideration here because the tradition we are dealing with is a modern one that developed and could only have developed after the invention of the printing press. Despite our habit of talking about the freedom of speech—a habit in which I myself shall frequently enough indulge—the significant questions more often concerned the freedom of publication, and these became more acute as literacy became more widespread. I have included Spinoza because he is a modern (a contemporary of Milton and Locke); he is, however, the only author treated here who did not write in English. Readers who wish a more comprehensive survey of the earlier part of the period covered here may find it, as Emerson indicates, in Leonard Levy's *Legacy of Suppression.* I believe in any case that, while other authors might have been and perhaps should have been included, the ones that are analyzed here are numerous enough to furnish an understanding of the groundlines on which the argument for freedom to speak and publish developed historically.

Parts of this book have previously appeared in print as articles, and I gratefully acknowledge the permission of the editors of the following journals to republish them in revised form. Chapter I appeared as "Freedom of Speech and Press: For What Purpose?" in *The American Journal of Jurisprudence,* 16 (1971); Chapter II as "John Milton and Freedom of Expression" in *Interpretation,* 7 (1978), and Chapter V as "J. S. Mill on Freedom of Expression" in *Modern Age,* 23 (1979).

The year in which I enjoyed—the word is not too strong—a sabbatical leave from Fordham University to complete this book was subsidized by a grant from the Earhart Foundation, for which I express my genuine and deep gratitude. I want also to express my thanks to the Jesuit Community at Fairfield University for their generous hospitality during the year that I lived and worked among them. I owe special thanks to Mrs. Edith L. Meyer for her untiring help in typing the manuscript.

FRANCIS CANAVAN
Fordham University

1

Freedom of Speech and Press

For What Purpose?

"The modern history of the guarantee of freedom of speech and press mainly has been one of a search for the outer limits of that right," said Justice Harlan of the U.S. Supreme Court in 1967. But the Court's concentration on the boundaries of freedom of expression, he felt, "has perhaps omitted from searching consideration the 'real problem' of defining or delimiting the right itself."[1] Justice Harlan's point was well taken. One examines the opinions of the Court in vain for a fully thought-out and consistent philosophy of the freedom of speech and press. It is not surprising that it should be so. The Court, after all, has the task of deciding cases at law and elaborates standards sufficient to the decision of the cases that come before it. It is not a philosophical academy and prudently abstains for the most part from trying to set forth the whole theory that lies behind its decision—if indeed there is a theory consciously acknowledged and accepted by all the justices who concur in those decisions.

The Court began to inquire into the limits of freedom of speech and press only in 1919. "No important case involving free speech was decided by this Court prior to *Schenck v. United States*, 249 U.S. 47 (1919)," according to Chief Justice Vinson,[2] and his statement is generally accepted. This chapter will draw upon the opinions of the Court and separate opinions of its members from 1919 to the end of the Court's term in July 1979, a period of six decades since the Schenck case. That the Court's interpretation of the freedom of speech and press is not brought up to date is, however, a matter of no importance because the aim of the chapter is *not* to present "the" philosophy of the Court in regard to that freedom. The opinions of the Court and of individual members will be copiously quoted,[3] but in the service of an analysis and an argument which is not theirs and with which some of them certainly and all of them possibly would disagree. In short, this chapter presents its author's thesis rather than an objective or complete study of the Court's point of view.

The thesis is that the "searching consideration" of "the 'real problem' of defining or delimiting the right" of free speech and free press, which Harlan suggested is needed, must start from the purposes which the right is intended to serve, taken in relation to other purposes which the Constitution also intends to achieve. For it is from these purposes that the norms and the limits of the exercise of freedom of speech and press must be derived.

In relation to its constitutional purposes, speech (taking it in a broad sense to include every kind of utterance and publication) is not always of the same kind or equally protected by the Constitution. Freedom of speech, without distinctions among kinds of speech, is no more defensible than an unqualified freedom of action, and no more desirable. A free society, after all, is as much a society in which people are free to act as one in which they are free to talk (unless one agrees with the *Dublin Opinion*'s sardonic comment that a free country is a country where you are free to complain about the restrictions). Yet freedom to act does not include freedom to perform every action, or any action in all circumstances, nor does it imply that every action is of equal value in the eyes of the law and, consequently, equally subject to or immune from restraint.

"Action," in fact, is an abstraction with little practical legal meaning until we know with what kind of action we are dealing, and the same is true of "speech." Utterances are of different qualities and unequal value in relation to the purposes for which freedom of speech is constitutionally guaranteed. A theory of freedom of speech must therefore make distinctions among kinds and grades of speech, and these distinctions will derive from the purposes which constitutionally protected speech is intended to serve.

A thorough discussion of freedom of speech would begin with the question whether this freedom should be legally protected. But let us begin where the Court begins, with the proposition that the freedom is constitutionally guaranteed[4] and is fundamental to the American political system. The Court and its members have long described freedom of speech and press as "basic to the conception of our government"[5] and as "essential to free government"[6] or to "the workings of a free society."[7] Freedom of thought and speech, as the Court said in 1937, "is the matrix, the indispensable condition, of nearly every other form of freedom."[8] Thirty years later the Court repeated the theme, "A broadly defined freedom of the press assures the maintenance of our political system and an open society,"[9] or of what, in another context, the Court once called "a scheme of ordered liberty."[10]

The chief function of the guarantee, then, in the eyes of the Court, is to serve the political needs of an open and democratic society. "The core value of the Free Speech Clause of the First Amendment," the Court has said, is "the public interest in having free and unhindered debate on matters of public importance."[11] Or, as Justices Black and Douglas said in a concurring opinion in *New York Times v. Sullivan*, "Freedom to discuss public affairs and public officials is unquestionably, as the Court holds today, the kind of speech the First Amendment was primarily designed to keep within the area of free discussion."[12] The hypothesis underlying the amendment is that "free debate of ideas will result in the wisest governmental policies."[13] Therefore, as an early authority said, the evil which the amendment was designed to obviate was "any action of the government by means of which it might prevent such free and general discussion of public matters as seems absolutely essential to prepare the people for an intelligent exercise of their rights as citizens."[14] In the words of Justice Black, "Whatever differences may exist about interpretations of the First Amendment, there is practically universal agreement that a major purpose of that Amendment was to protect the free discussion of governmental affairs."[15]

The further purpose, according to Chief Justice Hughes, was "that government may be responsive to the will of the people and that changes may be obtained by lawful means."[16] Justice Jackson was of the opinion that "the forefathers" protected freedom of speech and press "because they knew of no other way by which free men could conduct representative democracy."[17] On another occasion he explained: "It is our philosophy that the course of government should be controlled by a consensus of the governed. This process of reaching intelligent popular decisions requires free discussion."[18]

The primary purpose of the constitutional guarantee of free speech and press, then, is political; the means by which this purpose is to be achieved has been described by the Court, in the most general terms, as "communication of information or opinion."[19] The First Amendment assumes, according to the Court, "that the widest possible dissemination of information from diverse and antagonistic sources is essential to the welfare of the public."[20] "The predominant purpose of freedom of the press," the Court has said, "was to preserve an untrammeled press as a vital source of public information."[21] But, beyond the need for information about public affairs, the Court saw the constitutional guarantee as protecting a clash of opinions which fosters the pursuit of political truth and political good.

"Winds of doctrine should freely blow," declared Justice Frankfurter, "for the promotion of good and the correction of evil.... Because freedom of public expression alone assures the unfolding of truth, it is indispensable to the democratic process."[22] "It was the pursuit of truth which the First Amendment was designed to protect," agreed his frequent opponents, Justices Black and Douglas.[23] Echoed the Court in a later opinion: "It is the purpose of the First Amendment to preserve an uninhibited marketplace of ideas in which truth will ultimately prevail."[24] Or, as Justice Brennan put it, "our legal system reflects a belief that truth is best illuminated by a collision of genuine advocates."[25]

The metaphor of a "free trade in ideas," with the corollary notion that "the best test of truth is the power of the thought to get itself accepted in the competition of the market,"[26] has been a favorite of the Court since the days of Justice Holmes. The theory behind the metaphor received classic expression in an opinion by Chief Judge Learned Hand of the U.S. Court of Appeals, which was quoted as follows by Justice Frankfurter:

> "The interest which [the First Amendment] guards, and which gives it its importance, presupposes that there are no orthodoxies—religious, political, economic, or scientific—which are immune from debate and dispute. Back of that is the assumption—itself an orthodoxy, and the one permissible exception—that truth will be most likely to emerge if no limitations are imposed upon utterances that can with any plausibility be regarded as efforts to present grounds for accepting or rejecting propositions whose truth the utterer asserts or denies." *International Brotherhood of Electrical Workers v. Labor Board*, 181 F.2d 34, 40. In the last analysis it is on the validity of this faith that our national security is staked.[27]

The liberal orthodoxy thus expounded is, of course, no more exempt from criticism than any other orthodoxy. But let us take it as the prevailing faith of our liberal society. It asserts that the aim of freedom of expression is truth but, for that very reason, no idea enters the marketplace with a legal presumption that it is true or that the expression of opposing ideas may be legally prohibited. Government serves truth, not by teaching truth or repressing error, but by protecting the market in which truth will prevail. "It cannot be the duty, because it is not the right, of the state," Justice Jackson explained, "to protect the public against false doctrine. The very purpose of the First Amendment is to foreclose public authority from assuming a guardianship of the public mind through regulating the press, speech, and religion. In this every person must be his own watchman for truth, because the forefathers did not trust any government to separate the true from the false for us."[28] It follows, as the Court was to say years later, that "the Constitution protects expression ... without regard to ... the truth, popularity, or social utility of the ideas and beliefs which are offered."[29]

"Under the First Amendment there is no such thing as a false idea," the Court has said, but it immediately explained: "However pernicious an opinion may seem, we depend for its correction not on the conscience of judges and juries but on the competition of other ideas."[30] The Constitution evenhandedly protects the expression of ideas and beliefs, but not because it is indifferent to their truth and social utility. It does so because of a faith in "the power of reason as applied through public discussion"[31] to distinguish the true from the false, the good from the evil, without interference from government. "Back of the guarantee of free speech" there lies "faith in the power of an appeal to reason by all the peaceful means for gaining access to the mind."[32] The primary purpose of the First Amendment's guarantee, therefore, is to produce a government controlled by a public opinion that has been formed through free and rational debate on public issues.

The Court has also insisted that freedom of expression covers persuasion to action as well as exposition of ideas. The protection intended by the First Amendment, declared the Court, "extends to more than abstract discussion, unrelated to action. The First Amendment is a charter for government, not for an institution of learning. 'Free trade in ideas' means free trade in the opportunity to persuade to action, not merely to describe facts."[33]

Again, the Court said: "Abstract discussion is not the only species of communication which the Constitution protects; the First Amendment also protects vigorous advocacy, certainly of lawful ends, against governmental intrusion."[34] Thus, as the Court said in *New York Times v. Sullivan* in 1964 and often repeated, there is "a profound national commitment to the principle that debate on public issues should be uninhibited, robust, and wide-open, and that it may well include vehement, caustic, and sometimes unpleasantly sharp attacks on government and public officials."[35] The Court also declared in 1969 that it was "now well established that the Constitution protects the right to receive information and ideas."[36]

The end sought by constitutionally guaranteeing freedom of expression is not solely political, however. "The guarantees for speech and press are not the preserve of political expression or comment upon public affairs."[37] For one thing, freedom of speech and press "is as much a guarantee to individuals of their personal right to make their thoughts public and put them before the community ... as it is a social necessity required for the 'maintenance of our political system and an open society.'"[38] For another, the social goals of freedom of expression are broader than the merely political. Thus Justice Frankfurter said: "Freedom of expression is the well-spring of our civilization.... For social development of trial and error, the fullest possible opportunity for the free play of the human mind is an indispensable prerequisite."[39] Justice Harlan agreed that the Founders "felt that a free press would advance 'truth, science, morality and arts in general' as well as responsible government."[40]

For similar reasons, the Court extended the protection of freedom of speech and press to academic freedom. "Our Nation is deeply committed to safeguarding academic freedom, which is of transcendent value to all of us and not merely to the teachers concerned. That freedom is therefore a special concern of the First Amendment."[41] The Court even wrapped the mantle of freedom of expression around "mere entertainment," saying: "The line between the informing and the entertaining is too elusive for the protection of that basic right."[42] But in mentioning this position of the Court, we anticipate a problem that must be dealt with later, and which we therefore pass by for the moment.

From the dicta of the Court and of individual justices that have been quoted, one can elaborate a certain view of the purposes of the First Amendment's guarantee of freedom of speech and press. In this view, the guarantee was meant to protect and facilitate the achievement of rational ends by communication among free and ordinarily intelligent people. Chief among these ends is the successful functioning of the democratic political process. But freedom to express one's mind is an individual right as well as a means to social goals; and the social goods to be realized through free expression are much broader than the strictly political. They include the whole range of objects of the human mind, the esthetic as well as the logical and narrowly rational. It is the pursuit not only of the true and the good, but of the beautiful as well, that deserves constitutional protection. Yet what the Constitution intends to protect is always the free functioning of the rational human mind.

Abuses of freedom of speech and press must indeed be tolerated, but not for their own sake or as if there were no difference between use and abuse. As the Court said in *Cantwell v. Connecticut*, "the people of this nation have ordained, in the light of history, that, in spite of the probability of excesses and abuses, these liberties are, in the long view, essential to enlightened opinion and right conduct on the part of the citizens of a democracy."[43] The assumption is clear that not every opinion or principle of conduct is in itself enlightened or right and worth protecting.

The problem then is how to relate the constitutional guarantee of freedom of expression to the ends it is supposed to serve. The Constitution protects expression for the sake of those ends. But end or purpose is also a limiting principle, regulating and restricting the uses of means to those which in some way contribute to the end. If a freedom is guaranteed for the sake of a certain end, those uses of the freedom which make no contribution to that end, or are positive hindrances to its achievement, are abuses of the freedom and cease to enjoy the protection of the guarantee, *unless the effort to suppress the abuses would be an even greater hindrance to the end.*

There are many who feel that to authorize government to suppress any abuse of freedom of speech or press is necessarily and always a greater threat to the purposes for which the guarantee of freedom was established than it is to tolerate the abuses. The only acceptable solution to the problem, according to this view, is to absolutize the guarantee and to protect all utterances and publications without distinction or discrimination, so long as they remain in the realm of expression and do not pass over into the area of conduct. In the history of the Supreme Court, the names most prominently identified with this solution of the problem were those of Justices Black and Douglas.

Their position evolved over the years in the direction of an ever greater absolutism. Justice Douglas, for instance, once wrote: "The validity of the obscenity laws is recognition that the mails may not be used to satisfy all tastes, no matter how perverted."[44] In later years he and Justice Black abandoned that view.[45] By 1969 Douglas felt obliged to explain that he had consistently dissented from the decision that "'obscenity' is not protected by the Free Speech and Free Press Clauses of the First Amendment ... but not because, as frequently charged, I relish 'obscenity.'"[46] By 1973 he was saying that he had "always felt that 'obscenity' was not an exception to the First Amendment."[47]

The reason he gave for taking this position was that all standards for judging obscenity are purely subjective and cannot be made legal standards.[48] Most of the items that came before the Court as allegedly obscene, he conceded, "are in my view trash. I would find few, if any, of them, that had by my standards any redeeming social value. But what may be trash to me may be prized by others."[49] He recognized these items as ones "that did no more than excite man's base instincts."[50] Yet he seemed to have little faith in his own judgment that this material was trash which appealed to man's base instincts. All that mattered was that it "may be prized by others." Value was simply that which was valued by someone or other, and was not an object of knowledge or of rational judgment. There was, consequently, in Douglas's jurisprudence no distinction between base and noble instincts of which the law could take cognizance.

In a similar development, in *Beauharnais v. Illinois*, he was apparently willing, though reluctantly, to accept the power of a state to enact a group libel law.[51] Later he was to announce: "In my view the First Amendment would bar Congress (and the States) from passing any libel law,"[52] and in this view he was joined by Justice Black.[53] The latter made it explicit in another case that "the First Amendment does not permit the recovery of libel judgments against the news media even when statements are broadcast with knowledge they are false."[54] It was as impossible to accommodate the law of defamation with the freedom of speech and press, said Douglas, as it was to accommodate the law of obscenity.[55]

Finally, although Black and Douglas originally accepted the clear and present danger test as a norm for judging the limits of freedom of speech and press,[56] they came to "see no place in the regime of the First Amendment for any 'clear and present danger' test, whether strict and tight as some would make it, or free-wheeling as the Court in *Dennis* rephrased it."[57]

The ultimate Black-Douglas position was an absolutist interpretation of the freedom of expression guaranteed by the First Amendment. "The only line," said Douglas, "drawn by the Constitution is between 'speech' on the one side and conduct or overt acts on the other."[58] Again, the First Amendment "leaves, in my view, no room for governmental restraint on the press."[59] For a typical statement by Black we may take the following: "I think the Founders of our Nation in adopting the First Amendment meant precisely that the Federal Government should pass 'no law' regulating speech and press but should confine its legislation to the regulation of conduct. So too, that policy of the First Amendment made applicable to the States by the Fourteenth, leaves the States vast power to regulate conduct but no power at all, in my judgment, to make the expression of views a crime."[60]

The constitutional line, then, was between conduct and the expression of "ideas." The First Amendment, said Black, guarantees "complete freedom for expression of all ideas."[61] "Its aim was to unlock all ideas for argument, debate, and dissemination," Douglas agreed,[62] and it "leaves no power in government over *expression of ideas*."[63] They did not define, however, what constitutes an "idea." One gets the impression that for Black and particularly for Douglas, anything that was uttered by a human voice or came off a printing press, whether in the form of words, photographs or motion pictures, was an "idea" and as such was entitled to the protection of the First Amendment. According to Douglas, for example, the amendment gives people the right to know about sex in pictures (however "adult" they might be) as well as in words.[64] Certainly, for both of them obscene publications,[65] advocacy of the violent over-throw of the government,[66] and libellous statements, at least about the public conduct of public figures, enjoyed full constitutional protection.

Their willingness to give free rein to the expression of all "ideas," however mindless, was based on faith in the soundness of the popular mind. "I have the same confidence," said Douglas, "in the ability of our people to reject noxious literature as I have in their capacity to sort out the true from the false in theology, economics, politics, or any other field."[67] He also quoted with approval a writer who said: "The very interest in protection from injury from obscene material would be better served by allowing each individual to make a free appraisal of pornographic material."[68] Black felt a similar confidence that the American people could not be shaken in their devotion to free institutions by any amount of talk on the part of totalitarians.[69] The remedy for the danger posed by advocacy of the violent overthrow of the government, he said, "must be the same remedy that is applied to the danger that comes from any other erroneous talk—education and contrary argument." He was willing to add: "If that remedy is not sufficient, the only meaning of free speech must be that the revolutionary ideas will be allowed to prevail."[70]

Black and Douglas therefore insisted that, to be punishable under the First Amendment, mere speech or publication must be "shown to be part of unlawful action,"[71] or, in a phrase of which Douglas became fond, it must be proved to be "brigaded with illegal action."[72] The example of punishable speech usually given, that of a person who falsely shouts fire in a crowded theater, said Douglas, is "a classic case where speech is brigaded with action.... They are indeed inseparable and a prosecution can be launched for the overt acts actually caused. Apart from rare instances of that kind, speech is, I think, immune from prosecution."[73] Therefore he "would let any expression ... flourish ... unless it was an integral part of action."[74]

Black, as is well known, was criticized in his later years for apostatizing from his pristine liberalism and lapsing into the conservative heresy in regard to freedom of expression. Certainly he more than once shocked the faithful by uttering such sentiments as: "Uncontrolled and uncontrollable liberty is an enemy to domestic peace."[75] The criticism was chiefly inspired, however, by his willingness to restrict the right to engage in forms of expression that were not strictly and solely "speech," e.g., picketing and demonstrations, and by the vehemence with which he denied that aggrieved persons have the right "to use the public's streets, buildings, and property to protest whatever, wherever, whenever they want, without regard to whom such conduct may disturb."[76] But it must be emphasized that, as Black saw the issue, he denied only the right to certain kinds of conduct; speech and publication remained immune.[77]

Black, supported by Douglas, therefore continued to denounce what he called the "balancing test" for deciding freedom of speech and press cases.[78] He was once willing to say that the Court must "balance the Constitutional rights of owners of property against those of the people to enjoy freedom of press and religion," provided that the Court remained "mindful of the fact that the latter occupy a preferred position."[79] But his final position was that no balancing of rights was permissible where freedom of speech and press were involved, because there are no "more important interests" to which the freedom may constitutionally be subordinated.[80] "The men who drafted our Bill of Rights," he declared, "did all the 'balancing' that was to be done in this field."[81] The First Amendment is in itself a choice of freedom of expression over any values that can be weighed against it.[82] The question, therefore, whether in any given case the public interests to be achieved or safeguarded by limiting or suppressing expression outweighed the loss to freedom of speech or press was constitutionally illegitimate, because the First Amendment had already answered the question in the negative. After Black's retirement from the Court, Douglas continued to state this position in his place: "My belief is that all of the 'balancing' was done by those who wrote the Bill of Rights." They cast "the First Amendment in absolute terms."[83]

For Black and Douglas, it would seem, "expression" was a univocal term. If it was not "brigaded with illegal action," expression meant the same thing in relation to the First Amendment in every case, no matter what its content or the manner in which it was expressed. There could be no inquiry whether the expression had what Justice Brennan once called "saving intellectual content."[84] It was enough that something had been uttered rather than done. It followed that the Court might make no judgment on the relationship of the expression to the ends which freedom of speech and press is supposed to serve. On the contrary, according to Black and Douglas, the ends of the First Amendment were always served by guaranteeing absolute freedom of expression, and no further questions could constitutionally be raised.

The majority of the Court never accepted the Black-Douglas position. Despite considerable shifts of opinion among the members of the majority, the Court consistently maintained, in the words of Chief Justice Hughes, that "[l]iberty of speech, and of the press is also not an absolute right, and the State may punish its abuse."[85] Justice Harlan elaborated this principle in an opinion of the Court in 1961, in these terms:

> At the outset we reject the view that freedom of speech and association, ...as protected by the First and Fourteenth Amendments, are 'absolutes,' not only in the undoubted sense that where the constitutional protection exists it must prevail, but also in the sense that the scope of that protection must be gathered solely from a literal reading of the First Amendment. Throughout its history this Court has consistently recognized at least two ways in which constitutionally protected freedom of speech is narrower than an unlimited license to talk. On the one hand, certain forms of speech, or speech in certain contexts, has been considered outside the scope of constitutional protection....On the other hand, general regulatory statutes, not intended to control the content of speech, but incidentally limiting its unfettered exercise, have not been regarded as the type of law the First or Fourteenth Amendment forbade Congress or the States to pass, when they have been found

justified by subordinating valid governmental interests, a prerequisite to constitutionality which has necessarily involved a weighing of the governmental interest involved.[86]

In the majority view, some kinds of speech or publication were not protected at all by the Constitution. In a footnote to the passage quoted above, Harlan explained that the literalist view of freedom of speech and press "cannot be reconciled with the law relating to libel, slander, misrepresentation, obscenity, perjury, false advertising, solicitation of crime, complicity by encouragement, conspiracy and the like."[87] The classic statement on this point, which was often quoted in subsequent opinions, was made by Justice Murphy in 1942:

> Allowing the broadest scope to the language and purpose of the Fourteenth Amendment, it is well understood that the right of free speech is not absolute at all times and under all circumstances. There are certain well-defined and narrowly limited classes of speech, the prevention and punishment of which have never been thought to raise any Constitutional problems. These include the lewd and obscene, the profane, the libelous, and the insulting or 'fighting' words—those which by their very utterance inflict injury or tend to incite an immediate breach of the peace. It has been well observed that such utterances are no essential part of any exposition of ideas, and are of such slight social value as a step to truth that any benefit that may be derived from them is clearly outweighed by the social interest in order and morality.[88]

More specific statements of the kinds of speech and publication that are not constitutionally protected, and of the reasons why they are not protected, appeared in many opinions of the Court. We cite a few for illustration.

"Expressions found in numerous opinions indicate that this Court has always assumed that obscenity is not protected by the freedoms of speech and press," said Justice Brennan in *Roth v. U.S.*, because "implicit in the history of the First Amendment is the rejection of obscenity as utterly without redeeming social importance."[89] "Civil and criminal liability for defamation was well established in the common law when the First Amendment was adopted, and there is no indication that the Framers intended to abolish such liability," said Justice White.[90] Justice Frankfurter explained that "utterance in a context of violence can lose its significance as an appeal to reason and become part of an instrument of force. Such utterance was not meant to be sheltered by the Constitution."[91] According to Justice Roberts, "Resort to epithets or personal abuse is not in any proper sense communication of information or opinion safeguarded by the Constitution."[92]

In *New York Times v. Sullivan*, while insisting that the Constitution does not protect libellous statements, the Court proceeded to prohibit "a public official from recovering damages for a defamatory falsehood relating to his official conduct unless he proves that the statement was made with 'actual malice'—that is, with knowledge that it was false or with reckless disregard of whether it was false or not."[93] But even under this liberal rule, the deliberate or reckless lie was not protected. In later cases the Court explained: "Although honest utterance, even if inaccurate, may further the fruitful exercise of the right of free speech, it does not follow that the lie, knowingly and deliberately published about a public official, should enjoy a like immunity."[94] "Calculated falsehood," therefore, was not protected by freedom of the press,[95] because "[n]either lies nor false communications serve the ends of the First Amendment."[96]

From the passages cited above it is clear that the Constitution does not protect certain kinds of speech. They include, with the qualifications laid down by the Court in its opinions, libel, reckless or calculated lies, slander, misrepresentation, perjury, false advertising, obscenity and profanity, solicitation of crime and personal abuse or "fighting" words. The reason why such kinds of speech or publication are not protected is that they are of minimal or no value as an exposition of ideas, a communication of information or opinion, an appeal to reason or a step to truth, and therefore do not serve the ends of the First Amendment.

Advocacy of the forcible overthrow of the government may be taken as an example of the "speech in certain contexts," which, as Justice Harlan said above, "has been considered outside the scope of constitutional protection." The same would be true generally of advocacy of violation of the law. According to Chief Justice Vinson, "The important question that came to this Court immediately after the First World War was not whether, but how far, the First Amendment permits the suppression of speech which advocates conduct inimical to the public welfare." It was in answer to this question, he said, that Justices Holmes and Brandeis framed the clear and present danger test.[97]

The test was originally formulated by Justice Holmes in *Schenck v. U.S.* (1919) in these terms: "The question in every case is whether the words used are used in such circumstances and are of such a nature as to create a clear and present danger that they will bring about the substantive evils that Congress has a right to prevent."[98] "It is only the present danger of immediate evil or an intent to bring it about that warrants Congress in setting a limit to the expression of opinion where private rights are not concerned," he later explained in *Abrams v. U.S.*[99] In *Dennis v. U.S.* (1951), Chief Justice Vinson reviewed the cases since *Schenck v. U.S.*, and concluded: "The rule we deduce from these cases is that where an offense is specified in nonspeech or nonpress terms [i.e., where what the law forbids is an action] a conviction relying upon speech or press as evidence of violation may be sustained only when the speech or publication created a 'clear and present danger' of attempting or accomplishing the prohibited crime, e.g., interference with enlistment."[100] The results of constitutional adjudication since 1919 were again summarized by the Court in 1969 in the principle that "advocacy of the use of force or of law violation" may be forbidden or proscribed only "where such advocacy is directed to inciting or producing imminent lawless action and is likely to incite or produce such action."[101]

It is sufficient for our present purpose to remark that speech of a type that would, for example, deserve constitutional protection as an expression of political views loses its claim to protection, even though it remains speech, when it takes on a certain relationship to illegal action. But, whereas the Court has held that "obscenity is not protected expression and may be suppressed without a showing of the circumstances which lie behind the phrase 'clear and present danger' in its application to protected speech,"[102] a different situation is presented in a case where the clear and present danger test applies. "Many of the cases in which this Court has reversed convictions by use of this or similar tests have been based on the fact that the interest which the State was attempting to protect was itself too insubstantial to warrant restriction of speech," said Chief Justice Vinson in *Dennis v. U.S.*[103] Or, as Justice Brandeis had earlier said, "even imminent danger cannot justify resort to prohibition of these functions essential to effective democracy, unless the evil apprehended is relatively serious. Prohibition of free speech and assembly is a measure so stringent that it would be inappropriate as the means for averting a relatively trivial harm to society."[104] It followed that in order to decide whether a particular speech or publication threatened a valid social or governmental interest seriously enough to lose its constitutional immunity from punishment under the clear and present danger test, the Court must weigh the public interest involved.

In other words, the Court had to engage in what Justice Black so often denounced as "balancing" (and this doubtless explains why he and Justice Douglas eventually concluded that the clear and present danger test had no place in the interpretation of the First Amendment). The balancing process, however, was a severely limited one. On one side was set speech, without differentiation among kinds of speech, and it was given greater weight by the requirement that speech might not be punished unless it created a clear and present danger of a substantive evil that government could lawfully prevent. But, on the other side, there were grades of substantive evils that fell under the power of government. Some were more serious evils than others, and only the more serious ones warranted the suppression of speech, even under the conditions of clear and present danger. Implicit in this rule was the notion of a hierarchy of public interests which, in proportion to their importance, either did or did not outweigh the value of speech.

A balancing process was also involved in cases where the law's penalties fell, not on speech or publication, but on conduct, and restriction of the exercise of freedom of speech or press was an incidental effect of the regulation of conduct. Here again an essential question was whether a public interest of sufficient weight justified the restriction. Chief Justice Warren summarized a line of previous decisions on this point in *U.S. v. O'Brien* in 1968:

> This Court has held that when 'speech' and 'nonspeech' elements are combined in the same course of conduct, a sufficiently important governmental interest in regulating the nonspeech element can justify incidental limitations on First Amendment freedoms. To characterize the quality of the governmental interest which must appear, the Court has employed a variety of descriptive terms: compelling; substantial; subordinating; paramount; cogent; strong. Whatever imprecision inheres in these terms, we think it clear that a government regulation is sufficiently justified if it is within the constitutional power of the Government; if it furthers an important or substantial governmental interest; if the governmental interest is unrelated to the suppression of free expression; and if the incidental restriction on alleged First Amendment freedoms is no greater than is essential to the furtherance of that interest.[105]

"The mere fact that speech is accompanied by conduct does not mean that the speech can be suppressed under the guise of prohibiting the conduct," the Court once said.[106] On the other hand, the Court had also said that the First and Fourteenth Amendments do not "afford the same kind of freedom to those who would communicate ideas by conduct such as patrolling, marching, and picketing on streets and highways, as these amendments afford to those who communicate ideas by pure speech."[107] Borderline cases therefore arose. "We cannot accept the view that an apparently limitless variety of conduct can be labeled 'speech' whenever the person engaging in the conduct intends thereby to express an idea," said Chief Justice Warren in an opinion of the Court which rejected the claim that draft-card burning was entitled to constitutional protection as "symbolic speech."[108] But in another case the Court found that the wearing of black armbands to protest the Vietnam War by children attending a public school was "closely akin to 'pure speech' which, we have repeatedly held, is entitled to comprehensive protection under the First Amendment."[109] In other words, the more "pure" speech was, the more it escaped regulation aimed at conduct.

To refine a bit on Justice Harlan, there were at least three ways in which utterances could be found unprotected by the First Amendment. Some utterances, such as obscene or "fighting" words, were outside the ambit of the constitutional guarantee because they were of such slight social value that they did not merit the amendment's protection. Others bore so close a relationship to illegal action that they could be punished under the clear and present danger test. Still other expressions could be restricted, not directly, since they were in themselves protected, but incidentally to the regulation of conduct. In cases involving all three kinds of expression the underlying problem was that of accommodating the public interest in free speech and press with other public interests which government was also charged with safeguarding or promoting. Not all members of the Court cared to admit it, but it would seem that Harlan was right when he said that a "balancing of the competing interests at stake ... is unavoidably required in this kind of constitutional adjudication, notwithstanding that it arises in the domain of liberty of speech and press."[110]

The greatest exponent of "balancing" as the appropriate process in deciding freedom of speech and press cases, in the Vinson and Warren courts, was Justice Frankfurter. A typical expression of his view is found in his concurring opinion in *Dennis v. U.S.*, where he rejected the argument that "clear and present danger" was the only or the adequate norm for decision when freedom of expression was the issue. "A survey of the relevant decisions," he said, "indicates that the results which we have reached are on the whole those that would ensue from careful weighing of conflicting interests. The complex issues presented by regulation of speech in public places, by picketing and by legislation prohibiting advocacy of crime have been resolved by many factors besides the imminence and gravity of the evil threatened.... It were far better," he continued, "that the phrase [clear and present danger] be abandoned than that it be sounded once more to hide from the believers in an absolute right of free speech the plain fact that the interest in speech, profoundly important as it is, is no more conclusive in judicial review than other attributes of democracy or than a determination of the people's representatives that a measure is necessary to assure the safety of government itself."[111]

The "balancing test" supplied the Court with the rationale for its major anti-Communist decisions in the Cold War national security cases. Thus, for example, in *American Communications Ass'n. v. Douds*, the Court upheld a federal law that sought to discourage labor unions from choosing as their officials persons who were members or supporters of the Communist Party or of any other organization that believed in or taught the overthrow of the United States government by illegal or unconstitutional methods. In the opinion of the Court, Chief Justice Vinson admitted that the law restricted the exercise of First Amendment freedoms by Communists and other persons subject to it, but denied that it was necessarily unconstitutional for that reason. "When particular conduct is regulated in the interest of public order," he said, "and the regulation results in an indirect, conditional, partial abridgment of speech, the duty of the courts is to determine which of the two conflicting interests demands the greater protection under the particular circumstances presented." Regulation of "conduct," he granted, may be a cloak for censorship of ideas. "On the other hand, legitimate attempts to protect the public, not from the remote possible effects of noxious ideologies, but from present excesses of direct, active conduct [i.e., political strikes called by Communist union officials], are not presumptively bad because they interfere with and, in some of its manifestations, restrain the exercise of First Amendment rights."[112]

In *Dennis v. U.S.*, Vinson went even further in upholding the conviction of Communist leaders for conspiracy to advocate the violent overthrow of the United States government. Now the balancing test sustained the direct suppression of speech. "An analysis of the leading cases in this Court which have involved direct limitations on speech," he said, "will demonstrate that ... this is not an unlimited, unqualified right, but that the societal value of speech must, on occasion, be subordinated to other values and considerations."[113]

Justice Frankfurter's position and the "balancing test" generally were severely criticized. To regard the public interest in free speech as only one of several interests that have to be weighed in the balance, it was said, weakened the constitutional guarantee of freedom of expression which, if not absolute, at least enjoyed a "preferred position." Furthermore, it made the decisions of the Court in this area unpredictable, since no two cases were exactly alike, and one therefore did not know what balance the Court would strike in a future case. Finally, the criticism ran, the balancing test during the Cold War proved to be a handy device by which the Court could uphold Congressional legislation that impaired First Amendment rights, while loudly professing its devotion to those same rights in the abstract. It just happened that when the whole weight of "national security" was put on the scale against the claim of this or that "subversive" to a particular exercise of First Amendment freedoms, the government won.

One may as well admit the force that there was in this criticism. The Court has shown often enough that during the crisis of war, whether hot or cold, it will not blow the whistle on measures that the national government thinks necessary to national security, e.g., the "relocation" of Japanese-Americans during the Second World War, however much it may later deplore them in the cold, gray light of peace. It is also true that "balancing," carried far enough, would result in a case-by-case jurisprudence without predictable standards of decision. And no one can deny —certainly Frankfurter never did[114]—that a constitutionally guaranteed right is something more than merely one among many interests that the Court must take into account in assessing legislation.

But, when all of this has been said, it still remains that freedom of speech and press is not the only or in all circumstances the highest of constitutional values that the Court must weigh. The Warren Court moved far from the Vinson Court in its application of the balancing test. But it never abandoned the principle that the "societal value of speech" may sometimes be subordinated to other values by direct or incidental limitation of freedom of expression, and that such limitation involves a weighing and balancing of the competing interests. For example, in 1968, in the case of a teacher who had been dismissed for publicly criticizing the way his school board spent the taxpayers' money, the Court stated the issue in these terms: "The problem in any case is to arrive at a balance between the interests of the teacher, as a citizen, in commenting upon matters of public concern and the interest of the State, as an employer, in promoting the efficiency of the public services it performs through its employees."[115]

The Warren Court did not abolish the balancing test. What it did was to tip the balance in favor of freedom of speech and press and to become more reluctant to subordinate this freedom to other social values except in strictly defined and narrowly limited circumstances. The tipping of the balance appears most clearly in the opinions of Justice Brennan, the Warren Court's principal spokesman in freedom of speech and press cases. A typical majority in such a case, when the decision was on the liberal side, would include Justices Black and Douglas, concurring from their characteristic point of view. Added to them would be the chief justice, Justice Goldberg (succeeded by Justice Fortas) and Justice Brennan, who would write the opinion of the Court.

Justice Brennan's tendency was to approach the Black-Douglas position without actually joining it. Speech, for him, had a "transcendent value"[116] that was nearly, but not quite absolute. We may therefore take him as the leading exponent of the quasi-absolutist interpretation of freedom of expression. It was a position in which, in the Burger Court, he was regularly joined by Justice Marshall and frequently by Justice Stewart, though not usually by a majority. But, as we have indicated, it was the dominant position in the Warren Court.

According to Brennan, "the line between speech unconditionally guaranteed and speech which may legitimately be regulated, suppressed, or punished is finely drawn."[117] There was indeed such a line. But we must keep as much speech as possible inside the line of the unconditional guarantee and leave as little as we can outside it, because of

> the danger of tolerating, in the area of First Amendment freedoms, the existence of a penal statute susceptible of sweeping and improper application.... These freedoms are delicate and vulnerable, as well as supremely precious in our society. The threat of sanctions may deter their exercise almost as potently as the actual application of sanc-

tions....Because First Amendment freedoms need breathing space to survive, government may regulate in the area only with narrow specificity.[118]

The requirement of narrow specificity applied even to kinds of speech or publication that were *per se* outside the pale of constitutional protection. For example, having declared in *Roth v. U.S.* that "obscenity is not protected by the freedoms of speech and press," Brennan went on to emphasize that it was "vital that the standards for judging obscenity safeguard the protection of freedom of speech and press for material which does not treat sex in a manner appealing to prurient interest."[119] Hence, as he said in a later case, the Court's "insistence that regulations of obscenity scrupulously embody the most rigorous procedural safeguards" was only "a special instance of the larger principle that the freedoms of expression must be ringed about with adequate bulwarks."[120] Or, as Justice Fortas once phrased it, "An order issued in the area of First Amendment rights must be couched in the narrowest terms that will accomplish the pin-pointed objective permitted by constitutional mandate and the essential needs of the public."[121] There was still a balancing process by which competing interests were weighed against each other, but the balance was heavily weighted in favor of freedom of expression.

The balancing test as applied by the Vinson Court, we have remarked, was open to the criticism that it put the whole weight of "national security" on one side of the scale and "balanced" it against some individual or group claim to the exercise of First Amendment freedoms. The balancing test applied by Justice Brennan and the other "quasi-absolutists" on the Court was open to the opposite criticism. On one side of the scale they put, not the inane, indecent or obscene speech or publication which was in fact often all that was involved, but "our most precious freedoms,"[122] "the transcendent value to all society of constitutionally protected expression,"[123] and "our cherished First Amendment rights."[124] It was these weighty values that they "balanced" against some limited governmental interest. The result was predictable. What was expressed and how it was expressed virtually ceased to matter.

Brennan always recognized in principle "that there are governmental interests that may justify restraints on free speech,"[125] and that "the prohibition on encroachment of First Amendment protections is not an absolute."[126] In practice he sometimes, but seldom, discovered a public interest that overrode a First Amendment claim. For example, when an act of Congress required ex-President Nixon to turn his papers and tape recordings over to the custody of the Administrator of General Services, Mr. Nixon promptly challenged its constitutionality. One of the grounds he alleged was that some of this material concerned his partisan political activity; revelation of it would have a "chilling effect" on his own and other persons' future political activity; therefore the act violated the First Amendment. Brennan, writing for the Court, rejected this argument, pointing out that the act had provisions protecting Nixon "from improper public disclosures and guaranteeing him full judicial review before any public access is permitted." More to our point, he found that "the First Amendment claim is clearly outweighed by the important governmental interests promoted by the Act."[127]

But it was more typical of Justices Brennan and Marshall to claim, as they did, that the public interest in protecting the confidentiality of news sources outweighed the public interest in the investigating function of grand juries.[128] They would, they also said, never allow prior restraint on the right of the press to publish in order to secure a fair trial for a defendant, because they believed that other means of securing it were always available and adequate.[129] They believed, too, that the interest of prison authorities in maintaining order and security in prisons did not outweigh the First Amendment right of both inmates and the press to have news representatives enter prisons with television cameras and interview inmates.[130] Nor did they feel that the interest of the prison authorities overrode the First Amendment right of prisoners to associate freely by forming labor unions.[131]

They also dissented when the Court held that the First Amendment did not prevent military authorities from prohibiting political speeches and the distribution of political leaflets on a military post. As Brennan explained, "if the recent lessons of history mean anything, it is that the First Amendment does not evaporate with the mere intonation of interests such as national defense, military necessity, or domestic security."[132]

In an obscenity case he declared that "the bookseller has at stake ... an 'interest of transcending value'—protection of his right to disseminate and the public's right to receive material protected by the First Amendment."[133] In another case Marshall granted, "It may be that the Government has an interest in suppressing lewd or 'indecent' speech even when it occurs in private among consenting adults." He was in fact speaking of sexually explicit live entertainment and films which the California Department of Alcoholic Beverage Control prohibited in licensed bars and nightclubs, entertainment which the Court in its majority opinion described as "'performances' that partake more of gross sexuality than of communication."[134] But according to Marshall, the government's interest in keeping such entertainment out of places where liquor was sold "must be balanced against the overriding interest of our citizens in freedom of thought and expression."[135] When placed in the balance, freedom of expression won again, i.e., in the dissenting opinion of Justice Marshall.

It was also typical of the quasi-absolutists to find that a law regulating speech was unconstitutional because it was vague and overbroad, "overbreadth" being a lack of "narrow specificity." This was the premise on which the Court, in opinions written by Justice Brennan, struck down state and local laws against the use of opprobrious and abusive language.[136] It was also the premise on which Marshall and Brennan dissented from an opinion of the Court upholding a Massachusetts law that required state employees to take an oath to "oppose" the overthrow of the government of the United States or of the Commonwealth by force, violence or any other illegal means: the term, "oppose," was vague and overbroad.[137] On the same ground they asserted that the federal law against sending obscene material through the mails[138] and state laws against distributing obscene material were unconstitutional.[139] Indeed, they had already come to the conclusion "that the concept of 'obscenity' cannot be defined with sufficient specificity and clarity to provide fair notice to persons who create and distribute sexually oriented materials, to prevent substantial erosion of protected speech, and to avoid very costly institutional harms."[140] With these words Brennan abandoned the position he had taken in *Roth v. U.S.* and joined Justice Douglas in holding that no law against obscene speech or publication was constitutionally possible.

There is undeniably a need for a constitutional doctrine of overbreadth. As Marshall explained, "the overbreadth principle ... concerns the potential deterrent effect on constitutionally protected speech of a statute that is overbroad or vague on its face. The focus of the doctrine is not on the individual actor before the court [whose speech may in fact not be constitutionally protected] but on others who may forgo protected activity rather than run afoul of the statute's proscriptions."[141] But even granted the validity of this principle, vagueness and over-breadth can become handy weapons for striking down laws on doctrinaire grounds because, in the words of Justice Harlan, "almost any word or phrase may be rendered vague and ambiguous by dissection with a semantic scalpel."[142]

Justice Blackmun once accused the Court of invoking the doctrines of vagueness and overbreadth "indiscriminately without regard to the nature of the speech in question, the possible effect the statute or ordinance has upon such speech, the importance of the speech in relation to the exposition of ideas, or the purported or asserted community interest in preventing that speech." Consequently, he charged, "we are not merely applying constitutional limitations, ... but are invalidating state statutes in wholesale lots because they conceivably might apply to others who might utter other words."[143] Blackmun's accusation was exaggerated as directed against the majority of the Court, but not as addressed to Justices Brennan and Marshall. It would be hard to imagine a statute punishing obscene, indecent or opprobrious language which they would not find vague and overbroad.

This appears with striking clarity in Brennan's dissenting opinion in *Federal Communications Commission v. Pacifica Foundation* (1978). The foundation was the owner of a radio station which had broadcast a 12-minute monologue called "Filthy Words" by comedian George Carlin, in which he recited over and over a number of colloquial terms for sexual and execretory activities and organs. The FCC had imposed no sanctions for the broadcast but had said that it would decide on imposing them if further complaints were received about broadcasting the monologue during hours of the day when children might hear it. The majority of the Court held that the FCC had acted within its statutory powers and had not violated the First Amendment. Justice Brennan, joined by Justice Marshall, found the First Amendment in danger.

Fully to appreciate Brennan's dissenting opinion, one would have to read the full text of Carlin's "Filthy Words," which the Court thoughtfully provided in an appendix to its majority opinion.[144] But those who do not have easy access to it may use their imaginations without fear of being far off the mark about what the filthy words were. To Brennan they were "a message entitled to full First Amendment protection," and those who wanted to receive this message had a constitutional right to hear it on their radios, a right that was not outweighed by considerations derived from the privacy of people's homes or shielding their children from unsuitable language.[145]

The opinion of the Court by Justice Stevens and a concurring opinion by Justice Powell had suggested that those who felt a need to hear Carlin's monologue could go to a nightclub where he was appearing or buy a record of it. This suggestion, said Brennan, displayed "a sad insensitivity to the fact that these alternatives involve the expenditure of money, time, and effort that many of those wishing to hear Mr. Carlin's message may not be able to afford." But Stevens and Powell were guilty of an even more grievous fault. Their opinions betrayed "an acute ethnocentric myopia that enables the Court to approve the censorship of communications solely because of the words they contain." And this despite the fact that academic research—which Brennan cited—had shown that words like "----," "----," and "----" were commonplace and not considered obscene among blacks and young radicals.[146]

Justice Brennan may not have known it, but when he denounced the Court's decision in this case as "another of the dominant culture's inevitable efforts to force those groups who do not share its mores to conform to its way of thinking, acting and speaking,"[147] he was casting one vote against civilization. He was also exhibiting a kind of inverted snobbery. Since English is an Anglo-Saxon language, it may be that persons of Anglo-Saxon descent are more sensitive to its nuances than the rest of us. Still, one would like to think that Celts, Latins and Slavs, blacks, browns and redskins, Catholics and Jews could learn to appreciate the finer points of the language as well as white Anglo-Saxon Protestants. Or, at least, that we could come to understand that certain Anglo-Saxon four-letter words are crudities inappropriate to public discourse. Brennan seemed to doubt that we are up to it.

It is clear that by this time the idea of "saving intellectual content" had disappeared from Brennan's conception of freedom of speech. There was, he insisted, no constitutionally acceptable distinction between form and content, between the thought conveyed and the words used to convey it, because the very indecency of the words might be necessary to "convey the emotion that is an essential part of so many communications."[148] It was speech simply as speech that the First Amendment protected. Here it becomes plain that, with a few exceptions, the Brennan-Marshall position differed little from the Black-Douglas. There was the same separation of expression from any relation to the goals of the amendment, and the same tendency to presume that all speech, without regard to form or content, must be equally protected lest none of it should be protected at all.

"Freedom of speech," Brennan said in a later case, "is itself an end because the human community is in large measure defined through speech."[149] That was either a profound statement or an absurd one. It could be a restatement of Aristotle's insight that man is meant by nature to live in a polity because he is the thinking and therefore the talking animal, and rational speech, as distinct from the cries of other animals, implies the civil community. But if it meant, as one fears it did, that speech, any speech, any kind of speech or any manner of speaking, defines the human community, it was a shallow and specious proposition. Speech, understood without qualification or limit, is as capable of destroying as of establishing community among men.

If the Warren Court did not abandon the balancing test, the Burger Court may be said to have embraced it. With the retirement of Justice Black in 1971 and Justice Douglas in 1975, there was no one left on the Court who did not subscribe in principle to the balancing test. The members of the Court did not apply it in a uniform way: on one wing were Justices Brennan and Marshall, often joined by Justice Stewart; opposite them were Chief Justice Burger and Justices White and Rehnquist; and Justices Blackmun, Powell and Stevens moved about in the middle. Even this is a very rough description of the Burger Court, but it will do so long as the reader understands that it describes a planetary system and not a fixed constellation.

The members of the Burger Court named above were consistent, however, in recognizing that the decision of First Amendment cases required striking a balance among competing interests, however much they differed among themselves on what the right balance was. Hesitating and erratic though the course of their decisions was, they arrived on the whole at more sophisticated decisions than the Warren Court because they so often recognized that judgment in freedom of speech and press cases is contextual and is seldom derived from simple, sweeping principles.

The words of the Court's majority in a few sample cases will illustrate the extent to which it relied on the balancing test. When the president of a state college refused to grant recognition to a local chapter of Students for a Democratic Society, the Court saw the case involving "the mutual interest of students, faculty members, and administrators in an environment free from disruptive interference with the educational process" and "the equally significant interest in the widest latitude for free expression and debate consonant with the maintenance of order."[150] When newsmen claimed a First Amendment privilege against revealing confidential information and sources to grand juries, the Court stated the issue in these terms: "The heart of the claim is that the burden on newsgathering resulting from compelling reporters to disclose confidential information outweighs any public interest in obtaining the information" (a claim which the Court rejected).[151] In another case the Court granted that "a prison inmate retains those First Amendment rights that are not inconsistent with his status as a prisoner," but added that governmental interests may be balanced against First Amendment rights.[152] In a defamation case against a magazine the Court stated: "The First Amendment requires that we protect some falsehood in order to protect speech that matters." But it does not protect falsehood absolutely because "absolute protection for the communications media requires a total sacrifice of the competing value served by the law of defamation."[153] Finally, in passing on the constitutionality of the Federal Election Campaign Act of 1971, the Court admitted that the act's imposition of a ceiling on campaign contributions restricted "one aspect of the contributor's freedom of political association." But, it said: "Even a 'significant interference with protected rights of political association' may be sustained if the State demonstrates a sufficiently important interest and employs means closely drawn to avoid unnecessary abridgment of associational freedoms."[154]

This "balancing" process assumed that there were constitutionally relevant interests that could be weighed against each other, and the Court, at every stage of its history, recognized this whenever it applied the balancing test. The Court nowhere, however, set down the complete scale of interests that could be put in the balance. One finds statements indicating that some public interests are more important than others and hence more capable of justifying certain restrictions on freedom of speech and press. One does not find the whole hierarchy of public interests in their order of importance. More rarely one comes across suggestions that some kinds of utterance are less deserving of constitutional protection than others. The Court's opinions, therefore, did not furnish a satisfactory statement of all the elements that enter into the balancing process. It was sufficient for the Court's purposes, when balancing competing interests, to decide which of them should prevail in the case, or class of case, before it. The question before the Court was whether, in the context of the case, this sort of restriction on utterance (or on this *kind* of utterance) was justified by the kind and the magnitude of the public interest which the restriction was intended to serve. The Court needed to answer no further question.

Out of the decision of such cases arose a body of constitutional law in which the emphasis on freedom of expression or on government's right to restrict it shifted from decade to decade. Certainly, Chief Justice Vinson's Court struck the balance in the early 1950s differently from Chief Justice Warren's in the late 1960s, and Chief Justice Burger's Court struck it differently again in the 1970s. But there did not emerge a complete, coherent and fully articulated hierarchy of kinds of speech and levels of public interest in the light of which the Court made its decisions, and it would be fruitless to try to piece one together from the dicta of the Court and its individual members over a period of sixty years. Yet the hierarchy is there in the Court's opinions, though seen as in a glass, darkly, and it furnishes a basis for further reflection on the scales of value implicit in a regime of free speech and press.

For those who accept the Black-Douglas position, of course, no reflection on a hierarchy of constitutionally protected values and on the place of freedom of speech and press in that hierarchy is necessary or permissible. But it is submitted here that the Black-Douglas position is wrong, and the Brennan-Marshall position is little improvement on it. For it is simply not true that every kind of utterance, regardless of its content or mode of expression, or of the effects it may have on substantial and valid public interests is of equal intrinsic value or equally serves the ends of the First Amendment. Justice Frankfurter well said:

> Not every type of speech occupies the same position on the scale of values. There is no substantial public interest in permitting certain kinds of utterances: "the lewd and the obscene, the profane, the

libelous, and the insulting or 'fighting' words ..." It is pertinent to the decision before us to consider where on the scale of values we have in the past placed the type of speech now claiming constitutional immunity [i.e., advocacy of the forcible overthrow of the United States government] ... On any scale of values which we have hitherto recognized, speech of this sort ranks low."[155]

Failure or refusal to recognize that there are differences of kind and degree among utterances and modes of expression leads to the type of reasoning which Frankfurter derided in his concurring opinion in *Kovacs v. Cooper*: "It is argued that the Constitution protects freedom of speech; freedom of speech means the right to communicate, whatever the physical means for so doing; sound trucks are one form of communication; ergo, that form is entitled to the same protection as any other means of communication, whether by tongue or pen. Such sterile argumentation treats society as though it consisted of bloodless categories."[156] What is more to the point, it treats the key terms, such as "speech," "press," "expression," and "communication," as though they were mere abstractions which always mean exactly the same thing and can be applied to the decision of cases in constitutional law without regard to constitutional purposes or to the concrete realities to which they refer.

The effort so to apply them leads to such profundities as Justice Douglas's remark: "I seriously doubt the wisdom of trying by law to put the fresh, evanescent, natural blossoming of sex in the category of 'sin.'"[157] If one recalls that in the case in which Douglas made that remark the issue was the power of the state to forbid the sale of obscene literature to minors, one may be inclined more seriously to doubt the wisdom of trying by fiat of the Supreme Court to put the reading of pornography in the category of the fresh, evanescent, natural blossoming of sex. But what Douglas really meant was that the First Amendment permits neither the state nor the Court to tell the difference. It was enough that the magazines in question came off a printing press. That fact alone put them in the category of "expression" or even of "exposition of ideas," and should therefore render their sale immune from prosecution.

Admittedly, the absolutist (and to a lesser extent the quasi-absolutist) approach to freedom of speech and press has one great advantage: simplicity. It relieves legislatures and courts of any function other than that of drawing the line between utterance and conduct. In *Beauharnais v. Illinois*, for example, the Court, speaking through Justice Frankfurter, upheld Beauharnais's conviction for distributing a leaflet that exposed Negroes as a class to contempt, derision or obloquy in violation of a state group-libel law. "Every power may be abused," Frankfurter conceded, "but the possibility of abuse is a poor reason for denying Illinois the power to adopt measures against criminal libels sanctioned by centuries of Anglo-American law. 'While this Court sits,' it retains and exercises authority to nullify action which encroaches on freedom of utterance under the guise of punishing libel."[158] To which Justice Black replied: "We are told that freedom of petition and discussion are in no danger 'while this Court sits.' This case raises considerable doubt. Since those who peacefully petition for changes in the law [as Beauharnais was doing] are not to be protected 'while this Court sits,' who is? I do not agree that the Constitution leaves freedom of petition, assembly, speech, press, or worship at the mercy of a case-by-case, day-by-day majority of this court."[159]

Black's sincere concern for freedom is evident. Yet he ignored the wisdom in Justice Holmes's original coinage of the phrase: "The power to tax is not the power to destroy while this Court sits."[160] It is an ancient and useful maxim in constitutional law that the power to tax is the power to destroy. But, as Holmes saw and the Court eventually came to agree, the maxim inevitably leads to ridiculous results if it is applied mechanically without consideration of the end it is meant to serve and of the circumstances in which it is used. "There comes a point," as Justice Rehnquist said at a much later date, "when endless and ill-considered extension of principles originally formulated in quite different cases produces such an indefensible result that no logic chopping can possibly make the fallacy of the result more obvious."[161] Some human mind or minds must apply the First Amendment to the decision of cases. In the American constitutional system, that function is assigned in the highest instance to the Supreme Court and will have to be performed by it "while this Court sits." If we may be pardoned for pressing some words of Justice Stewart's into a service of which he might not approve, no doubt the Court will "be required to make some delicate judgments.... But that, after all, is the function of courts of law."[162]

When deciding whether an exercise of the taxing power or any other power of government exceeds constitutional limits, the Court cannot draw a conclusion from the letter of the Constitution as though it were deriving a theorem in geometry. It must decide what the letter of the document means in the light of history, precedent and other relevant considerations; what ends it was designed to achieve or evils to avert; how they are to be reconciled and combined with other constitutional ends; and how the attainment of these ends is affected by the facts of the case. Therefore, in freedom of speech and press cases, the First Amendment, to borrow a phrase from Justice Frankfurther, "is not a self-wielding sword." It is a sword that the Court has to wield in the exercise of its "duty of closer analysis and critical judgment in applying the thought behind the phrase."[163]

Such a process of analysis and judgment can issue in error, of course, and it will never result in conclusions so demonstrably true or decisions so manifestly right that they impose themselves on the mind of every honest and intelligent man. Yet it is the process in which not only the Court but its critics must engage. Constitutional rules are not self-explanatory and self-enforcing to the point of eliminating the need for judgment.

The First Amendment indeed commands Congress (and, by decision of the Supreme Court, the states, too) to make no law abridging the freedom of speech or of the press. This command, however, does not relieve the Court of the obligation of deciding what "the freedom of speech, or of the press" is and what exercises of governmental power "abridge" it. The Court can be influenced by public opinion, checked to some extent by the other branches of the government or overruled by the exercise of the amending power. But in the performance of its function of judicial review, it is the ordinary final judge of the meaning, purpose, and limits of freedom of speech and press, as of other constitutional guarantees. If the Court is to perform its function, it must be granted a certain degree of confidence that "while this Court sits," it will exercise its authority to nullify action which encroaches on freedom of expression under the guise of punishing libel or other crimes that can be committed by words. After all, even Justices Black and Douglas had to rely on the Court to nullify action which encroached on freedom of utterance under the guise of punishing conduct, because there was normally no other body on which to rely.

These two justices maintained, as we have seen, that while the Court could adequately distinguish speech from conduct, to allow it to make distinctions among utterances put freedom of expression at the capricious mercy of a majority of the Court. Other justices, who took positions less extreme than theirs, nonetheless shared their fears, as appeared in a debate that broke out in the Court in the 1970s.

In an opinion of the Court handed down in 1972, Justice Marshall declared that "above all else, the First Amendment means that government has no power to restrict expression because of its message, its ideas, its subject matter, or its content."[164] Echoed Justice Brennan in 1974: "Subject matter or content censorship in any form is forbidden,"[165] and Justice Stewart repeated in an opinion of the Court in 1976 that it was constitutionally impermissible "to discriminate in the regulation of expression on the basis of the content of that expression."[166]

In the same year, 1976, the recently appointed Justice Stevens raised the question whether the First Amendment really imposed such an absolute prohibition. The Court, indeed, had said so, but "we learned long ago that broad statements of principle, no matter how correct in the context in which they are made are sometimes qualified by contrary decisions before the absolute limit of the stated principle is reached." The fact is that "whether speech is, or is not, protected by the First Amendment often depends on the content of the speech." Whether a speaker was merely advocating an idea or inciting to violence depends, not only on when and where he said it, "but also on exactly what the speaker had to say." So, too, with "fighting words" or publishing military information in time of war. "Even within the area of protected speech, a difference in content may require a different governmental response." For example: "The measure of constitutional protection to be afforded commercial speech will surely be governed largely by the content of the communication."[167]

Stevens acknowledged the validity of "the underlying reason for the rule which is generally described as a prohibition of regulation based on the content of protected communication. The essence of that rule," he explained, "is the need for absolute neutrality by the government; its regulation of communication may not be affected by sympathy or hostility for the point of view being expressed by the communicator."[168] But this was not to say that government might never take the content of speech into account when regulating it.

Stevens made these remarks in an opinion of the Court, but on this particular point he lost his majority. Justice Stewart wrote a dissenting opinion protesting against "selective interference with protected speech whose content is thought to produce distasteful effects."[169] He was joined, as one might expect, by Justices Brennan and Marshall, but also by Justice Blackmun; and Justice Powell, without explaining why, refused to concur with the rest of the majority in what it said about the content of speech as a permissible basis for regulation.

Powell did explain in a later case in which Stevens repeated his proposition that regulation of speech may be based on its content.[170] In an opinion joined by Justice Blackmun, Powell said: "I do not subscribe to the theory that the Justices of this Court are free generally to decide on the basis of its content which speech protected by the First Amendment is most 'valuable' and hence deserving of the most protection, and which is less 'valuable' and hence deserving of less protection."[171] Yet in the same year he himself also said: "Expression concerning purely commercial transactions has come within the ambit of the Amendment's protection only recently," and even then was not put on the same plane with other kinds of expression. The reason he gave for the distinction was this:

> To require a parity of constitutional protection for commercial and noncommercial speech alike could invite dilution, simply by a levelling process, of the force of the Amendment's guarantee with respect to the

latter kind of speech. Rather than subject the First Amendment to such a devitalization, we have afforded commercial speech a limited measure of protection, commensurate with its subordinate position in the scale of First Amendment values, while allowing modes of regulation that might be impermissible in the realm of noncommercial expression.[172]

Blackmun had already said: "In concluding that commercial speech enjoys First Amendment protection, we have not held that it is wholly undifferentiable from other forms."[173] Even Justice Stewart agreed: "Ideological expression, be it oral, literary, pictorial, or theatrical, is integrally related to the exposition of thought—thought that may shape our concepts of the whole universe of man.... Commercial price and product advertising differs markedly from ideological expression because it is confined to the promotion of specific goods or services."[174]

It is difficult to see how these justices could make such distinctions among kinds of speech without recognizing the contents that distinguish kinds of speech from one another. One understands their fear of allowing government to pass judgment on the content of expression. But it would seem that Stevens was right in maintaining that, in order to make judgments about the protection of expression, government must take its content into account.

At any rate, distinctions among kinds of expression must be made. Bawling invectives is not the same as presenting reasoned arguments, a gossip columnist does not do the same thing as the author of a treatise on physics, and a pornographic film is not a Shakespearean play written by a lesser genius. To pretend that these and a host of other types of speech and publication are all simply and without qualification instances of "expression" is, in the words of Justice Jackson, "to endanger the great right of free speech by making it ridiculous and obnoxious."[175]

If freedom of speech and press is to be preserved from that danger, the Court must distinguish among kinds of expression in the light of the purposes which the constitutional freedom is intended to serve. The Court's judgment in the matter will presuppose what no one denies, that the United States is committed by the First Amendment to a regime of free speech and free press and that, as Justice Harlan said, "where the constitutional protection exists it must prevail." But rational determination of where this protection prevails must include the application of several scales of value. There is a scale of kinds of utterance in relation to the ends that freedom of expression is designed to promote. Opposite it is another scale of the personal and societal values to which freedom of expression may be subordinated because they, too, merit protection by the Constitution and the laws. There is also a scale of modes or manners of expressing oneself, of very unequal value.

There is, in addition, a variety of media of communication (spoken or printed words, photographs and paintings, motion pictures, radio and television) which, whether or not they can be arranged in a hierarchy, cannot be regarded as identical with each other in constitutional adjudication. "Each medium of expression," according to the Court, "must be assessed for First Amendment purposes by standards suited to it, for each may present its own problems."[176] Similarly, there is a variety of fora (public streets and parks, auditoriums, schools, etc.) that cannot be governed by identical standards, and some places are not fora at all, e.g., "a prison is most emphatically not a 'public forum.'"[177]

All of these scales of value do or can enter into a judgment on freedom of speech or press. Some kinds of speech and publication enjoy no constitutional protection and so stand at the bottom of the scale of the types of utterance of which the law takes cognizance. Other kinds of speech and publication, however, are above the bottom of the scale and *per se* merit protection. But they stand low on the scale and may be sacrificed to public interests which stand rather low on their own scale and would not justify suppressing utterances of higher value. The higher the kind of expression, the higher the level of public interest required to limit or suppress it.

Freedom of expression figures on this scale not only as a means to other ends but as an end or value in itself. The ability to speak and publish without fear of punishment is desirable for its own sake and apart from whatever other purposes it may serve. Our law favors liberty, as Bracton said in the thirteenth century, and our Constitution today considers freedom of expression as a good in itself and protects it as such, though not absolutely.

Even taken as an end in itself, however, expression is not always deserving of the same protection, since making an obscene phone call does not quite rank with affirming one's deepest beliefs. Furthermore, the First Amendment does not protect the right to speak and publish merely or principally because liberty-loving Americans cherish being able to talk and publish freely. The guarantee is in the Constitution chiefly as a means to ends beyond self-expression. Freedom to express oneself, therefore, while it ranks as one of the ends of the First Amendment, is not the highest of them and consequently, as Justice Harlan said, "constitutionally protected freedom of speech is narrower than an unlimited license to talk."

There are higher ends which the right of free speech and press is intended to promote. The primary purpose is to serve the political needs of a representative democracy which depends on free discussion of public affairs. The guarantee also broadly serves all the social needs that can be satisfied by communication. These needs determine the relative constitutional value of the several kinds of communication.

It should therefore be possible to arrange the kinds of utterance in a scale for purposes of constitutional interpretation. Harry M. Clor cites an example of such an effort from *Roth v. U.S.*, as argued before the Supreme Court:

> The government's brief urged that the value of obscene speech be judged in the light of a comparative scale of First Amendment values based on the purpose of the amendment as interpreted in Supreme Court decisions. This scale of values was tendered as illustrative:
>
>   Political speech
>   Religious
>   Economic
>   Scientific
>   General News and Information
>   Social and Historical Commentary
>   Literature
>   Art
>   Entertainment
>   Music
>   Humor
>   Commercial Advertisements
>   Gossip
>   Comic Books
>   Epithets
>   Libel
>   Obscenity
>   Profanity
>   Commercial Pornography
>
> The public interest required to justify restraint would diminish as one moves down the scale and increase as one moves up. The brief then proceeds to the "weighing." Expression characterized by obscenity has extremely low value in the light of basic First Amendment purposes. Arrayed against this expression are social interests in the preservation of moral standards.[178]

As Mr. Clor points out, while the government won its case in *Roth v. U.S.*, the Court rejected its proposed rationale for the decision and refused to accept the scale of values suggested in the government's brief.[179] Rather than commit itself, even by implication, to the proposition that political, religious, economic, scientific, literary, and artistic expression are related to one another in a descending order of value, the Court, in an opinion written by Justice Brennan, simply ruled obscenity outside the pale of constitutional protection on the ground that it was "utterly without redeeming social importance."[180] Obscenity, so to speak, was declared to have no place at all on the scale of First Amendment values.

One understands the Court's reluctance to become involved, even remotely, in determining the relative merits of political and religious speech, or of scientific and literary publications. There is, in fact, little

reason why it should do so. For most practical purposes, these fields of
expression stand constitutionally on the same plane. The Founding
Fathers, as we have seen, felt that freedom of the press (and therefore of
speech as well) would advance "truth, science, morality and arts in
general" as well as responsible government. Not only the expression of
political and religious belief, but the cultivation of all the arts and
sciences is protected by the guarantee of freedom of speech and press. To
allow the free operation of the human mind in all of these fields is the
global end of the First Amendment, and the Court has little or no
occasion to determine their relative merits and to decide whether a
treatise on economics is of higher value than one on physics, or political
speech ranks above a poem.

It is possible, nonetheless, that the Court might some day face the
necessity of making some such determination. One might argue, for
example, that while national security would in certain circumstances
justify suppressing the publication of news or of scientific findings, it
would not in the same circumstances justify suppressing the expression
of political opinion, and this because the latter stands higher on the scale
of First Amendment values. But, generally speaking, it is not necessary
to determine what order of value obtains among the kinds of utterance
that serve the higher ends of the amendment.

It might well be relevant, however, for the Court to inquire whether a
speech or publication is an effort to attain any of these higher ends and,
if so, to what degree. Can the utterance be taken as an attempt to pursue
the truth, to argue for a conception of morality, or to communicate an
esthetic experience? Or is the dominant purpose of the utterance to
amuse and entertain, to sell goods, to satisfy idle curiosity, to express
hatred, or to furnish a vicarious experience which is subhuman and
degrading? These questions imply a scale of values that puts political,
religious, economic and scientific speech, the communication of general
news and information and the cultivation of literature and the arts on a
superior plane to mere entertainment, commercial advertising, gossip,
epithets and pornography. The latter kinds of utterance serve either
inferior ends of the First Amendment or no constitutional ends at all,
and so may be more readily subordinated to overriding public interests
or suppressed altogether.

The pursuit of truth is, by universal agreement among the justices of
the Supreme Court who have spoken on the matter, a chief end of the
Freedom of Speech and Press Clause. If we assume, with Chief Judge
Learned Hand, "truth will be most likely to emerge if no limitations are
imposed upon utterances that can with any plausibility be regarded as
efforts to present grounds for accepting or rejecting propositions whose
truth the utterer asserts, or denies," then we may insist that there should

at least be some plausibility. Government may not pass upon the truth of propositions in matters of belief or doctrine. But it can, and sometimes must, distinguish efforts, however mistaken, to get at truth from utterances which tend toward or reach the merely trivial or the irrational. If freedom of speech and press are meant to protect the "exposition of ideas," it is fair to require that what is exposed be an idea and not a mindless appeal to passion or to vulgar curiosity.

For example, in 1959, the Court declared unconstitutional a New York law under which a license had been denied for showing the film, *Lady Chatterley's Lover.* "What New York has done," the Court said, "is to prevent the exhibition of a motion picture because it advocates an idea—that adultery under certain circumstances may be proper behavior."[181] That adultery may be engaged in with propriety is indeed an idea—if not a true one, at least a consoling one—and, like any other idea, it may be advocated through the medium of an art form. It does not follow that if a film included a clinically explicit depiction of the act of sexual intercourse as performed by partners in adultery, it would be "advocating an idea." As *Time* once remarked, voyeurism is a vice, not a point of view.

Admittedly, the Court has upon occasion denied that "saving intellectual content" is necessary for constitutional protection of publications. In *Winters v. New York* in 1948 it said:

> We do not accede to appellee's suggestion that the constitutional protection for a free press applies only to the exposition of ideas. The line between the informing and the entertaining is too elusive for the protection of that basic right. Everyone is familiar with instances of propaganda through fiction. What is one man's amusement, teaches another's doctrine. Though we can see nothing of any possible value to society in these magazines [described as exploiting "criminal deeds of bloodshed or lust"], they are as much entitled to the protection of free speech as the best of literature.[182]

The Court was careful to add to the above passage the statement that the magazines in question "are equally subject to control if they are lewd, indecent, obscene or profane." But twenty-one years later, the Court went farther and said: "Nor is it relevant that obscene materials in general, or the particular films before the court, are arguably devoid of any ideological content. The line between the transmission of ideas and mere entertainment is much too elusive for this Court to draw, if indeed such a line can be drawn at all."[183]

This latter declaration merits even more strongly Justice Frankfurter's comment in the *Winters* case: "The essence of the Court's decision is that it gives publications which have 'nothing of any possible value to society' constitutional protection but denies to the States the power to prevent the grave evils to which, in their rational judgment, such publications give rise."[184] To maintain that publications that contain no ideas and are of no possible value to society deserve protection against the claims of a substantial public interest is tantamount to saying that speech or publication need have no rationally discernible relation to the ends of the First Amendment in order to come under its mantle.

Besides, while the line between the transmission of ideas and mere entertainment may be too elusive for a court of law to draw, it need not be assumed that this line coincides with the boundary between constitutionally protected and unprotected speech. In *Roth v. U.S.*, for example, having declared that obscenity is constitutionally unprotected, the Court laid it down that the test for finding material obscene was "whether to the average person, applying contemporary community standards, *the dominant theme of the material taken as a whole* appeals to prurient interest."[185] If the First Amendment was intended to foster and protect an appeal to reason, but not to prurient interest, then the clear dominance of the latter appeal over the former in a given work is enough to disqualify it for constitutional protection, even though it may contain some elements that can be called transmission of ideas. In other words, the question of proportion is constitutionally relevant.

Although Justice Brennan wrote the opinion of the Court in *Roth v. U.S.*, he later rejected proportionality as a constitutional criterion in obscenity cases. For a work to be obscene under the First Amendment, he insisted, it must be "*utterly* without redeeming social value."[186] This interpretation of the meaning of the *Roth* test never won the agreement of more than two other members of the Court but, because of the concurrence of Justices Black and Douglas from their own absolutist point of view, it effectively became the norm that the Court applied in obscenity cases from 1966 to 1973. What was wrong with it as a test of obscenity was precisely the word "utterly," because it made the question of the dominant theme of the material irrelevant and rendered the *Roth* definition of obscenity useless. By refusing to consider the question of proportion, the Court for several years was led into a doctrinaire ignoring of the reality with which it was dealing. The Court ended up protecting blatant pornography because it was not demonstrably devoid of "ideas." *Redrup v. N.Y.*,[187] a per curiam opinion that summarized the position of the Court's majority in 1967, may justly be called the Magna Carta of the American pornography industry.

Redrup was reversed in 1973, though without noticeable effect, it must be said, on the prosperity of the burgeoning pornography industry. Pornography had become an established part of American life, not fully accepted by society at large, but tolerated by most citizens and, in the minds of many, the very hallmark of liberal democracy and all that it stood for. Having let the djinn out of the bottle, the Court could not get him back in again in social practice. But in constitutional law it made a determined effort to do so in a group of cases decided on the same day in June, 1973, the leading one of which was *Miller v. California.*

In this case, in an opinion by Chief Justice Burger, the Court reinstated the criterion of proportionality, and explicitly rejected "as a constitutional standard the *'utterly* without redeeming social value' test." "At a minimum," said the Court, "prurient, patently offensive depiction or description of sexual conduct [which alone would constitute 'obscenity' in the constitutional sense] must have serious literary, artistic, political, or scientific value to merit First Amendment protection." The proportion between the element of obscenity and the serious value was therefore determinative, and it was not beyond the ability of courts to judge what the proportion was. To think otherwise would "assume that courts cannot distinguish commerce in ideas, protected by the First Amendment, from commercial exploitation of obscene material."[188]

Distinctions could be made, therefore. As Burger said in a companion case to *Miller v. California,* "Preventing unlimited display or distribution of obscene material which by definition lacks any serious literary, artistic, political, or scientific value as communication ... is distinct from a control of reason and the intellect."[189] Moreover, distinctions must be made, because "in our view, to equate the free and robust exchange of ideas and political debate with commercial exploitation of obscene material demeans the grand conception of the First Amendment and its high purposes."[190]

It is true, as the Court said in the *Winters* case, that everyone is familiar with instances of propaganda through fiction. But works of literature and of the arts aim principally at communicating an esthetic experience rather than a version of the truth. To speak of them primarily in terms of the transmission or exposition of ideas, as justices of the Supreme Court have frequently done, and as this writer has done in the preceding paragraphs, is often to misconceive their principal function. Nevertheless, the quality of the esthetic experience which a work intends to communicate is itself an object of rational judgment which may serve as the basis for deciding whether the work is protected by the constitutional guarantee of freedom of the press.

To take a hypothetical example, let us suppose that three directors film the same battle scene in three distinct films. The first director films the battle as an adventure and wishes to communicate the experience of danger faced and overcome, of victory achieved and glory won. His film may also be intended to serve as propaganda for a "hawkish" U. S. foreign policy. The second director films the battle in order to communicate an experience of the horrors of war and to induce a revulsion against it. His film may, in addition, be intended to serve as propaganda for a "dovish" U. S. foreign policy. But, whatever one may think of either director's point of view, his filming of the battle scene communicates an acceptable vicarious experience and is a legitimate exercise of freedom of the press.

In contrast, the third director films the battle as an exercise in sadism. What he communicates is a vicarious experience of the pleasure of inflicting pain, death and degradation on human beings. To picture soldiers beating their enemies to death with their rifle butts is shocking but, properly handled, it can be a realistic portrayal of war and can serve a legitimate artistic end. But at some point of gruesomeness, such a portrayal will pass beyond any legitimate end. If the camera dwells long and lovingly on a man's face being beaten into a bloody and shapeless mass until it is no longer recognizably human, the suspicion and finally the certainty grows that what is being appealed to is nothing more than a sick appetite for violence. It is submitted that, with all due presumptions in favor of artistic freedom, reason can sometimes recognize such an appeal so clearly and unmistakably as to judge it unworthy of constitutional protection. For, if freedom of expression is not an absolute end in itself, judgment must be passed on that which is expressed, and not everything that can be expressed serves the ends of the First Amendment.

It is too narrow an interpretation of freedom of speech and press to confine its protection to appeals to the mind through reasoned discourse. Appeals to the imagination and emotions through literature and the arts also deserve protection. But there is a sense in which every kind of utterance ought to be subject to reason under the First Amendment. To decide the constitutionality of limiting or suppressing an utterance requires passing rational judgment on the ends which the utterance serves and rational evaluation of those ends in the light of the purposes of the First Amendment. Literary and artistic criticism are presumably exercises of the rational human mind and so, too, is legal judgment when it bears upon works of literature and art. The refinements of literary and artistic criticism are doubtless beyond the ordinary competence of courts, for the law is far too blunt an instrument to be used as a scalpel in that kind of intellectual surgery. But rational judgment sufficient for the purposes of constitutional adjudication ought not to be beyond the abilities of the legal mind.

The purposes of the First Amendment are ends that reason recognizes and approves. Those who think that asking, "Whose reason?" is a crushing reply that effectively disposes of that proposition should be prepared to explain on what grounds they defend the amendment. Since the question they ask implicitly denies that there is a commonly-shared human reason, they cannot present arguments that appeal to the reason of mankind. By their definition reason is always someone's reason, and therefore individual and private. The only grounds they can offer, therefore, are a private preference for freedom of expression and a corresponding distaste for limiting it. Justice Brennan spoke for them when he said: "A given word may have a unique capacity to capsule an idea, evoke an emotion, or conjure up an image. Indeed, for those of us who place an appropriately high value on our cherished First Amendment rights, the word 'censor' is such a word."[191] The sentiment, as sentiments go, is admirable. But does an emotional revulsion against "censorship" furnish a sufficient explanation of why we have and should maintain freedom of speech? One may reasonably doubt it and continue to believe that the First Amendment stands upon our trust in reason or on nothing at all.

There is no need to rush to the other extreme and make the amendment the charter of a dogmatic rationalism. Reason can approve of much that it cannot prove. Religious belief depends on faith rather than on rational demonstration, and the same can be said of political and other kinds of belief. But belief can be advocated and defended rationally. Even a false idea or, for that matter, an evil idea can serve the cause of truth if an effort is made to present the grounds for it (however specious) in the manner appropriate to rational argument and it is subjected to rational criticism. Literature and the arts, as we have said, appeal to the imagination and the emotions as much or more than to naked reason, yet they, too, are subject to rational judgment and should serve ends of which reason can approve. All of these, as well as the kind of expression that seeks to engender complete rational conviction through demonstrative argument, deserve constitutional protection. But the appeal to mere passion, uncontrolled by reason and directed to irrational or anti-rational purposes, does not deserve protection because it does not serve what Justice Jackson called "the great end for which the First Amendment stands."[192]

The objection usually alleged against allowing the law any power over speech or publication that appeals to sexual lust is that "obscenity" is beyond the ability of law adequately to define. Justice Stewart, for example, was laughed at for saying that, while he could not define hardcore pornography, "I know it when I see it."[193] But consider the following lines from *Time* for April 6, 1970. After the fall of Prince Sihanouk from power in Cambodia, the magazine reported, the "local press mocked him savagely and his half-Italian wife Princess Monique even more. Some newspapers ran composite photos of her head on anonymous nude bodies in obscene poses." The editors of *Time* evidently assumed that their readers would have no difficulty in understanding what those words meant, and the people in Cambodia who made up and published the composite photographs took it for granted that their readers would know an obscene pose when they saw one. To bring the matter closer to home, if one's sister, wife or daughter posed in the nude for a photographer, would it make any difference what poses she was asked to assume? Or would one feel obliged to maintain that a truly liberal and objective mind could recognize no meaningful differences among poses? Anyone who would honestly have to admit that he could recognize differences and find them significant should be willing to admit that a jury could do so, too. It was, in fact, to juries, properly instructed in the legal norms and subject to review by appellate courts, that the Supreme Court assigned the function of recognizing obscenity for what it is.[194]

The Court also found a public interest important enough to justify state regulation or suppression of obscene material. "The sum of experience, including that of the past two decades," it said in June, 1973, "affords an ample basis for legislatures to conclude that a sensitive, key relationship of human existence, central to family life, community welfare, and the development of human personality, can be debased and distorted by crass commercial exploitation of sex." In an implicit rejection of *The Report of the [Presidential] Commission on Obscenity and Pornography*, [195] the Court added: "Nothing in the Constitution prohibits a State from reaching such a conclusion and acting on it legislatively simply because there is no conclusive evidence or empirical data."[196] After all, it pointed out, legislatures had acted in many fields on indemonstrable assumptions, yet the Court had upheld their legislation.[197] In saying this, far from abandoning reason, the Court realistically recognized the way in which reason acts and must act in the regulation of human affairs.

Ultimately, then, the line drawn by the First Amendment is not simply between speech and conduct but between irrational and more or less rational speech. The presumption in every case favors freedom of utterance. But the presumption must sometimes yield to the claims of competing public interests. In such cases, the Court must take into account, not only the weight and value of the public interest alleged, but also the quality and comparative value of the kind of speech involved. This value will depend on the rationally discernible relationship of the speech in question to one or more of the ends of the First Amendment. In this sense, the unifying principle of the hierarchy of kinds of speech, for purposes of constitutional adjudication, is rationality.

In addition to the two basic scales—kinds of speech and levels of public interest—that are weighed against each other in constitutional adjudication, we may postulate another scale, that of the manners or modes of expression. Independently of the content of an utterance, the way in which it is uttered may make it more or less deserving of constitutional protection. Justice Stewart once wrote that "the Constitution protects coarse expression as well as refined, and vulgarity no less than elegance."[198] It is true that the Constitution was not written for a nation made up exclusively of ladies and gentlemen, and that it protects a large range of expressions that are neither refined nor elegant. It does not follow that there are and ought to be no limits on the kind of language one is permitted to use in public, on the visual imagery that one may set before the public's eyes, or on the kind and volume of noise which one may inflict on the public's ears. The more offensive an utterance becomes in its manner of expression (as distinct from its content), the more easily it may be subordinated to public propriety and comfort, and the more nearly it approaches the point where it loses its claim to constitutional protection.

This, it must be remarked, is a point that the Burger Court several times overlooked, e.g., in *Cohen v. California, Rosenfeld v. New Jersey,* and *Papish v. University of Missouri.*[199] A Rosenfeld, getting up at a public school board meeting and using "the adjective 'm——f——' on four occasions to describe the teachers, the school board, the town, and his own country,"[200] was not furthering public discussion but making it impossible. As not every kind of utterance, so not every mode of utterance equally serves the ends of the First Amendment, and it is not really helpful constantly to fall back on the doctrine of "overbreadth" in order to deny this.

Law, as we have acknowledged, is a blunt instrument and not a surgeon's scalpel. But despite its necessary rigidity and bluntness, law can and must make distinctions and recognize degrees of difference in applying its general rules to the decision of particular cases. The distinctions will be more easily and more accurately made in regard to freedom of speech and press if we get back to asking, more insistently than we have in recent years, what are we trying to protect and why. Not everything that can be labelled "speech," or "expression," or "utterance" is worth protecting. Much of it must be granted immunity for the sake of preserving the freedom of speech and press that serves the ends of the First Amendment. But not all of it need be or should be rendered immune from legal regulation for the general good. The ends of the First Amendment, broad though they are, are not compatible with everything that it enters into the mind of man to utter, in any way in which he chooses to utter it. The quest for rationality in interpreting the amendment's guarantees of freedom of speech and press forces us to ask, in the end, what the freedom is for.

Divorced from their original purpose, Walter Lippmann once wrote, "freedom to think and speak are not self-evident necessities. It is only from the hope and the intention of discovering truth that freedom acquires such high public significance." But, he warned,

> when the chaff of silliness, baseness, and deception is so voluminous that it submerges the kernels of truth, freedom of speech may produce such frivolity, or such mischief, that it cannot be preserved against the demand for a restoration of order or of decency. If there is a dividing line between liberty and license, it is where freedom of speech is no longer respected as a procedure of the truth and becomes the unrestricted right to exploit the ignorance, and to incite the passions, of the people. Then freedom is such a hullabaloo of sophistry, propaganda, special pleading, lobbying and salesmanship that it is difficult to remember why freedom of speech is worth the pain and trouble of defending it.[201]

Lippmann's words state the contemporary problem well. It is not to push back ever farther the outer limits of freedom of speech and press, but to remember ever more clearly why the freedom was worth defending in the first place. For when the purpose of freedom is forgotten, freedom cannot long survive.

2

The True Wayfaring Christian
John Milton

The argument of the previous chapter was that the norms and limits of the freedom of speech and press must be derived from the purposes which it is intended to serve, taken in relation to other purposes which the Constitution also intends to achieve. The purposes of the constitutional right to speak and publish can be summed up, in the most general terms, as the liberation of the human mind to pursue through thought and communication all the objects that it can propose to itself as goals of rational endeavor. The line drawn by the First Amendment, therefore, is not simply between speech and conduct but between irrational and more or less rational speech.

Interpreting the First Amendment is a uniquely American problem because the amendment is a part of the Constitution of the United States and has no force outside its borders. But the interpretation requires some theory of the nature and function of the freedom which is guaranteed by the Constitution, and it cannot be extracted from the mere words of the document. They were themselves the product of a long historical development, and we may take it that their meaning was not frozen when the amendment was adopted in 1791. Nor is it enough to recur, as we did in the previous chapter, to what the U.S. Supreme Court has said on the matter.

In this and the following chapters, therefore, we shall examine "the literature" on the meaning of freedom of speech and press, and on the reasons why it should be recognized as a legal right. For, as Willmoore Kendall has said,

> We may ... speak properly of a *literature* of the problem of freedom of thought and speech, one easy to identify in the sense that most scholars in the field of political theory, regardless of their views on that problem ..., would name the same list of "must" items dealing with the problem, and cite those items over and over again when they address themselves

to the problem.... [T]he items are: Plato's *Apology* and *Crito*, Locke's *Letters concerning Toleration*, Spinoza's brief discussion of the problem in the *Tractatus*, Milton's *Areopagitica*, and above all ... Mill's *Essay on Liberty*.[1]

For reasons stated in the Introduction, we will omit Plato's writings from consideration here. If we did consider them, we should find what any undergraduate philosophy major knows: that, for Plato, only the philosophically-trained intelligence, inspired by love of Being under its aspects of the True, the Good, and Beauty, is fit to govern either itself or others. Freedom, therefore, to the extent that Plato advocated it, is for the sake of that kind of intelligence. Rightly or wrongly, he did not hesitate to banish poets from his republic.

We shall analyze the other items in the literature mentioned by Kendall and a number of other writings that can be regarded as major contributions to the theory of freedom of speech and press. As I said in the Introduction, in deciding what these major contributions are, I have let myself be guided largely by Professor Emerson because he believes that the works he names point to an absolute freedom of expression, and I hope to show that they do not. They may be taken, on either interpretation, as having shaped the modern tradition of freedom of expression. It is, as we have said, a tradition that developed only after the invention of the printing press. Modern ideas of intellectual freedom, of course, have been formed as much at least by the Reformation and the Enlightenment as by Gutenberg's invention. Yet freedom to publish one's views has been a major object of the struggle for intellectual freedom in the modern period and has furnished the occasion for most of the writings dealt with here.

We may, then, appropriately begin with John Milton's *Areopagitica*, which is said to be "the first work devoted primarily to freedom of the press."[2] The question usually asked concerning *Areopagitica* is what was the freedom of the press for which Milton contended. But the question of greater importance to our inquiry is, whatever may have been Milton's immediate objective, how broad are the conclusions regarding freedom of expression that can be drawn from his arguments.

Neither of them is an easy question to answer. As its subtitle declares, *Areopagitica* is a plea "for the liberty of unlicenc'd printing." But it is not clear, nor is it universally agreed among scholars, how far Milton meant to go in his attack on censorship. As Arthur Edward Barker has remarked, "In spite of the radical tone of its arguments, ... the extent of the freedom Milton demands remains uncertainly restricted."[3]

What Milton openly advocated in *Areopagitica* was considerably less than full freedom of the press as it is understood in modern liberal democracies. This fact does not of itself exclude the possibility that a greater freedom than he contended for was implicit in his premises and arguments. But all that he explicitly demanded was the abolition of the official prior censorship of books that had been established by an Order of Parliament in June 1643, somewhat over a year before Milton published his pamphlet.

The key phrase of this Order required that no "Book, Pamphlet, paper ... shall from henceforth be printed ... by any person or persons whatsoever, unlesse the same be first approved of and licensed under the hands of such person or persons as both, or either of the said Houses [of Parliament] shall appoint for the licensing of the same."[4] Milton's declared object in *Areopagitica* was to persuade Parliament to revoke this requirement of licensing (as Parliament finally did only in 1695). It was compatible with this purpose to accept the punishment of authors and printers of books subsequent to publication and to set limits to the views that could be published without punishment. That was in fact Milton's explicit position[5] — though it remains possible that he really wanted more than he openly asked for.[6]

Milton asserts that the licensing of books was an invention of the Council of Trent and the Spanish Inquisition, imported into England by Romanizing Anglican bishops.[7] "Till then," he says, "Books were ever as freely admitted into the World as any other birth; the issue of the brain was no more stifl'd than the issue of the womb ...; but if it prov'd a Monster, who denies, but that it was justly burnt, or sunk into the sea."[8] Again, Milton approves an earlier parliamentary order

> that no book be Printed, unlesse the Printers and the Authors name, or at least the Printers be register'd. Those which other wise come forth, if they be found mischievous and libellous, the fire and the executioner will be the timeliest and the most effectuall remedy, that man's prevention can use.[9]

Milton, then, opposes prior censorship or licensing but accepts subsequent punishment for "mischievous" (without defining the term) and libellous publications. He also indicates in the following passage that the toleration of the publication of diverse opinions that he proposes has limits.

> Yet if all cannot be of one mind, as who looks they should be? this doubtles is more wholesome, more prudent, and more Christian that many be tolerated, rather than all compell'd. I mean not tolerated Popery, and open superstition, which as it extirpats all religions, and civill supremacies, so it self should be extirpat ...: that also which is impious or evil absolutely either against faith or maners no law can possibly permit, that intends not to unlaw it self: but those neighboring differences, or rather indifferences, are what I speak of, whether in some point of doctrine or of discipline.[10]

Milton has often been hailed as a herald of the modern liberty of the press.[11] But, because of the restrictions he placed on toleration, others have taken a dim view of his liberalism. Thus Leonard W. Levy says:

"Unquestionably several passages in the *Areopagitica*, which are ritualistically quoted to the exclusion of all else, carry implications of majestic breadth, but no one who reads him with care should refer to 'Milton's dream of free speech for everybody.' " In fact, Levy claims, Milton's tolerance extended only to "Protestantism in a variety of Puritan forms."[12]

Willmoore Kendall, in the article previously quoted, contends that *Areopagitica* does not belong at all among the classics of freedom of thought and speech. Rather, it is really an anti-freedom tract.[13] It lends itself easily to misinterpretation, Kendall concedes, because it "abounds in passages, highly quotable because of their intoxicating rhetoric, which when wrenched from context do indeed seem to commit Milton to the libertarian 'side' on the freedom of thought and speech issue." But Milton is arguing only for tolerance within an essentially closed society whose members are in such full agreement about important things that they can afford to tolerate one another. "The 'principles' that should have 'led Milton on' to demand a still broader toleration," says Kendall, "are simply not there."[14]

Enough has been said to indicate that there is considerable disagreement about the extent of the freedom that Milton advocated in *Areopagitica*. One source of the disagreement is the nature of *Areopagitica* itself. It was not a dispassionate and exhaustive investigation of the whole question of freedom to think and to publish one's thoughts. It was a pamphlet aimed at an immediate practical result: the repeal of the parliamentary Licencing Order. There is no reason to doubt Milton's sincerity, but in a pamphlet written with such an object, a man may well say both more and less than he would say in a philosophical treatise.

But for our purpose we may leave unanswered the question of what Milton "really meant" and how far he wanted to go in *Areopagitica* and may proceed upon a different premise. We shall borrow it from a paper read by the Dean of St. Paul's, W. R. Matthews, at a conference held in London in 1944 to commemorate the tercentenary of the publication of *Areopagitica*, where he said:

> We must own that Milton's conception of the nature of tolerable books was limited, and it appears that many who have not recently read his book have an exaggerated notion of what he urges as reasonable liberty.... Are we wrong, then, in venerating Milton as a pioneer of intellectual freedom? Certainly we are, if we regard only what he himself intended, but we are right if we regard the arguments he used, for they carry us beyond the limits which he would have imposed.[15]

Now, to accept Dean Matthews's position is to do what Willmoore Kendall has told us we must not do, namely, to find "principles" that should have "led Milton on," but which are simply not there in his work.

Let us assume Dean Matthews's reading of Milton nonetheless, not as demonstrably the correct reading, but as the most liberal one that can reasonably be sustained. Let us agree, for the sake of argument, that the arguments Milton used "carry us beyond the limits which he would have imposed." We may then ask to what limits, or lack thereof, they carry us in regard to freedom of expression.

Milton states in general terms two chief goals to be achieved by allowing the publication of books without prior censorship. He says that "books freely permitted are [a means] both to the triall of vertue, and the exercise of truth."[16] In more modern terminology, reading a wide range of books that have been published without previous restraint helps men to develop their moral characters and to pursue truth.

Since that is the substance of Milton's case against censorship, he of course devotes his efforts to showing that freedom to publish really does serve the ends he states for it. But to argue for a freedom on the basis of the ends it serves is to make the freedom less than absolute. For those uses of a freedom that do not promote—still more those which actually inhibit—the achievement of the end are not justified by the end and may even be prohibited by it. We may therefore ask how much freedom to publish can be inferred from the goals that Milton alleges to be served by the unrestrained publication of books.

Let us first consider the "exercise of truth." Truth, for Milton, is to be pursued by the use of human reason. Books are important because they embody, as it were, reason. Thus he says:

> Books are not absolutely dead things, but doe contain a potencie of life in them to be as active as that soule was whose progency they are; nay they do preserve as in a violl the purest efficacy and extraction of that living intellect that bred them.

It is for this reason that Milton admits that Church and Commonwealth may keep a vigilant eye on books and may "confine, imprison, and do sharpest justice on them as malefactors": they are like the dragon's teeth in the fable, and "being sown up and down, may chance to spring up armed men."[17]

Milton's real point, however, is that suppressing books is an attack on reason and on truth. He therefore immediately adds:

> And yet on the other hand unlesse warinesse be us'd, as good almost kill a Man as kill a good Book; who kills a Man kills a reasonable creature, Gods image; but hee who destroyes a good Booke, kills reason it selfe, kills the Image of God, as it were in the eye.[18]

In this line of argument, then, books are valuable as expressions of reason. The function of reason is to seek truth. It is not necessary that the books that reason produces or uses should express only true opinions, since even erroneous ones have their uses. On this point Milton appeals to the authority of the eminent and learned member of Parliament, John Selden, who, he says, has proved "that all opinions, yea errors, known, read, and collated, are of main service & assistance toward the speedy attainment of what is truest."[19]

Milton therefore is thinking primarily of the writing and the reading of books by intelligent and learned men. Having argued at length that the licensing system does not and cannot achieve the goal at which it aims, namely the protection of the people against intellectual and moral corruption, he continues: "I lastly proceed from the no good it can do, to the manifest hurt it causes, in being first the greatest discouragement and affront, that can be offer'd to learning and to learned men." Milton means those who "evidently were born to study, and love lerning for it self, not for lucre, or any other end, but the service of God and of truth."[20]

When such "a man writes to the world, he summons up all his reason and deliberation to assist him; he searches, meditats, is industrious, and likely consults and conferrs with his judicious friends; after all which done he takes himself to be inform'd in what he writes, as well as any that writ before him."[21] What, then, can be more fair than to let a man of this kind "openly by writing publish to the world what his opinion is, what his reasons, and wherefore that which is now thought cannot be sound"?[22]

When a man has done hard intellectual labor "only that he may try the matter by dint of argument," for his opponents to silence him by prior censorship "is but weaknes and cowardise in the wars of Truth. For who knows not that Truth is strong next to the Almighty; she needs no policies, nor stratagems, nor licencings to make her victorious."[23]

The liberty that Milton seeks to defend is that of sincere, though possibly erring, seekers after truth. His argument assumes that truth, while never completely grasped, is attainable, that progress in finding it can be made, and that truth will emerge from open and honest intellectual debate. This is so even in regard to religious truth, from the discovery of which reason is by no means excluded. According to Barker, in the group of pamphlets of which *Areopagitica* forms a part,[24] "the emphasis is not on reformation and divine prescript [as it was in Milton's earlier pamphlets] but on liberty and free reasoning. Instead of a rebuilding according to the clearly revealed pattern, reformation becomes a progressive search for truth."[25]

What, then, is Milton's conception of truth? "Truth," he says, "indeed came once into the world with her divine Master, and was a perfect shape most glorious to look on." But after the death of His apostles, "a wicked race of deceivers" arose who hewed the body of Truth into pieces. Since that time "the sad friends of Truth" have been "gathering up limb by limb." But we shall not find them all "till her Masters second comming; he shall bring together every joynt and member, and shall mould them into an immortall feature of lovelines and perfection." In the meantime, we must not prevent men by licensing laws from trying "to unite those dissever'd peeces which are yet wanting to the body of Truth." On the contrary:

> To be still searching what we know not, by what we know, still closing up truth to truth as we find it (for all her body is *homogeneal*, and proportionall) this is the golden rule in *Theology* as well as in Arithmetick, and makes up the best harmony in a Church; not the forc't and outward union of cold, and neutrall, and inwardly divided minds.[26]

Milton was neither a skeptic nor a relativist. Sirluck points out: "What must be emphasized is that although the truth is now known only in part, this part is absolutely known."[27] We search for what we know not by what we do know. Nor need we fear that the search will end in anything other than the truth. Milton assures us:

> And though all the winds of doctrin were let loose to play upon the earth, so Truth be in the field, we do injuriously by licencing and prohibiting to misdoubt her strength. Let her and Falshood grapple; who every knew Truth put to the wors, in a free and open encounter. Her confuting is the best and surest suppressing.[28]

At least in the part of *Areopagitica* in which Milton contends that freedom to publish will certainly forward the pursuit of truth, he seems open to B. Ifor Evans's comment:

> His conception is based ultimately on the conditions which might have prevailed in a small Athenian community had printing been then invented. It presupposes a small audience, all of them capable of forming their own judgments, with ample discussion to correct false views. He has in mind the formulation of adequate conclusions by a Socratic method. Even the England of his own day did not fit that picture altogether, and the world of our own does not fit it at all. A small group of men in full command over the machinery of the press, or of the radio, effect a secret tyranny over the minds of millions.[29]

Whatever one may think of the alleged tyranny of the communications media, as we now call them, it would seem that Milton's argument is most applicable to academic publications. Its applicability diminishes steadily as one moves out of the academic world, in which a reasoned presentation of one's views must at least appear to be made, into a world of writing in which there is far less, and often no, pretense at the rational pursuit of truth. If one wishes to defend an unqualified freedom of expression in such publications as gossip columns, commercial advertisements, comic books, pornographic magazines and films, and other forms of popular entertainment, one must look for arguments elsewhere than in this part of *Areopagitica*. An argument proves no more than it proves, and all that Milton is here trying to prove is that freedom to present a reasoned exposition of one's views will aid the pursuit of truth. He is not speaking of catering to tastes that have little or nothing to do with a desire for the truth.

There is, however, another line of argument in *Areopagitica* that may be more to the purpose of defending an absolute freedom of expression, the one concerned with "the triall of vertue." Here Milton argues that the knowledge of good depends upon the knowledge of evil, and the development of virtue upon confrontation with vice. This state of affairs is the result of original sin:

> It was from out the rinde of one apple tasted, that the knowledge of good and evill as two twins cleaving together leapt forth into the World. And perhaps this is that doom which *Adam* fell into of knowing good and evill, that is to say of knowing good by evill.[30]

We are no longer living in the Garden of Eden, and this has important consequences for our moral lives.

> As therefore the state of man now is; what wisdome can there be to choose, what continence to forbeare without the knowledge of evill? He that can apprehend and consider vice with all her baits and seeming pleasures, and yet abstain, and yet distinguish, and yet prefer that which is truly better, he is the true wayfaring Christian.[31]

Because we are born in sin, "we bring not innocence into the world, we bring impurity much rather." We can no longer, therefore, seek the vanished virtue of a prelapsarian innocence: "that which purifies us is triall, and triall is by what is contrary." We must not flee the knowledge of evil: "That vertue therefore which is but a youngling in the contemplation of evill, and knows not the utmost that vice promises to her followers, and rejects it, is but a blank vertue, not a pure." And this, says Milton, "was the reason why our sage and serious Poet *Spencer* ... describing true temperance under the person of *Guion*, brings him in with his palmer through the cave of Mammon, and the bowr of earthly blisse that he might see and know, and yet abstain."[32]

It might seem to follow that true wayfaring Christian should perform his own rite of passage through such bowers of earthly bliss as are available by frequenting taverns, brothels, gaming houses and opium dens in order to see and know, and yet abstain. But Milton does not draw that conclusion. Instead, he says:

> Since therefore the knowledge and survay of vice is in this world so necessary to the constituting of human vertue, and the scanning of error to the confirmation of truth, how can we more safely, and with less

danger scout into the regions of sin and falsity then by reading all manner of tractats, and hearing all manner of reason? And this is the benefit which may be had of books promiscuously read.[33]

The unrestricted reading of books, and therefore their unrestrained publication, is a positive aid to moral growth, with which wise and good men cannot dispense. Milton does not deny that to the many who are weak, reading bad books may be a temptation or at best a waste of time. He is content to say that "bad books ... to a discreet and judicious Reader serve in many respects to discover, to confute, to forewarn, and to illustrate,"[34] and to insist that to mature men

> such books are not temptations, nor vanities; but usefull drugs and materialls wherewith to temper and compose effective and strong med'cins, which mans life cannot want. The rest, as children and childish men, who have not the art to qualifie and prepare these working minerals, well may be exhorted to forbear, but hinder'd forcibly they cannot be by all the licencing that Sainted Inquisition could ever yet contrive.[35]

This leads Milton into his next contention, namely, that the attempt to protect the masses from temptation by licensing publications simply will not succeed. Furthermore, he argues, if we hope "to rectifie manners" by regulating printing, in consistency "we must regulat all recreations and pastimes, all that is delightful to man," but that will only "make us all both ridiculous and weary, and yet frustrat."[36] We must accept the fact that all the pleasures of life are subject to abuse, and that it is not the licensing of books or of anything else that will restrain the abuses. We must rather rely on "those unwritt'n or at least unconstraining laws of vertuous education, religious and civill nurture ...; these they be which shall bear chief sway in such matters as these, when all licensing will be easily eluded."[37]

God Himself, after all, showers us with "all desirable things," while commanding us to be temperate, just, and continent. "Why should we then affect a rigor contrary to the manner of God and nature, by abriding or scanting those means, which books freely permitted are, both to the triall of vertue, and the exercise of truth." We should rather "learn that the law must needs be frivolous which goes to restrain things, uncertainly and yet equally working to good, and to evill."[38]

Milton's thesis is no more than that the effort to protect morals by prior censorship is bound both to be ineffective and to deprive good men of a positive benefit. But the arguments he presents for his thesis would seem to sustain the further conclusion that the publication of books should not be subject on moral grounds to subsequent punishment. For the latter, too, is and is intended to be a restraint on publication. If, then, the publication of books that present vice in its most alluring forms is on the whole a benefit to mankind, it ought to be free of any legal restraint either previous or subsequent.

One reason for not accepting this conclusion is that, as one writer has put it, Milton himself allows for the suppression as well as the publication of books and his "opposition seems to be not so much against a policy which will permit suppression as against a policy which would put the power of restraint into the hands of unfit persons."[39] This much is true, that throughout *Areopagitica* Milton's wrath is directed chiefly against the requirement that a writer's work, before it can appear in print, must be subject to what in one place he calls "the hasty view of an unleasur'd licencer, perhaps much his younger, perhaps far his inferiour in judgement, perhaps one who never knew the labour of book-writing."[40]

But it can be replied to this that in *Areopagitica* Milton was preoccupied with licensing and prior censorship precisely because a Licencing Order was in effect and the immediate need was to have it repealed. It does not follow that he would have been willing to have writers and printers subject to subsequent penalties for publishing the kind of "bad books" that he defended.

That leads to the more basic question, how wide a range of books did Milton defend? A French writer, Jean-Jacques Mayoux, has described the liberty that Milton advocated in very broad terms, but none the less with significant limitations. The important theme of *Areopagitica*, he says, is the urgent plea that it makes for freedom to write everything, to read everything, and to experience everything at least in imagination, as a necessary element of the moral liberty of a responsible person.[11] Milton, he says, defends not only man as the rational and autonomous master of himself, but man as the experiencer of pleasure. Himself a Puritan, Milton takes a malicious pleasure in ridiculing all puritans from Plato onwards. This is Milton the artist and man of sensibility speaking.[12] And yet, Mayoux adds, we must not make Milton into the kind of contemporary critic who pleads the cause of *The Story of O* or the writings of the Marquis de Sade. "The idea that one can read or write without bearing one's responsibility in mind never occurred to him, would have seemed to him devoid of sense."[43]

In *Areopagitica* Milton discusses what Herbert Read calls the "scurrilous writers of antiquity" and, according to Read, "is clearly of the opinion that there never was a case for suppressing any of them." He refers also to "Milton's tolerance of the printing even of obscenities."[44] But tolerating the occasional scurrility or obscenity of acknowledged classics seems to be about as far as Milton was willing to go.

Allen H. Gilbert devoted an article to Milton's views on obscenity, and concluded with the following remarks, which are worth quoting *in extenso*.

Milton deals with the use of plain or bawdy language in two situations. The first is the instance of strong feeling, as when God denounced the wickedness of the Jews. The second is the comic employment of such language....

The comic authors Milton liked suggest what his practice would have been had he attempted comedy. Aristophanes he calls the "loosest" of the old comedians and a book "of grossest infamy," yet he refers to the Greek as though not unfamiliar with him, and annotators have traced to him passages in *Paradise Regained*. He had no objections to the reading of "scurrill Plautus" and thought his jests, like those of the old Greek comedians, "elegant, urbane, clever, and witty." The bawdry of Shakespeare and Jonson did not cause Milton to withhold his admiration. The sexual double meaning jocosely employed [by Milton himself] in the attack on [Alexander] More is quite such as a comic author familiar with Italian literature might employ.

Altogether, Milton's literary background, his theory of what is allowable in stirring up laughter, and his practice in both verse and prose ... lead one to suppose that had he attempted comedy, he would when required by decorum—"the grand masterpiece to observe"—not have hestitated to set down passages as bawdy as some of those in Jonson and Shakespeare, his favorite English comedians.[45]

But there is a considerable distance between the bawdiest passages in Aristophanes, Plautus, Shakespeare or Jonson and *The Story of O* or *Deep Throat*. That is to say, there is a difference between the occasional and, in Milton's eyes, justified use of obscenity in literature and works that pander to prurience, morbid curiosity, lust and the appetite for violence.

There remains the question of the literature that, according to Milton, reveals "vice with all her baits and seeming pleasures" and presents "the utmost that vice promises to her followers."[46] Milton does not name it. Presumably it is the same scurrilous literature, largely of antiquity, that he has been discussing up to that point in his text. Furthermore, most of it was not in English and so could be read only by the learned who presumably would read it with the same detachment as John Milton.

Milton wrote *Areopagitica* at the end of an age when, as Donald Thomas points out, "the erotic or bawdy classics of European literature were not English nor, as a rule, available in English translations." That era was coming to a close, as is indicated by a petition organized by the Puritans in 1640 against "[t]he swarming of lascivious, idle, and unprofitable books and Pamphlets, Play-Books, and Ballads." Yet all the works that Thomas mentions as examples of the new wave of obscenity appeared in English after the publication of *Areopagitica*[47] and so were hardly in Milton's mind as works available to the general public or even to that small part of it which was literate in English but in no other tongue.

Be that as it may, it is worth remarking that the conclusion of his defense of freely permitting books as a means to "the triall of vertue and the exercise of truth" is that "the law must needs be frivolous which goes to restrain things, uncertainly and yet equally working to good, and to evill."[48] A literature that works equally to good and to evil may indeed contain passages that offend pious ears or create temptations for the immature. But it is surely something less than a massive and sustained solicitation to vice.

Milton's defense of "books promiscuously read" is that they serve a moral as well as an intellectual end: "the knowledge and survay of vice [that] is in this world so necessary to the constituting of human vertue."[49] One must ask, then, how much and what kind of survey of vice is needed to constitute human virtue. The works that set before the reader the utmost that vice promises to her followers must be compatible with this end. If one wishes to use Milton's argument in favor of absolute freedom of expression, one must show that it serves the moral end by which he justifies reading "bad books." Today, that would require a demonstration that every possible presentation of vice, complete with audio-visual aids, is necessary or at least useful for the development of moral character.

It would not be necessary to show that the works protected by absolute freedom of expression are *intended* to serve a moral end. Milton defended reading works which he regarded as immoral in their intention. But it would be necessary to show that the works protected *do* in fact serve a moral end. Milton clearly thought that the immoral works of literature that were available in his day served such a purpose, at least for a judicious reader. It does not follow that he would have thought the same about all of the immoral or merely trivial publications available today. More importantly—since what Milton would have thought is not the controlling consideration—it is taxing credulity to maintain that we can stretch his justification of "bad books" to cover the whole range of publications on our contemporary market. That would be asking us to believe that pandering to the lowest tastes of a mass audience performs the function of helping the true wayfaring Christian—or, for that matter, the highminded agnostic—to see and know, and yet abstain.

Granted Milton's contention that one cannot be truly temperate who has not experienced and learned to master the enticements of pleasure, it does not follow that an unrelenting assault on the passions is an aid to temperance. Milton's thesis, after all, is that "passions within us, pleasures round about us ... *rightly temper'd* are the very ingredients of vertue."[50] There must be some proportion between the means and the end if one wishes to remain within the framework of Milton's thought. But today there is a vast quantity of publication—including photographs, films, records, and other products of modern technology—that makes no pretense or only the flimsiest pretense of serving any end other than the uninhibited satisfaction of desire. One finds in it no proportion between the means employed and a moral (or, for that matter, an aesthetic) end. It is this kind of publication, above all, that is defended by the plea for absolute freedom of expression, because the meaning of the plea is that expression is a value in itself and needs no relationship to a justifying, and potentially limiting, purpose.

To absolutize freedom of expression by detaching it from purpose is therefore not only to go beyond anything that Milton advocated but beyond anything that can reasonably be inferred from his premises. In *Areopagitica,* Milton was contending for the removal of certain limits on publication, and therefore gave only passing attention to the limits that he would maintain. Those that he mentioned were certainly more stringent than would be generally acceptable today. But even if we agree with Dean Matthews that Milton's arguments carry us beyond the limits which he would have imposed, his arguments do not lead to the conclusion that there should be no limits. To the extent, then, that Milton represents or, on a liberal interpretation of his thought, can be made to represent the intellectual tradition in favor of freedom of the press, the contemporary absolutist position on freedom of expression is not a development but a perversion of that tradition.

3

The Liberal
Christian Conscience

John Locke

"To the extent that modern liberalism can be said to be inspired by any one writer, Locke is undoubtedly the leading candidate." So says Sheldon Wolin,[1] and not many will dispute with him. Locke's contribution to the theory of freedom of speech and press is indirect, however. He wrote little on that subject and is relevant to the broader campaign for freedom of thought chiefly through his argument in favor of religious toleration. Nonetheless his influence in establishing the liberal doctrine of freedom to express opinions was so large that he must be considered here.

According to Ernst Troeltsch, Locke's "advocacy of freedom of worship also meant freedom for philosophical and theological interests, and security for freedom of thought outside the churches."[2] The implications of Locke's plea for religious toleration no doubt extended that far. Leonard Levy's more jaundiced interpretation of Locke's objective, however, is also more accurate. Locke, he says, "evinced sustained interest in the problems of freedom of expression only in connection with his preoccupation for protecting liberty of conscience, the subject of his four *Letters on Toleration* ... [and] addressed himself mainly to freedom for sectarian rather than secular expression."[3]

Levy nevertheless sees Locke as "adding a new dimension to the arguments for civil liberty" in his *Essay Concerning Human Understanding.*[4] He employed the same arguments for intellectual tolerance that his predecessors had used, but "relied mainly on the contention that the mind is so frail, its understanding so limited, its beliefs so involuntary, that truth is inaccessible to it."[5] That Locke thought truth simply inaccessible is an exaggeration. Yet we may agree with Richard Ashcraft, that "[w]hat is striking about the *Essay Concerning Human Understanding* is not the claims it advances on behalf of human reason, but rather, its assertion of the meagreness of human knowledge."[6] It was the meagreness of knowledge in the strict sense, i.e., of what men could know by direct experiential intuition or by reasoned demonstration, and the consequent "necessity of believing, without knowledge, nay, often upon very slight grounds," that led Locke to say that "it would methinks become all men to maintain peace, and the common offices of humanity and friendship, in the diversity of opinions."[7]

Some critics see his *Essay* as so severely limiting human reason that it can no longer serve as the source of moral and political theory. Thus, Ellis Sandoz says that in the *Essay* "reason" is taken

> in the narrow sense of discursive intelligence or the inferential faculty; it thereby becomes synonymous with *reasoning*, exclusive of common sense, on the one hand, and of the intuitive or noetic intelligence, on the other, on which all rationality ultimately depends. Such "reason" becomes the new test of all knowledge on the basis of the sensationalist (empirical) epistemology of the *Essay*.[8]

According to Sandoz, Locke has a "systematic intention to break with the classical and Christian tradition in philosophy and religion while appearing to be the true advocate of that tradition."[9] In saying this, Sandoz echoes the well-known criticism of Locke made by the late Leo Strauss.[10] Locke, says Strauss, revolutionized the theory of natural law to such an extent that his "law of nature is not a law in the proper sense of the term." The goals of human life are no longer objective goods discoverable by reason but are simply the objects of men's passionate desire for pleasure and aversion from pain. Reason is thus reduced to the instrumental role of finding effective means to nonrational ends, and the "law of nature is nothing other than the sum of the dictates of reason in regard to men's 'mutual security' or to 'the peace and safety' of mankind." The law of nature, therefore, is not founded on the natural constitution of man but is "a creature of the understanding," a mere mental construct that enables men to achieve their goals in mutual peace and security.[11]

"Consequently," as another writer, James W. Byrne, puts it, "the conclusion of Locke's *Essay* ultimately eliminates the use of the 'law of nature' as a consistent principle of Locke's moral philosophy ... Locke's moral judgments in political affairs are a real expediency based on utilitarian considerations."[12] In the same vein F. E. Devine concludes: "The validity of laws for Locke—as for Hobbes—comes to rest, not on reason, but on consent."[13]

These criticisms of Locke's conception of reason and of the law of nature are by no means without substance. Throughout the *Essay*, Locke expounds a nominalist metaphysics. "Metaphysical truth," he says in one place, "... is nothing but the real existence of things, conformable to the

ideas we have annexed to their names. This, though it seems to consist in
the very beings of things, yet, when considered a little nearly, will appear
to include a tacit proposition, whereby the mind joins that particular
thing to the idea it had before settled with a name to it."[14] We do not
know "the internal constitution and true nature of things, being destitute
of faculties to attain it."[15] Substances do indeed have real essences, but we
do not know them. All that we know is the nominal essence ("the idea ...
before settled with a name to it") that our mind has framed for a
substance.[16]

Furthermore, the real essence of a thing is not a specific essence. It is
the particular constitution of the thing, which makes it *this* thing,
nothing more. From it flow properties (qualities, accidents) that certain
other things also have, and on the basis of which we can classify them in
the same species. But the common essence that we attribute to the
members of the species is a merely nominal essence, an abstract idea.
Men *make* such abstract ideas and "thereby enable themselves to consider things, and discourse of them as it were in bundles," for reasons of
convenience.[17] But "universality belongs not to things themselves, which
are all of them particular in their existence." General ideas "are the
inventions and creatures of the understanding, made by it for its own
use."[18]

Our abstract ideas of the natures or essences of substances are composed from sense impressions; they "are such combinations of simple
ideas [immediate sense impressions] as are really united, and co-exist in
things without us."[19] The same is true of our idea of the nature of man.
We base it on the way human beings ordinarily look and on how we see
them act, but we do not know any objectively real, specific nature of man.
"For though perhaps voluntary motion, with sense and reason, joined to
a body of a certain shape, be the complex idea to which I, and others,
annex the name man, and so be the nominal essence of the species so
called; yet nobody will say that complex idea is the real essence and
source of all those operations which are to be found in any individual of
that sort."[20] Accordingly, it is impossible to say that an idea of man which
makes rationality his defining characteristic is a better description of his
real essence than one based on his outward appearance.[21]

Locke is even more thoroughly a nominalist in his moral philosophy.
"The names of simple ideas and substances, with the abstract ideas in the
mind which they immediately signify, intimate also some real existence,
from which was derived their original pattern," he says. "But the names
of mixed modes terminate in the idea that is in the mind, and lead not
the thoughts any farther."[22] Now, virtues and vices are mixed modes. But
the essence of each species of mixed mode, therefore of every virtue and
vice, is made by the human mind alone, since it is only a voluntary

combination of simple ideas, with "no other sensible standard existing anywhere but the name itself," to which we may conform it. Consequently, when a man is said to have a false idea of justice or gratitude, it means only that his idea does not agree with the one commonly in use.[23]

Morality is thus a mental construct, and an arbitrary one at that. The "essences of the species of mixed modes are not only made by the mind, but made very arbitrarily, made without patterns, or reference to any real existence."[24] So, for example: "What the word murder or sacrilege, &c. signifies, can never be known from things themselves," because the visible part of the action has no necessary connection with the other ideas that make up the complex idea of the crime. "They have their union and combination only from the understanding, which unites them under one name: but uniting them without any rule or pattern," the mind produces "arbitrary ideas."[25] "And hence we see," says Locke, "that in the interpretation of laws, whether divine or human, there is no end; ... and of limiting, distinguishing, varying the signification of these moral words, there is no end."[26] One begins to see why Locke was disposed in favor of religious toleration.

Not surprisingly, Locke is also a hedonist. He says, for instance:

> Things then are good or evil only in reference to pleasure or pain. That we call good, which is apt to cause or increase pleasure or diminish pain in us; or else to procure or preserve us the possession of any other good, or absence of any evil. And, on the contrary, we name that evil, which is apt to produce or increase any pain or diminish any pleasure in us; or else to procure us any evil, or deprive us of any good.[27]

All men, to be sure, desire happiness and therefore pursue the good. But the good is pleasure, and different men have different pleasures. Hence, if we confine ourselves to this world alone, the philosophic inquiry into the *summum bonum*, that which is by nature the highest good for man, is vain.[28] We get a different view, however, if we think of happiness in the light of God's law and of His rewards and punishments in the next life.

All law, Locke explains, supposes penalty and reward, i.e., "some good and evil that is not the natural product and consequence of the action itself. For that being a natural convenience, or inconvenience, would operate of itself without a law."[29] Morality thus becomes a matter of penal law. "Moral good and evil then is only the conformity or disagreement of our voluntary actions to some law, whereby good or evil is drawn upon us by the will and power of the law-maker; which good and evil, pleasure or pain, attending over our observance or breach of the law by the decree of the law-maker, is what we call reward and punishment."[30]

The highest law, of course, is "the divine law, whereby I mean that law which God has set to the actions of men, whether promulgated to them by the light of nature, or the voice of revelation." God's law, therefore "is the only true touchstone of moral rectitude" because by it alone can men judge whether their actions "are like to procure them happiness or misery from the hands of the Almighty."[31]

Men commonly live in a state of uneasiness caused by their desire for the worldly goods that they think would make them happy. They are apt to conclude that they can be happy without "the greatest absent good," and are little moved by the thought of "the joys of a future state." But to him who can check his present desires and take time to reflect, a different conclusion suggests itself.

> Change but a man's view of these things; let him see that virtue and religion are necessary to his happiness; let him look into the future state of bliss or misery, and see there God, the righteous judge, ... to him, I say, who hath a prospect of the different state of perfect happiness or misery that attends all men after this life, depending on their behaviour here, the measures of good and evil, that govern his choice, are mightily changed.[32]

Or, as Locke put it more pointedly in *The Reasonableness of Christianity*, when the eternal reward is put on one side of the scale, "virtue now is visibly the most enriching purchase, and by much the best bargain."[33]

Locke thus appears as ultimately a voluntarist: it is the *will* of God that makes his moral philosophy hang together. One understands, therefore, why a number of scholars have seen him as making a break with the tradition of natural law. Locke's nominalism and hedonism, with the individualism that is implicit in them, would, if pushed to their logical conclusions, lead to the abandonment of the idea of a moral law founded on the nature of man.

Later generations of liberals did abandon it. But, if Locke was a founder of liberalism, he was a pious liberal.[34] As J. W. Gough says, "The God of Christianity was the unquestioned ultimate presupposition of all his thought, and the faculty of reason really operated within a sphere conditioned by his religious faith.... Granted this faith, the whole structure hangs together."[35] Consequently, says Gough, "Locke's account of the law of nature as a whole ... might not unfairly be described as roughly equivalent to the moral duties normally expected of a Protestant Chrisitian in the seventeenth century" and "its real meaning for him" was "the dictates of the conscience of contemporary Protestantism."[36]

Nonetheless, Locke was in his own way supremely a rationalist. Hans Aarsleff, who insists that Locke was a consistent natural-law philosopher, says: "It is Locke's fundamental belief, stated again and again, and indispensable to his entire philosophy, that man is 'by nature rational' and hence capable of knowledge, gained by the play of reason on the materials provided by sense-experience and reflexion, and gained to varying degrees, by different men in proportion to their native endowments, their efforts, and their opportunities."[37] That, of course, is the point at issue: whether knowledge, gained by the play of reason on the materials provided by sense experience and reflection, as Locke uses these terms, is sufficient to found a doctrine of natural law or, indeed, any moral philosophy other than a species of utilitarianism. There are those who hold that Locke himself came to doubt it.[38] Yet, whatever his ultimate misgivings, Locke in his major works is confident that reason is, in principle, adequate for the guidance of human life.

We shall return to this point below. First, however, it is necessary to point out an even deeper sense in which Locke is a rationalist, namely, that for him the norm of reason's judgment is simply the perception of the agreement or disagreement among its own ideas. The world that human reason knows is very largely a world that reason has constructed according to the laws of logic. But, Locke believes, this is enough to enable man to cope with the world and to save his soul.

It is true that Locke is also an empiricist. The building blocks of all human knowledge are "simple ideas," and these are furnished by direct experience. We receive them, that is, "from corporeal objects by sensation, and from the operations of our minds as the objects of reflection."[39] Sensation and reflection "are the fountains of knowledge, from whence all the ideas we have, or can naturally have, do spring."[40]

The empirical starting point leads to a limited knowledge of real existences: "we have the knowledge of our own existence by intuition ["an internal infallible perception that we are"]; of the existence of God by demonstration; and of other things by sensation."[41] Some people, Locke says, doubt whether we can with certainty infer the existence of external objects from the simple ideas that we have of them. But Locke himself is certain that we have knowledge "of the existence of particular external objects, by that perception and consciousness we have of the actual entrance of ideas from them."[42]

These three—God, ourselves and sense objects—exhaust our knowledge of existence, since "real existence ... has no connection with any other of our ideas."[43] For the rest, "all general knowledge lies only in our thoughts, and consists barely in the contemplation of our own abstract ideas."[44] Locke goes farther. "Knowledge," he says, "seems to me to be nothing but the perception of the connexion and agreement, or disagreement and repugnancy, of any of our ideas. In this alone it consists."[45] "It is the first act of the mind," he explains, "when it has any sentiments or ideas at all, to perceive its ideas; and so far as it perceives them, to know each what it is, and thereby also to perceive their difference, and that one is not another." Without this perception, "there could be no knowledge, no reasoning, no imagination, no distinct thoughts at all."[46]

This perception is gotten

> 1. Either by intuition, or the immediate comparing any two ideas; or, 2. By reason, examining the agreement or disagreement of two ideas, by the intervention of some others; or, 3. By sensation, perceiving the existence of particular things.[47]

All knowledge, then, is knowledge of ideas. Sensation, strictly speaking, is the perception of the simple idea produced in our mind by an external object when it impinges on our senses and therefore is "intuitive knowledge."[48] The mind's immediate perception of the identity or difference of two ideas is also intuition. If the mind must reason to their agreement or disagreement by using intermediate ideas, it is engaged in demonstration. Yet demonstration itself depends on intuition, because "in every step reason makes in demonstrative knowledge, there is an intuitive knowledge of that agreement or disagreement it seeks with the next intermediate idea, which it uses as a proof."[49] He concludes: "These two, viz. intuition and demonstration [which depends on intuition], are the degrees of our knowledge; whatever comes short of one of these, with what assurance soever embraced, is but faith, or opinion, but not knowledge, at least in all general truths."[50]

As will appear later, this distinction between opinion (faith) and knowledge is essential to Locke's theory of toleration. It should be added here that there is a degree of probability, short of knowledge, that amounts to virtual certainty. It belongs to propositions based on constant and widespread experience such as "the stated constitutions and properties of bodies, and the regular proceedings of causes and effects in the ordinary course of nature. This we call an argument from the nature of things themselves."[51] Science, therefore, is safe from rationalist criticism. Yet, though "we may conclude" that "things that, as far as observation reaches, we constantly find to proceed regularly, ... do act by a law set them," we must admit that they act "by a law that we know not" and so "we can have but an experimental knowledge of them."[52]

To return to the point, knowledge may be reduced to the intuition we have of the agreement or disagreement of our own ideas. But this is objective knowledge, for while one may choose to think or not to think, one cannot think whatever he pleases: "so far as men's thoughts converse with their own determined ideas, they cannot but, in some measure, observe the agreement or disagreement that is to be found amongst some of them, which is so far knowledge ... For what a man sees, he cannot but see; and what he perceives, he cannot but know that he perceives."[53]

Reason, understood as the power of the mind to perceive the agreement and disagreement of its ideas and to move through intermediate ideas to new perceptions, is the standard of truth.

> Light, true light, in the mind is or can be nothing else but the evidence of the truth of any proposition; and if it be not a self-evident proposition, all the light it has, or can have, is from the clearness and validity of those proofs upon which it is received. To talk of any other light in the understanding, is to put ourselves in the dark, or in the power of the Prince of Darkness."[54]

Locke here attacks the view of fideists who make religious faith rest upon faith itself. We must indeed, he says, believe what God has revealed, and God may reveal truths that are "beyond the discovery of reason."[55] Revelation nevertheless rests on reason, since "our assurance can be no greater than our knowledge is, that it is a revelation."[56] and "it still belongs to reason to judge of the truth of its being a revelation, and of the signification of the words wherein it is delivered."[57] The certainty of faith, therefore, cannot be greater than the certainty of reason, and nothing can be accepted on faith which is contrary to reason, i.e., "contrary to the clear perception of the agreement or disagreement of any of our ideas."[58] In short: "Reason must be our last judge and guide in every thing."[59]

Locke was keenly aware of the limitations of human knowledge. But he also had, or at least professed, an enormous confidence that, however short men's "knowledge may come of an universal or perfect comprehension of whatsoever is, it yet secures their great concernments, that they have light enough to lead them to the knowledge of their Maker, and the sight of their own duties."[60] After all, "morality and divinity" are "those parts of knowledge that men are most concerned to be clear in,"[61] and "the goodness of God hath not been wanting to men ... since he hath furnished man with those faculties, which will serve for the sufficient discovery of all things requisite to the end of such a being."[62]

The first thing requisite is a knowledge of God, and this reason gives us. "For the visible marks of extraordinary wisdom and power appear so plainly in all the works of the creation, that a rational creature, who will but seriously reflect on them, cannot miss the discovery of a Deity."[63] Nay more: "It is as certain that there is a God, as that the opposite angles, made by the intersection of two straight lines, are equal." This language may appear strong, but it is not surprising in a writer who derives all knowledge from the perception of the agreement and disagreement of ideas and therefore takes mathematics as the model form of knowledge. So convinced is Locke that the existence of God and a theorem in geometry are equally certain that he says: "There was never any rational creature, that set himself to examine the truth of these propositions, that could fail to assent to them." The obvious fact that "many men ... are ignorant both of the one and the other" is due to their "having not applied their thoughts that way."[64]

Next, men need to know the moral law, and this, too, can be known by reason. Locke devotes Book I of the *Essay* to refuting the notion that there are ideas or principles innate in the human mind. But this does not mean that he rejects "a law of nature." Rather, he says, "they equally forsake the truth, who, running into contrary extremes, either affirm an innate law, or deny that there is a law knowable by the light of nature, i.e. without the help of positive revelation."[65]

The law of nature is knowable by reason, but this is not to say that it is known by everyone, everywhere. An impartial survey of the world and its history will show "that there is scarce that principle of morality to be named, or rule of virtue to be thought on ... which is not, somewhere or other slighted and condemned by the general fashion of whole societies of men."[66] This consideration leads to the argument of *The Reasonableness of Christianity*, that the Christian revelation was necessary to teach men the moral law. On the other hand, Locke feels that enlightened self-interest carries men a long way toward a knowledge of the law of nature. Despite the variations, through time and space, in men's views of virtue and vice, on the whole their understanding of their own interest led them to a conception of virtue and vice that corresponded with the true standard of right and wrong, the law of nature and of God.[67] For, he says, "it is no wonder that esteem and discredit, virtue and vice, should in a great measure every where correspond with the unchangeable rule of right and wrong, which the law of God hath established: there being nothing that so directly and visibly secures and advances the general good of mankind in this world as obedience to the laws he has set them."[68]

But, though a view of morality based on esteem and discredit may correspond with the true standard, it gives us only "the law of opinion or reputation"[69] rather than a knowledge of the law of nature. "We must, therefore," says Locke, "if we will proceed as reason advises, adapt our methods of inquiry to the nature of the ideas we examine, and the truth we search after. General and certain truths are only founded in the habitudes and relations of abstract ideas."[70] So, too, in the realm of morals. "The idea of a Supreme Being ... and the idea of ourselves, as understanding rational beings ... would, I suppose, if duly considered and pursued, afford such foundations of our duty and rules of action, as might place morality amongst the sciences capable of demonstration."[71] This is, to borrow a phrase from Spinoza, ethics demonstrated in the manner of geometry, on the premise that morality, like mathematics, works out "the discoverable connexion and agreement" of abstract ideas whose nominal essence is there only essence.[72]

Locke, in fact, according to John Dunn, "never completed any such demonstration" of the contents of the law of nature, "although he seems to have tried frequently enough." The reason for his failure is "that such a demonstration is not in principle possible and that the development of Locke's ideas had drawn the difficulties of such an effort sharply to his attention."[73] The difficulties, no doubt, were real enough. Still, in the *Essay*, Locke professes a general optimistic rationalism: "I imagine that men, who abstract their thoughts, and do well examine the ideas of their own minds, cannot much differ in thinking, however they may perplex themselves with words."[74] In regard to moral reasoning, Locke admits that though it is modelled on mathematical reasoning, it is more difficult and more prone to error. But this, he says, "may in a good measure be remedied by definitions."[75] Whatever his private doubts, in his published works Locke maintained that a demonstrated ethics is in principle possible, if we will confine ourselves to clear and distinct ideas and to words that correspond to them exactly.

We come thus to a natural religion and a natural morality. Everything in the Old and New Testaments is "infallibly true, yet the reader may be, nay cannot choose but be, very fallible in the understanding of it." But God "hath spread before all the world such legible characters of his works and providence, and given all mankind so sufficient a light of reason, that they to whom this written word never came, could not (whenever they set themselves to search) either doubt of the being of a God, or of the obedience due to him ... the precepts of natural religion are plain, and very intelligible to all mankind, and seldom come to be controverted."[76]

Locke was not a Deist who was prepared to throw out the Christian revelation as unnecessary. But as Gough puts it, "his theology was in fact what would now be called Unitarian."[77] H. McLachlan, himself a Unitarian, agrees with this, and adds that Locke was an Arian.[78] Be that as it may, what Locke offers us in his apologia for Christianity, *The Reasonableness of Christianity*, is a stripped-down, desupernaturalized, rationalized version of the Christian revelation, with the argument that mankind needed it to do what in principle reason could and should have done, but in fact did not do.

Locke argues throughout the first hundred or so pages of *The Reasonableness* that in the New Testament the only doctrine required to be believed is that Jesus is the Messiah. He does not explicitly deny, but neither does he mention, the doctrines of the Trinity, the Incarnation, the Atonement, or the necessity of saving grace. In fact, he says, for those who have never heard of the Messiah, "the light of reason, revealed to all mankind" is sufficient for salvation.[79] The question naturally arises, and Locke poses it himself: "What need was there of a Saviour? What advantage have we by Jesus Christ?"[80] His answer comes down to the need of a Teacher sent by God to teach the natural religion clearly and with authority.

"Though the works of nature, in every part of them," he says, "sufficiently evidence a Deity; yet the world made so little use of their reason, that they saw him not, where, even by the impressions of himself, he was easy to be found." The reason for this was that "vice and superstition held the world ... the priests [heathen, of course], every-where, to secure their empire, having excluded reason from having any thing to do in religion." The one true God was found by the "rational and thinking part of mankind" when they searched for Him, but they "had never authority enough to prevail on the multitude."[81] But when our Savior came, "the clear revelation he brought with him dissipated this darkness."[82]

Again, although natural reason in principle could work out the principles of morality, it turns out "that it is too hard a task for unassisted reason to establish morality in all its parts, upon its true foundation, with a clear and convincing light." Once moral principles have been revealed, "they are found to be agreeable to reason." But "[e]xperience shows, that the knowledge of morality, by mere natural light (how agreeable soever it be to it) makes but a slow progress, and little advance in the world." Men were too sunk in their "necessities, passions, vices, and mistaken interests" to develop a complete natural morality. The plain fact is "that human reason unassisted failed men in its great and proper business of morality. It never from unquestionable principles, by clear deductions, made out an entire body of the 'law of nature.'"[83]

In accordance with his rationalism, Locke understands natural law as a code deduced by a method analogous to that of mathematics, and it appears that no one, either before or after Christ, has worked out "any such code" of natural morality. "It is true, there is a law of nature: but who is there that ever did, or undertook to give it us all entire, as a law; no more, nor no less, than what was contained in, and had the obliga-tions of that law?" No one;[84] yet men need "such a morality; such a law" to guide them, and this is what Christ supplies. "Such a morality Jesus Christ hath given us in the New Testament," not, however, by rational demonstration but "by revelation." The rule he gives us is "conformable to that of reason," but "the truth and obligation of its precepts" rest upon "the authority of God."[85]

Nor could it really have been otherwise. Reason, it is true, had discovered "[t]hose just measures of right and wrong" on which the

existence of human society depends. But they were not seen as obliga-
tory precepts of "the highest law, the law of nature," because prior to
Christ men were "without a clear knowledge and acknowledgment of the
law-maker, and the great rewards and punishments for those who would
or would not obey him." This knowledge of the true character and
binding force of the law of nature we have from revelation, not because it
is totally beyond the power of reason, but because "some parts of that
truth lie too deep for our natural powers easily to reach, and make plain
and visible to mankind; without some light from above to direct them."[86]

Furthermore, even if philosophy "should have gone farther, as we see
it did not, and from undeniable principles given us ethics in a science like
mathematics, in every part demonstrable; this yet would not have been
so effectual to man in this imperfect state, nor proper for the cure." A
demonstrated ethics might serve for "a few who had much leisure,
improved understandings, and were used to abstract reasonings." But
most men would be incapable of following the demonstration. "The
greatest part cannot know, and therefore they must believe." Consequently "the instruction of the people were best still be left to the
precepts and principles of the Gospel."[87]

It would be misleading to present Locke as a Voltaire before his time,
content to leave the shoemakers and the serving girls to the apostles, so
long as the educated few were free to live by reason alone. Locke sincerely
wanted to save Christianity. But, as Gough points out, he was in
"fundamental sympathy" with the rationalist spirit "which became more
widespread as the seventeenth century advanced." He therefore sub-
scribed to the view "that the essentials of religious faith could be reduced
to a few broad tenets which were a kind of lowest common factor between
all the Christian churches."[88] He may also have hoped to win back the
Deists by showing them that "essential Christianity," purged of the
corruptions of superstition and priestcraft, was the same as, but more
efficacious than, their "natural religion" in achieving the one thing
necessary, a good moral life.

Locke's understanding of the essentials of religious faith is the premise of his plea for religious toleration in his four letters on that subject.
Like Milton, he felt that it is "for the most part ... frivolous things ...
which breed implacable enmities among Christian brethren, who are all
agreed in the substantial and truly fundamental part of religion."[89]
George Sabine remarks that Locke wrote on toleration in the aftermath
of the Puritan Revolution, which "in its own understanding of itself, was
a contest between religious sects each bent on finding freedom for its
own beliefs ..., and too often equally bent on forcing its beliefs ... on
other bodies that also were convinced of their own divine mandate." The
outcome of the struggle, however, was a standoff: "What was most

obviously achieved in 1688 was religious toleration." Writing a generation after the Revolution, "John Locke was able to see quite clearly what had been accomplished and to state it quite dispassionately."[90]

Unlike Milton, however, Locke did not confine his doctrine of toleration to Protestant brethren disagreeing on "frivolous things," but extended it to men of all religions, Jews, Moslems and pagans as well as Christians. "No man whatsoever ought ... to be deprived of his terrestrial enjoyments, upon account of his religion," he said, and generously added: "Not even Americans, subjected unto a Christian prince, are to be punished either in body or goods, for not embracing our faith and worship."[91] Locke therefore needed a universal principle on which to base his theory of toleration and could not find it simply in the line between the essential and nonessential elements of Christianity.

The only people whom Locke excepts from the general rule of toleration are Roman Catholics (because of their hierarchy's claim to supremacy in civil matters) and atheists.[92] "Promises, covenants, and oaths, which are the bonds of human society," he explains, "can have no hold upon an atheist."[93] Locke does not mention it here, but we must remember his repeated insistence elsewhere that the existence of God can be demonstrated (and therefore *known*) and is indispensable to perceiving the law of nature as a law. He does say in this place: "The taking away of God, though but even in thought, dissolves all." He also holds that "no opinions contrary to human society, or to those moral rules which are necessary to the preservation of civil society, are to be tolerated by the magistrate."[94] We may infer, therefore, that Locke's doctrine of toleration was not intended to extend to attacks on the basic truths which reason can know and on which society depends.

Locke rejected the charge made by his Anglican critic, Jonas Proast, that his argument for toleration must depend on one or other of these premises: "That no religion is the true religion," or "That though some one religion be the true religion, yet no man can have any more reason than another man of another religion may have to believe his to be the true religion."[95] Locke took a somewhat different line: there is "but one truth, one way to heaven,"[96] and one man may have more reason than another to believe his religion to be that single truth and way. But he cannot demonstrate it, nor are governments any more capable of doing so than private citizens. Therefore, where we cannot demonstrate, we ought to tolerate.

Locke's case for toleration in matters of religion proceeds from a double distinction: on the one hand, between the purpose of civil society and the purpose of religion; on the other hand, not so much between faith and reason as between opinion and knowledge. As to the first distinction, Locke's intention, as he tells us at the beginning of his first

letter on toleration, is "to distinguish exactly the business of civil government from that of religion, and to settle the just bounds that lie between
the one and the other." A "concernment for the interest of men's souls" is
not the business of civil government because the end and goal of the
commonwealth is men's "civil interest" alone. This comprises "life,
liberty, health, and indolency of body; and the possession of outward
things, such as money, lands, houses, furniture, and the like."[97] To
promote and preserve these goods, the "civil magistrate" has power "to
give laws, receive obedience, and compel with the sword," and such
power "belongs to none but the magistrate." But "[t]he care of souls
cannot belong to the civil magistrate, because his power consists only in
outward force," and its use does not extend to matters of conscience,
faith and worship.[98] "The business of laws is not to provide for the truth
of opinions, but for the safety and security of the commonwealth and of
every particular man's goods and person."[99]

Civil power is purely secular and therefore "is the same in every place:
nor can that power, in the hands of a Christian prince, confer any greater
authority upon the church, than in the hands of heathen; which is to say,
just none at all."[100] It follows that "there is absolutely no such thing,
under the Gospel, as a Christian commonwealth."[101] A commonwealth is
by definition a society of men banded together to promote their welfare
in this world, and its government's coercive power, given by them for that
purpose, does not extend beyond it.

True religion, on the other hand, "is not instituted in order to the
erecting an external pomp, nor to the obtaining of ecclesiastical
dominion, nor to the exercising of compulsive force; but to the regulating of men's lives according to the rules of virtue and piety."[102] That men
should live good lives, Locke admitted, "concerns also the civil government," because the safety of the commonwealth as well as of men's souls
depends on it. "Moral actions belong therefore to the jurisdiction both of
the outward and inward court; ... both of the magistrate and conscience."
But he contented himself with acknowledging that there was "great
danger" of the two jurisdictions encroaching on one another, and said no
more on the point.[103]

Drawing the line between the temporal and spiritual jurisdictions was
scarcely a new problem in Locke's day but one as old as Christendom.
But Locke was saying something new in urging that religion was no
business of the civil government, and what he urged was by no means
obviously true. After all, if the safety of the commonwealth lies in the
good lives of the citizens, the most effective way to promote such lives is
to foster and protect the true religion. Locke himself, as we have seen,
argued in *The Reasonableness of Christianity* that the Christian revelation is
practically necessary for a knowledge of God and the full moral law of

nature. In its own interest, therefore, one might argue, the common-wealth should protect the true religion and penalize the practice of false ones.

Locke met this argument with a triple response. First, there is no way in which religious intolerance can be made to serve the true religion alone. Secondly, the use of coercive force in religious matters is contrary to the nature of religion. Finally (and here we come to the second distinction mentioned above), once we get beyond the existence of God and the moral law, religious truth is an object of belief, i.e., of opinion, not of knowledge.

As to the first point, Locke argues throughout the letters on toleration that "every one is orthodox to himself,"[104] and "every church is orthodox to itself; to others, erroneous or heretical."[105] Granted that there is only one true religion, it must also be granted that "whoever believes any thing, takes it to be true, and as he thinks upon good grounds."[106] He therefore replies to his Anglican critic, "it is of no advantage to your cause, for you or any one of it, to suppose yours to be the only true religion; since it is equally unavoidable, and equally just for any one, who believes any other religion, to suppose the same thing."[107] Therefore, "whatever privilege or power you claim, upon your supposing yours to be the true religion, is equally due to another, who supposes his to be the true religion, upon the same claim."[108] The use of governmental power in the service of the true religion necessarily means, in practice, the service of the religion that the government believes is true.

"I do not think all religions equally true or equally uncertain," Locke insisted.[109] He also insisted that there is no judge on earth who can decide between men who have conflicting understandings of religious truth. No government and no church can do it, since they could only decide in favor of their own versions of the truth. "The decision of that question," then, "belongs only to the Supreme Judge of all men, to whom also alone belongs the punishment of the erroneous."[110]

This further follows from the very nature of "true and savings religion," which "consists in the inward persuasion of the mind, without which nothing can be acceptable to God."[111] Saving faith is an individual and personal conviction of the truth, so much so that "although the magistrate's opinion in religion be sound, and the way that he appoints be truly evangelical, yet if I be not thoroughly persuaded thereof in my own mind, there will be no safety for me in following it. No way whatsoever that I shall walk in against the dictates of my conscience, will ever bring me to the mansions of the blessed."[112] The supreme norm of religious truth thus becomes the individual conscience. As Wolin remarks, Locke made "a decisive shift in the notion of conscience," from "one controlled by the 'objective' standard of Scripture" to one that meant "the subjective *beliefs* held by an individual."[113]

Yet what the individual believes, he believes as true, and this in the most important concern of life, where whim and fancy have no place. For he has "an immortal soul, capable of eternal happiness or misery," and his happiness depends "upon his believing and doing those things in this life, which are necessary to the obtaining of God's favour, and are prescribed by God to that end." The individual's right to follow his conscience is founded upon his duty to seek the truth, for "the observance of these things is the highest obligation that lies upon mankind, and ... our utmost care, application, and diligence, ought to be exercised in the search and performance of them."[114] Locke does not defend the individual's right to think as he pleases, but his right to think as he must: "the light and persuasion a man has at present, is the guide he ought to follow, and which in his judgment of truth he cannot avoid to be governed by."[115]

Diversity of opinions in religion must be tolerated, then, because religious belief cannot be forced. At a deeper level, Locke's argument is that religious belief is, after all, only opinion because it concerns things about which there is, strictly speaking, no proof. Locke admitted that some beliefs were more rationally grounded and had better evidence in their favor than others: if we consider "the ground of any one's supposing his religion true, ... men of all religions cannot be equally allowed to suppose their religions true."[116] But doctrines that go beyond the demonstrable truths of natural religion are objects of opinion, not of knowledge.

This premise is basic to Locke's theory of toleration. He stresses it throughout the letters on toleration, particularly in the second and third. For example, we can believe but not demonstrate that Christ died at Jerusalem and rose again from the dead. "This is the highest the nature of the thing will permit us to go in matters of revealed religion, which are therefore called matters of faith: a persuasion of our own minds, short of knowledge, is the last result that determines us in such truths." But this, says Locke, "is all that God requires in the Gospel for men to be saved," for "[k]nowledge, ... properly so called," is not "to be had of truths necessary to salvation."[117] In the light of *The Reasonableness of Christianity,* one may wonder how many indemonstrable truths, if any, Locke himself thought necessary to salvation. But in this place, against his Anglican adversary, he argued that salvation depends on assent to the necessary truths; but their truth is not demonstrable; therefore it must be left to the sincere judgment of the individual.

This conclusion, however, does not follow with rigid necessity from the stated premises, but requires still another premise that grows out of

Locke's individualism. This is that in the affair of salvation, "[e]very man ... has the supreme and absolute authority of judging for himself ... because nobody else is concerned in it, nor can receive any prejudice from his conduct therein."[118] Given this, it follows that the individual must be left to his own judgment, without coercion by others.

"Every man," Locke grants, "has commission to admonish, exhort, convince another of error, and by reasoning to draw him into truth."[119] Argument "is the only right method of propagating truth, which has no such way of prevailing, as when strong arguments and good reason, are joined with the softness of civility and good usage."[120] Locke does not exclude truth and reason from religious belief because he does not exclude them from the area of opinion. But he does insist that, since religious beliefs are opinions, not demonstrated knowledge, they cannot be made public truths imposed by law. "Speculative opinions, therefore, and articles of faith, as they are called, which are required only to be believed, cannot be imposed on any church by the law of the land."[121] As Sterling Lamprecht paraphrases Locke: "The limits of human understanding do not comprise such doctrines as go to make up the rival faiths of most Christian sects. Hence, since neither the truth nor the falsity of these doctrines can be clearly determined, the need for toleration is obvious."[122]

That Locke made a fully coherent case for toleration is somewhat less obvious. For the case was based on a philosophy that suffers from profound internal strains. Locke's philosophy may be seen as a step forward in the Western mind's march toward the discovery of the distinction between facts and values or, what comes to the same thing, as a stage in the collapse of the mind's confidence in its own ability to find meaning in reality. However one reads the sequel to Locke, it seems clear that his attempt to meld Christianity and natural law with the abstract rationalism of his age was predestined to fail. It therefore furnishes no secure foundation for a theory of toleration.

But the question immediately relevant here is not how good Locke's argument is, but what he is arguing for, and the answer to that is reasonably clear. Locke built his theory of toleration within a framework of natural moral law, established by God the Creator and knowable by human reason, even though in practice it needed illumination by the Christian revelation. Within this framework he advocated freedom for the individual mind to seek, to put into practice and peacefully to propose to others those truths that God wishes to be believed, and to judge what they are according to its own inward light and persuasion. The most basic truths—God and the moral law—are demonstrable. The rest are not demonstrable; concerning them, therefore, the individual must be free to decide for himself. He may in fact decide for irrational reasons, and often does. But, as Locke insisted, men are obliged to use their reason to decide whether a proposition has been revealed and, if so, what it means, because ultimately they have no other standard of judgment. Locke's case for toleration thus is a plea for men's freedom to use their individual reason to seek for and assent to the truth in the matters of highest concern to them. One can stretch the case to cover the search for truth in other serious matters, but hardly beyond that.

What Locke would have said about the freedom of the press, had he written a treatise on it, we can only guess. He did make a small contribution to the subject when Parliament allowed the Licensing Act (which required censorship before publication) to lapse in 1695 by refusing to renew it. The Commons overcame the initial resistance of the Lords to this step by presenting them "with a list of reasons for not renewing the Act, a list composed by John Locke himself." But the reasons given were all purely pragmatic ones. As Macaulay later complained, the Licensing Act was condemned, "not as a thing essentially evil but on account of the petty grievances, the exactions, the jobs, the commercial restrictions, the domiciliary visits which were incidental to it." These, no doubt, were the reasons that the Commons (and Locke) felt the Lords would respond to.[123] Locke's document, therefore, does not present a theory of the freedom of the press. Presumably, however, if he had written one, it, too, would have been an argument for freedom to seek the truth through the expression and exchange of opinions.

We do have a brief essay entitled *Some Thoughts Concerning Reading and Study for a Gentleman* which indicates what Locke's view of the proper use of reading was. "Reading," he begins, "is for the improvement of the understanding." In the several pages that follow, he outlines the kind of reading a gentleman should do to improve his understanding. On the last page he mentions "another use of reading, which is for diversion and delight. Such are poetical writings, especially dramatic, if they be free from profaneness, obscenity, and what corrupts good manners; for such pitch should not be handled."[124] One is left with the feeling that Locke was still some distance from the regime of uninhibited freedom of expression.

4

Political Rationalism:

Spinoza and Wortman

Juxtaposing the names of Benedict de Spinoza and Tunis Wortman requires some justification. Spinoza was a major figure in the history of philosophy, Wortman an obscure New York lawyer, and they published their works more than a century apart. Even when it is explained, as it will be in the proper place, that Wortman appears here as a stand-in for Thomas Jefferson, he still hardly belongs in the same chapter with a man of Spinoza's intellectual stature. The reason for so joining them is, candidly, a practical one. Since the treatment of each is brief, they fit neatly into one chapter. But this much further can be said for it: each of them was moved to argue for the free expression of ideas by an enormous confidence in the power of reason, once freed, to arrive at truth. Let them stand together, then, as exponents of the rationalism that characterized Western thought in the seventeenth and eighteenth centuries.

Benedict de Spinoza

Among the seventeenth-century founders of the tradition of freedom of speech and press, Spinoza stands high. According to Lewis Feuer, "Spinoza was the first political philosopher of modern times to avow himself a democrat." He was a democrat, however, not because of any "mystic faith in the common man," but because of his belief in liberty. "Majority rule, in his opinion," says Feuer, "would interfere least with minority rights, with the rights of the individual."[1] Spinoza's views are important, then, for a grasp of the original liberal understanding of the meaning and purpose of the freedom to speak and publish.

He presented his views on this subject most fully in his *Tractatus Theologico-Politicus,* published anonymously in 1670, and in the *Tractatus Politicus,* which was published in 1677 after his death in that year. Feuer sees the first of these works as "the great philosophic statement of the Republican party" in the Netherlands, whose leader was Jan DeWitt. In it Spinoza emerged as the "practical political philosopher ... the optimistic advocate of Amsterdam liberalism, the analyst of the problems of the Dutch Republic." But after the murder of DeWitt in 1672, "the Republican optimism of Spinoza vanished in the bloodshed and reaction," and he became a less confident advocate of democracy. "He was at the end concerned with showing how every governmental form could be made consistent with the life of free men."[2]

Yet in relation to freedom of expression this development in Spinoza's political thought is of minor importance. Robert McShea remarks: "Except for the apparent fact that the *Tractatus Politicus,* written after the murder of DeWitt in 1672, reflects a more sober or pessimistic political outlook, the dates of composition [of Spinoza's works] are of interest only to the specialist. Spinoza's writings show no significant change of outlook in time."[3] Whatever happened to Spinoza's faith in democracy, his belief in liberty, and especially in intellectual liberty, remained unchanged.

He takes up the subject of freedom of speech and publication in chapter 20 of the *Tractatus Theologico-Politicus.* The scope of the freedom that he advocates is indicated by the chapter's title, "That in a free state everyone may think what he pleases, and say what he thinks."[4] He does not mean by this, however, that society and its sovereign government are without any right to control the expression of thought. Indeed he says, in accordance with his general philosophy in which power and right are identical, that the sovereign's right in the matter is coextensive with his power, and so "he has the right to treat as enemies all who are not in complete agreement with him" and "to rule with the utmost violence." On the other hand, since the sovereign (which could be a democratic government) cannot do these things without weakening his power, we may "deny that he has a full right to do them either."[5] Everyman's right to think as he pleases and to say what he thinks must be understood, therefore, in relation to the sovereign's rights.

As Spinoza says, "it must be admitted that words can be treasonable as well as deeds; and so, though it is impossible to deprive subjects of such freedom entirely, it will be quite disastrous to grant it to them in full." He therefore poses the question in these terms: "Hence we must inquire how far it can and must be granted to everyone if the peace of the state and the right of the sovereign are to be preserved."[6]

He addresses himself to this question with a reference to the theory of the founding of the state which he had spelled out in chapter 16 of this *Tractatus.* There he began with a state of nature even more radically atomistic and amoral than Hobbes's.[7] Since right is power, every man in the state of nature had a sovereign right to do everything he had the power to do; however irrational it may have been, it could not be unjust. In the state of nature injustice and wrong were impossible to commit, because justice and right are entirely the products of an organized civil community or state which has the power to make and enforce laws defining what is just and unjust in the relations among individuals. The state, of course, when it comes into existence holding sovereign power, cannot do wrong by doing anything that is within its power to do, for power and right remain by nature identical.

Yet the sacrifice of absolute natural liberty to the power of the state is made because "without mutual help men live in utter wretchedness, and are inevitably debarred from the cultivation of reason." Hence, "to live safely and well men had necessarily to join together. They therefore arranged that the right to do everything which each had by nature should be held collectively, and should be determined no longer by the force and appetite of each but by the power and will of all together."[8] This is to say that, in their own interest, men must create by covenant or compact the sovereign state.

To return to chapter 20, Spinoza explains how freedom of thought and expression are compatible with the power of the state, in these terms:

> We also saw that to create a state the one thing needful was that all power to make decisions should be vested either in all collectively, or in a few, or in one man; for the great diversity of men's free judgments, the claim of each to have a monopoly of wisdom, and their inability to think alike and speak with one voice made it impossible for men to live at peace unless everyone surrendered his right to act entirely as he pleased. Thus it was only his right to act as he pleased that everyone surrendered, and not his right to think and judge. This means that while a subject necessarily violates his sovereign's right by acting contrary to its decree, there is no violation whatever in his thinking and judging, and therefore also saying, that the decree is ill-advised; as long as he does no more than express or communicate his opinion, and only defends it out of honest rational conviction, and not out of anger, hatred, or a desire to introduce any change in the state on his own authority.... But if he breaks the law in order to accuse the magistrate of injustice and to stir up mob hatred against him, or makes a seditious attempt to repeal the law against the magistrate's will, he is simply an agitator and a rebel. This shows how everyone can express and communicate his opinions without infringing the right and authority of the sovereign, i.e. without disturbing the peace of the state; he must leave the determination of all actions to the sovereign, and do nothing contrary to its decree, even though the actions required are frequently in conflict with what he thinks, and declares, to be good.[9]

Since for Spinoza the basic reality is power, he does not mean that in forming the compact which brings the state into being men reserved their moral right to think and speak, and surrendered their right to make decisions. He means, rather, as he explained in the *Tractatus Politicus,* that "nobody *can* give up his power of judgement; for by what rewards or threats can a man be led to believe that a whole is no greater than its part, or that God does not exist, or that a body which he sees to be finite is an infinite being; and, in general, to believe anything contrary to what he perceives and thinks?"[10] Conversely, the state has no right to coerce men's judgments, because it lacks the power to do so. Indeed, as Spinoza labors at some length to show in chapter 20 of the *Tractatus Theologico-Politicus,* the very attempt to force men's minds and stop their mouths weakens the power of the state and by that fact alone is beyond its right. For the state's right, like that of every other being, is its power.

Nonetheless, there are some opinions which the state can punish and must suppress, namely, seditious beliefs. Spinoza explains:

> A consideration of the basis of the state ... enables us to determine just as easily which beliefs are seditious; they are those which, when accepted, immediately destroy the covenant whereby everyone sur-rendered the right to act as he pleased. For instance, if anyone believes that the sovereign does not have absolute right, or that nobody is bound to keep promises, or that everyone should live as he pleases, or holds other similar views which directly contradict the said covenant, he is seditious; not so much, to be sure, because of his judgement and opinion as because of the action which it involves, i.e. because merely by thinking in this way he breaks the promise he has given either tacitly or expressly to the sovereign.[11]

Lying behind the power of the state to suppress seditious opinions is a general principle that Spinoza enunciates in the *Tractatus Politicus:* "A commonwealth, then, does wrong when it does, or allows to be done, things that can be the cause of its own downfall."[12] But to tolerate seditious opinons would be to allow the dissolution of the covenant on which the state is founded. It must therefore be within the power of the state to suppress them or at least to punish their expression.[13]

With this limitation Spinoza's thesis is, however, that freedom to say what one thinks "not only can be granted without danger to public peace, piety, and the right of the sovereign, but actually must be granted if they are all to be preserved."[14] Or again: "If honesty, then, is to be valued above servility, and sovereigns are to retain full control, without being forced to yield to agitators, it is necessary to allow freedom of judgement, and so to govern men that they can express different and conflicting opinions without ceasing to live in harmony."[15] In Robert Duff's paraphrase of Spinoza, "As free thought, free speech, and free-dom of religious belief will exist in spite of all the State could do to suppress them, the path of true safety for it is to welcome what it cannot change, and to enlist on its side, and in its interest, the forces that would else become its worst enemy."[16] But this result, Spinoza thought in 1670, is best achieved in a democracy where men agree to abide by majority decisions while retaining their freedom of judgment and the possibility of changing the decisions.[17] For the fact is, as he still thought in the posthumous *Tractatus Politicus*, that "human wits are too blunt to get to the heart of all problems immediately; but they are sharpened by the give and take of discussion and debate, and by exploring every possible course men eventually discover the measures they wish, measures which all approve and which no one would have thought of before the discussion."[18]

Spinoza was a philosopher, and some scholars have taken his argument for a free and open society as a plea for the freedom of philosophy. Stanley Rosen, for example, says: "It is important to remember that the political regime has as its highest good the preservation of philosophy.... The free society is absolutely dependent, not on freedom of speech in the sense of anyone's speech, but on freedom of philosophical speech."[19] He therefore concludes: "The defense of democracy is essentially a defense of those conditions which make possible the development of philosophy."[20] This is true enough insofar as for Spinoza the fully human life is the life fully in accord with reason and therefore with philosophy. But we should unduly narrow the scope of the freedom for which Spinoza argued if we saw it as exclusively or primarily the freedom to engage in philosophical thought and discussion.

Lucien Mugnier-Pollet is nearer to the mark when he says that the whole *Tractatus Theologico-Politicus* has as its object to win from the sovereign complete and full freedom for rational thought. Spinoza undoubtedly is concerned with freedom to philosophize, but not with that alone. Freedom to express one's thought, a right recognized as belonging to all men, cannot be limited to that fraction of the population which is capable of philosophizing. The best state, the one that Spinoza wants, does not reserve a privileged treatment for philosophy. It is a state in which the greatest freedom of opinion reigns, since it is through political discussion and the practice of making decisions by majority vote that men educate themselves and become citizens.[21]

In addition, everyone has "a perfect right and authority to judge freely about religion, and hence to explain and interpret it for himself."[22] Spinoza also held that freedom of opinion "is quite indispensable for the advancement of the arts and sciences, for these are cultivated with success only by men whose judgement is free and unbiassed."[23] As Mugnier-Pollet says, Spinoza affirms freedom of judgment in its fullest extent, identifies it with the free use of reason and extends it to every aspect of human life.[24] His claim is for *"la liberté d'expression à portée universelle."*[25]

Even under this broad interpretation of the freedom for which Spinoza contended, however, his argument is still very much a plea for the liberty of *rational* thought and its expression. For reason is the essence and the perfection of man and, therefore, of human society.

It is not that Spinoza had a high esteem for the rationality of his fellowmen. On the contrary he said: "All men certainly seek their own advantage, but seldom as sound reason dictates; in most cases appetite is their only guide, and in their desires and judgements of what is beneficial, they are carried away by their passions, which take no account of the future or anything else."[26] But this is their imperfection, not their true freedom, for "the man who is captivated by his pleasures, and can neither see nor do anything advantageous to himself, is really the greatest slave of all, and the only free man is one who has a sound mind and lives wholly by the guidance of reason."[27] More than that: "A man's true happiness and blessedness lies simply in his wisdom and knowledge of truth."[28] Therefore, "[s]ince the better part of us is our understanding, it follows that, if we really wish to seek our own good, our primary aim must be to make our understanding as perfect as possible; for it is in its perfection that our supreme good must lie."[29]

All of this is compatible, in Spinoza's mind, with his basic and universal determinism. He claims to have deduced his political doctrines from "the essential nature of man, irrespective of how he is considered, i.e. from the universal urge of all men to preserve themselves."[30] But this urge is a passion and that is why "their natural power, or natural right, must not be defined in terms of reason, but must be held to cover every possible appetite by which they are determined to act, and by which they try to preserve themselves."[31] Hence the law of nature forbids nothing that anyone wants to do, and is not identical with the laws of human reason. On the other hand, man can be happy only by following the laws of reason, for they aim at "men's true interest and preservation," and declare things to be good or bad "not in relation to the order and laws of nature as a whole, but only in relation to the laws of our nature in particular."[32]

The cultivation of reason, then, is the goal to be aimed at. Not only that, once achieved it is determinative: if a man knows by reason the right and good thing to do, he *must* do it, because the basic law of all nature determines him to do everything he can to preserve his own being and therefore, since he is a human being, to preserve his "sound mind."[33]

Thus are reconciled freedom and necessity:

the more free we conceived a man to be, the more should we be compelled to maintain that he must necessarily preserve himself and have a sound mind; as everyone who does not confuse freedom with chance will readily grant me. For freedom is virtue or perfection: and so nothing that betokens weakness in a man can be put down to his freedom. In consequence, it is quite impossible to call a man free because he can fail to exist, or fail to use reason; he can be called free only in so far as he has the power to exist and act in accordance with the laws of human nature. So the more free we conceive a man to be, the less we can say that he can fail to use reason, and choose evil in preference to good; and this because God, who exists, understands, and acts with complete freedom, also exists, understands, and acts by necessity; i.e. by the necessity of his own nature.[34]

Whether Spinoza's reconciliation of freedom and necessity is successful is a question on which the opinions of commentators have varied, and we need not try to answer it here. It is enough to say that, for Spinoza, as reason is the perfection of man, and freedom understood as obedience to reason is the only firm foundation of his happiness, so rational freedom is the law and the goal of the state. Spinoza says that "a commonwealth is most fully possessed of its own right when it acts in accordance with the dictate of reason ...; in so far, then, as it acts against reason, it fails to realize its true nature, or does wrong."[35]

Moreover, the state's

ultimate purpose is not to subject men to tyranny, or to restrain and enslave them through fear, but rather to free everyone from fear so that he may live in all possible security, i.e. may preserve his natural right to exist and act in the best possible way, without harm to himself or his neighbour. It is not, I say, the purpose of the state to change men from rational beings into brutes or puppets; but rather to enable them to exercise their mental and physical powers in safety and use their reason freely, and to prevent them from fighting and quarrelling through hatred, anger, bad faith and mutual malice. Thus the purpose of the state is really freedom.[36]

Therefore, "when I say that the best state is one in which men live in harmony, I am speaking of a truly human existence, which is characterized, not by the mere circulation of blood and other vital processes common to all animals, but primarily by reason, the true virtue and life of the mind."[37] The purpose of the state, as Spinoza says, is really freedom. But freedom consists in following reason, since only the rational man is truly free.

In terms of what is predictable, however, the state's constitution cannot be framed on the expectation that most men will in fact follow reason. The state cannot be governed by persuading men to live wisely —for with most of them that is impossible—but by so arranging the state's institutions that, in following their common passions, men will in practice promote the welfare of the commonwealth.[38] It follows that "a constitution cannot be kept intact unless it is supported both by reason and by the common passions of men; otherwise, of course, i.e. if it depends on the support of reason only, it is weak and easily over-thrown."[39] But this is only to say that the passions of the mass of men must be enlisted in the cause of reason, if reason is to prevail and to preserve the state.

In a complete treatise on Spinoza's political thought, more would need to be said about the relationship between reason and appetite.[40] For the present purpose, however, it is enough to point out the close connec-tion that he posits between the freedom of expression and the promo-tion of the life of reason. As Duff says, "That the fostering and develop-ment of human intelligence and will is the one supreme end for the sake of which the State exists at all—this is the dominating principle of Spinoza's whole theory of Politics."[41] Stuart Hampshire adds: "For Spinoza, the exercise of reason is not merely the means to self-preservation and the satisfaction of desire, but constitutes in itself the supreme end to which everything else must be a means; ... The criterion by which a political organization is to be judged is whether it impedes or makes possible the free man's rational love and understanding of Nature."[42] We may therefore conclude with McShea that

> Spinoza thought that the suppression of free speech would entail the suppression of thought itself and the defeat of man's struggle to realize his essential need to understand, and further, that in diminishing the power of the subject, it weakened the state power it meant to support.... His belief that freedom of speech should be allowed was based not on any notion of right but on the pragmatic judgment that the interests of both nation and citizen were thus advanced.[43]

If one wishes to maintain that freedom of speech and press is the freedom to express opinion in the pursuit of truth and a knowledge of the good, he will find in Spinoza an intellectual forebear. But one cannot find in Spinoza the thesis that freedom of speech and press can be reduced to an unqualified freedom of expression or to the right to express whatever one finds within himself for no other reason than a desire to express it. Spinoza, like Locke, was an exponent of rationalism, though certainly a more intelligent and consistent one. It was a particu-lar kind of rationalism, to be sure, and by no means the only kind. Nevertheless, Spinoza believed supremely in reason, and it is an abuse of his argument to appeal to it in support of forms of "expression" that do not and cannot serve the goals of reason.

Tunis Wortman

The name of Tunis Wortman is scarcely a household word. According to Leonard Levy, he was "a New York lawyer who was prominent in Tammany politics."[44] He was also one of the Jeffersonian Republican spokesmen who responded to the challenge of the Federalists' Sedition Act of 1798 by constructing "a new theory of freedom of speech and press."[45] But what makes him worth discussing here is, quite frankly, simply Professor Levy's word for it that his *A Treatise, Concerning Political Enquiry, and the Liberty of the Press,* published in 1800,[46] "is, in a sense, the book that Jefferson did not write but should have."[47]

Jefferson, with his oath upon the altar of God against every form of tyranny over the mind of man, is America's hero of the freedom of thought. But, Levy says, one looks to him in vain for a developed and consistent theory of the freedom of the press. In the controversy over the Sedition Act, which made defamation of the U. S. government or its leading officials a crime,

> Thomas Jefferson ... contributed only tired clichés. The philosopher of freedom, unreflective and uninventive as a theorist, bound by the high-minded formulations of the Enlightenment, had his philosophy handed to him by his more liberal, more critical, followers. And it is doubtful that the new libertarianism meant much to Jefferson, for it scarcely altered his own thinking.[48]

Jefferson's Kentucky Resolutions of 1798 contain a single paragraph dealing with the freedom of the press, and this is "one of his most extended statements on the subject."[49] Wortman's treatise, on the other hand, is a "masterful analysis of freedom"[50] and "a work of political philosophy that systematically presents the case for freedom of expression."[51] It is, says Levy, "surely the preeminent American classic, because of its scope, fullness, philosophical approach, masterful marshalling of all the libertarian arguments, and uncompromisingly radical views."[52]

It is possible to make a less favorable assessment of the merits of Wortman's work. Walter Berns, for example, says: "Its outstanding characteristics in fact are its naive presentation of the sentiments, arguments, and hopes of the Enlightenment and its adoption of the views of Thomas Paine."[53] Still, there is little reason to think that Jefferson would have written a better or even a greatly different book, for he, too, was a man of the Enlightenment. Wortman's treatise is admittedly a minor work, but we may take it as the book Jefferson should have written or, at least, as the most thorough argument for the freedom of speech and press to emerge from the Jeffersonian camp.

It is clear that Wortman's mind was formed in the same intellectual milieu that produced Jefferson and Paine and, for that matter, the Englishman, Joseph Priestley. Like Priestley, Wortman believed that "[i]mprovement is a constant law of our intellectual nature,"[54] and that "it must become a source of exquisite consolation, to consider Man as destined to perpetual improvement."[55] Like Paine and Jefferson, he held: "Government is, strictly speaking, the creature of society originating in its discretion, and dependent on its will; ... It must ever remain the inherent and incontrovertible right of society, to dissolve its political constitution, whenever the voice of public opinion has declared such dissolution to be essential to the general welfare."[56]

Wortman gave all power to public opinion because he had in full measure the Enlightenment's confidence in reason, as that age understood reason. This understanding did not include the noetic intelligence that operates in the field of metaphysics. Wortman explains:

> Metaphysics and polemics abound in obscurity, they are fraught with incertitude, and pregnant with inexplicable mysticism. Many who have been most profoundly conversant with the subtleties of THOMAS AQUINAS, or the laborious researches of a BENTLEY, or MALEBRANCHE, have been constrained to lament the sacrifice of time, in frivolous and unsatisfactory pursuits.[57]

University departments of philosophy will please note. Then he adds, in a passage that seems designed to cheer the heart of a political scientist: "Not so with rational politics. Every truth is luminous; every principle is clear, perspicuous, and determinable; its doctrines are established in the common sentiments and feelings of mankind; its positions are maintained and enforced by universal experience."[58]

Wortman's point here is the same as Paine's: politics is not mysterious or arcane. Since "the character of political institution depends upon the application of simple and perspicuous principles,"[59] it is open to the understanding of ordinary men, if they will but think. For think they can. "Mind is the common property of man, and the capacity of knowledge is the inseparable attribute of mind."[60] This capacity is pretty evenly distributed among men, for there is a "striking uniformity that exists in the human understanding."[61]

Granted, as Wortman reluctantly does grant, that the discoveries of an Isaac Newton may have required native genius of a kind not commonly found in men,[62] he nonetheless insists: "However great may be the diversity in human genius and talents, in the subjects of moral disquisition, there is but little inequality.... The laws of morality are correspondent at Paris and Hindostan, and the standard of decision is the common property of mankind."[63]

Men's equality in moral understanding founds their political equality, because for Wortman politics is a branch of ethics.[64] Political questions are ultimately questions of justice and natural law,[65] on which the multitude of ordinary men is as competent to judge as the few who staff the offices of government.[66] Questions of policy must be decided under, not outside of, the natural laws of justice which are known or knowable to all men. Nor is it beyond the capacity of the people to evaluate government's handling of policy matters, since it "requires only the exercise of that judgment, which is the common attribute of humanity, combined with such information, as every intelligent Being can with application acquire."[67]

Society, therefore, composed of the mass of men, not only has the right but the competence to control government. Wortman does not "venture to decide" whether in a representative system of government, social control must entail universal suffrage.[68] That for him is an incidental question because his thesis applies to all forms of government.[69] It is that public opinion is, and of right ought to be, the ruling power in society.[70] Public opinion must therefore be free:

> The general will, which is the necessary result of Public Opinion, being superior to Political Institution, must of consequence remain independent of its control. Governments are entrusted with the exercise of the ordinary powers of sovereignty, but Society is, nevertheless, the real and substantial sovereign.[71]

Public opinion, it should be noted, is not the expression of a mass mind, but "an aggregation of individual sentiment." The collectivity as such does not think; rather it is "the individual who is to reflect and decide,"[72] and therefore "every man should be left to the independent exercise of his reflection; all should be permitted to communicate their ideas with the energy and ingenuousness of truth."[73] Public opinion grows out of private judgment and is "that general determination of private understandings which is most extensively predominant." In practice, this means "the opinion of the majority."[71]

It follows that government cannot perform its functions properly without the control of an enlightened and truly public opinion. A reading of history makes us "tremble at the deplorable catastrophes which have ensued from political ignorance and imposture.... Disgusted or appalled by the sad recital of human miseries and crimes, we abandon the affecting volume, or efface its pages with our tears."[75] To these woes "the only antidote which can be applied, is the progress of information.... By enlightening the understanding, you lay the foundation of positive virtue and benefit."[76]

The functions of government, fortunately, are easily open to ordinary understanding because they are few. "Political dominion is established for no other purpose than to suppress the commission of crimes, and to afford protection to the community." All the rest should be left to society acting, and above all thinking and discussing, freely. Thought control, therefore, is simply not a function of government. "The coercion of Thought, and the restriction of Intellectual Intercourse, are entirely foreign to the sphere of rational jurisdiction."[77]

Wortman's book is directed to establishing the freedom of "political enquiry," and to this he naturally devotes the greater part of his pages. But he maintains also that the benefits of a regime of free discussion extend to every sphere of social life. "Society," he says, "is possessed by the absolute right to investigate every subject which relates to its interests,"[78] and "a liberty of investigation into every subject of thought ... is indispensable to the progression and happiness of mankind."[79] It is to society, not to government, that we owe "the cultivation of intellect, and the progress of literature, ... the arts, ... [and] the numerous truths of science.... It is society that has laid the foundation of knowledge [and] furnished all the means of improving the human faculties."[80] Government's role is negative: "It is only to be wished that with respect to the improvement of general Science it would observe strict neutrality."[81] To put it more forcefully, "The government that interferes with the progress of opinion, subverts the essential order of the social state."[82]

If government will refrain from impeding thought and discussion, society will improve of itself. "One truth will infallibly lead to another, and the laws of percipient causation, will inevitably operate in perpetual geometrical progression."[83] In words that anticipate John Stuart Mill's argument in *On Liberty* by six decades, Wortman proclaims:

> In proportion as investigation continues free and unrestricted, the mass of error will be subject to continual diminution, and the determinations of distinct understandings will gradually harmonize. Upon every subject that can become presented to our attention, it is the province of Reason to deliberate and determine. The uninterrupted progression of Truth demands that the intellectual intercourse between men, should remain entirely unshackled....
>
> It is likewise to be remarked, that diversity of sentiment in the earlier stages of enquiry, is far from being unfavorable to the eventual reception of Truth. It produces Collision, engenders Argument, and affords exercise and energy to the intellectual powers; it corrects our errors, removes our prejudices, and strengthens our perceptions; it compels us to seek for the evidences of our knowledge, and habituates us to a frequent revisal of our sentiments. In the conflict between opinions we are enured to correctness of reflection, and become taught in the school of Experience to reason and expatiate. It cannot surely be visionary to predict the ultimate triumph of Truth ... Mind has already proceeded too far to retrograde ... [and] the rays of Intellectual Light will still

proceed to brighten and increase, and the days of Liberty and Science succeed to the gloomy night of Ignorance and Despotism.[84]

As ignorance and despotism go together, so do liberty and knowledge. Wortman's thesis no more depends than Mill's on intellectual scepticism or an indifference to the distinction between truth and error. But Wortman's chief concern was not with the advancement of science. He was as thoroughgoing a moralist as Mill. Like Mill, he saw knowledge and virtue as advancing hand in hand, though he had not arrived at Mill's conviction that public opinion itself, and not merely government, was the major obstacle to intellectual and moral progress. For Wortman, it would be enough to remove the heavy hand of government from the public discussion of moral and political topics to bring about the improvement of mankind.

"The suppression of Vice," he declared, "must ever be necessary to the public welfare."[85] Furthermore, we all know or can become enlightened enough to know what vice and virtue are. "There is abundant evidence to prove, that all men are possessed of what is termed the MORAL SENSE.... Our perceptions concerning the nature of moral and social obligation, are entirely similar, and our decisions with respect to them, will in general be uniform and correspondent."[86] Moral education, of course, is needed: "To discriminate between virtue and vice, forms an essential part of the education of every intellectual Being."[87] But it is society, not government, that will give the moral education, and it will give it through a process of free discussion.[88]

Virtue is conduct governed by reason, and the obstacle to it is passion. Passion can mean "propensities arising from physical organization, such as hunger and sexual desire," but "in this sense it is certainly foreign to the present subject of enquiry." As Wortman uses the term, passion is "any extraordinary or vehement excitement of the mind," or more particularly, an emotion "such as revenge or anger, ambition or avarice." To the argument that free discussion is politically dangerous because it allows demagogues to exploit these passions, he replies that "knowledge is the only preservative against the inordinate excitement of the passions."[89]

If we frequently err by yielding to the impulse of the passions,

> it is because we have not sufficiently advanced in the school of knowledge and experience: it is because our minds have not been habituated to the salutary discipline of moral discussion. If the period should ever arrive, in which it shall become a general practice to investigate the subjects of morality and politics, society will then become enabled to decide with accuracy upon the merits of human action. Every man will partake, in some degree, of the benefit of such general illumination:

reason will become the universal standard of decision, and the empire of judgment will succeed to the pernicious dominion of the passions.[90]

This, in sum, is Wortman's faith. Men, by and large, are substantially equal in their ability to form judgments on the matters of most concern to them, i.e., morality and its subdivision, politics. To form and refine their judgments, they need freedom to express and discuss them. A government that allows this complete freedom of discussion, far from finding itself endangered, will discover that it is strengthened by an enlightened public opinion. "Tyranny alone," therefore, "should tremble at the sternly inquisitive glance of enlightened investigation."[91]

Wortman wrote his book as a general treatise on political enquiry, but its immediate objective was to attack the Sedition Act of 1798. He therefore applies his general thesis to the particular conclusion that, while no one "can have a right ... to misrepresent the public measures of a government,"[92] such misrepresentation nevertheless should not be made a crime. Government, that is, should not enjoy the power "to punish men for their assertions concerning itself." It is in this sense that Wortman says: "Public prosecutions for libels are ... more dangerous to Society than the misrepresentation they are intended to punish."[93]

The defamation of particular persons is a different matter. It does personal injury and real damage to individuals. Libel suits to redress this wrong create no political danger, since "prosecutions commenced for Personal Slander ... are entirely the objects of civil jurisdiction, and are not liable to become converted into instruments of oppression."[94] But "a virtuous Government cannot become materially injured by Misrepresentation,"[95] whereas the power to prosecute for seditious libel enables government to stifle the free discussion on which the welfare and progress of society depend.[96]

Wortman argues at length that the Sedition Act is unconstitutional because "the restriction of Political Opinion, or the coercion of Libels" are not within the powers given to the government of the United States by the Constitution.[97] "Wherever such Coercion is proper or necessary," he says, "our State legislatures and tribunals are possessed of sufficient authority to remedy the evil."[98] Walter Berns takes this as meaning that "Wortman's position was essentially Jefferson's,"[99] namely, that what was wrong with the Sedition Act was that it had been enacted by the U.S. Congress instead of by a state legislature that had the constitutional power to make such a law.[100] But Wortman expressly argued throughout his book against allowing government as such, therefore at any level, to restrict political opinion by prosecuting people for criticizing itself. The reservation to the states of such coercion of libel as may be "proper or necessary" thus means no more than that civil suits for personal libel should be conducted under state, not federal, laws.

Wortman did not believe that even the states had power to legislate against seditious libel. It is probable, though he does not say so, that he believed that the states had power to prosecute obscene publications.[101] His doctrine might allow state laws against incitement to racial or religious hatred, as a kind of group libel, but such laws did not enter his mind in 1800. The question whether Nazis have a right to march through a Jewish neighborhood is one that he could not have imagined. His sole concern was with the freedom of *opinion*.

In his final chapter, on the liberty of the press, Wortman grants that it "would, doubtless, be desirable to controul the Licentiousness of the Press, if any means could be pursued for that purpose without endangering its Liberty." But the licentiousness of the press turns out to consist in going to one or the other of two extremes, either "an interested partiality towards the Government," or "a wanton or designing misrepresentation of its measures."[102] Government has no interest in controlling the former and cannot be trusted with power to control the latter. Therefore, we must and "we may securely trust to the wisdom of Public Opinion for the correction of Licentiousness."[103] But this is the only licentiousness that Wortman contemplates. His argument for the freedom of the press, like the rest of his book, is an expression of his belief that the open exchange of opinions, free from governmental control, will lead to knowledge of the truth, and especially of that moral and political truth in which the public welfare consists. He argues for nothing more.

Wortman's rationalistic faith may seem today to have been overly optimistic and even shallow. No doubt it was. So was Jefferson's; so was Paine's. But there is no denying that a belief in the power of reason to arrive at moral and political truth furnished the premise of Wortman's entire argument for freedom of speech and press. Destroy the premise, and the conclusions are destroyed with it. Wortman's thesis therefore provides no intellectual ancestry to those who contend that moral and political scepticism is the rock on which the edifice of freedom is built. Still less can Wortman be claimed by those who demand freedom for a kind of "expression" that is devoid of rational content and serves no rational ends. Every demand for freedom raises the question: freedom for what? To that question Wortman's answer, whatever its flaws, is at least clear. It is: for Reason.

5

The Marriage of Liberalism and Utilitarianism

John Stuart Mill

John Stuart Mill's essay *On Liberty* has been severely criticized from the time of its publication in 1859 to the present day. Yet it continues to be republished in numerous paperback editions, is read by thousands of students every year, and is considered to be the classic statement of the liberal position on individual freedom. As Willmoore Kendall puts it, it is widely assumed that there is "an unanswerable 'pure case'" for the "open society," which is "to be found in the literature of political philosophy, especially in the writings of John Stuart Mill."[1] One may even say, with Gertrude Himmelfarb, "Like all successful textbooks, [*On Liberty*] no longer has to be read to make itself felt. We imbibe its 'truth' by osmosis, so to speak, from the culture at large."[2]

Mill himself later in life described *On Liberty* as "a kind of philosophic textbook of a single truth."[3] He strove with great acumen and skill to expound that truth in his essay. Yet we may still ask what the application of his truth was to freedom of expression. The answer is less clear than many have assumed.

The reason for the obscurity lies in the tension between Mill's individualism and the rationalistic utilitarianism that he inherited from Jeremy Bentham and his own father, James Mill. One writer on Mill, Thomas Woods, has said that Mill's "task was to harmonize philosophy —the philosophy of his father and Bentham—with human feelings, particularly human feelings as revealed in poetry which, he came to believe, represented a kind of direct contact with truth."[4] From this effort of Mill's to recognize the claims of both feeling and thought, poetry and philosophy, Karl Britton adds, "we can trace the beginnings of his own moral and political theory; his personal emphasis on the intrinsic value of the individual character and individual differences."[5] It is this that lies

behind the attempted marriage between liberalism and utilitarianism in
On Liberty. Mill believed deeply in the value of individuality, but felt
obliged to show that it was socially useful. We thus come to the question
of immediate interest to us: how much utility for individual freedom of
expression did Mill try to establish in his essay?

In chapter 1, Mill says that his object in the essay is "to assert one
very simple principle, as entitled to govern absolutely the dealings of
society with the individual in the way of compulsion and control,
whether the means used be physical force in the form of legal penalties
or the moral coercion of public opinion." (On the whole he regards
public opinion as the greater threat to liberty.) The principle is that "the
only purpose for which power can be rightfully exercised over any
member of a civilized community, against his will, is to prevent harm to
others. His own good, either physical or moral, is not a sufficient
warrant." Other-regarding actions, which justify restraint by either law or
social censure, are those that harm others.[6] In chapter 4 it is further
explained that the kind of harm that is meant is done only by conduct
which violates "a distinct and assignable obligation to any other person
or persons." All that part of a person's conduct, therefore, "which neither
violates any specific duty to the public, nor occasions perceptible hurt to
any assignable person except himself," remains in the class of self-
regarding actions and is immune from social control.[7]

The right to self-regarding actions includes absolute freedom of
thought and opinion on all subjects and absolute freedom to express and
publish opinions. Freedom of expression admittedly "belongs to that
part of the conduct of an individual which concerns other people, but
being almost of as much importance as the liberty of thought itself and
resting in great part on the same reasons, is practically inseparable from
it."[8] This is the only reason for freedom of expression that Mill offers in
chapter 1. The argument so far, then, seems to be that what a man
thinks does not concern others, and what he says is inseparable from his
thinking it; therefore, it does not concern others either, in the sense of
doing the kind of harm that they have a right to prevent.

Chapter 2 is devoted expressly to the liberty of thought and discussion, and here the argument shifts its ground. The right to the
"expression of opinion" is again proposed as absolute; in Mill's oft-
quoted words, "If all mankind minus one were of one opinion, mankind
would be no more justified in silencing that one person than he, if he
had the power, would be justified in silencing mankind."[9] But as R. P.
Anschutz points out, Mill's argument for freedom of expression does
not really rest on the premise that the individual should be free in
self-regarding actions, as chapter 1 would have led one to expect.
It proceeds, rather on "the assumption that there is to be the freest

interchange of opinions among men. It is an argument for interaction rather than insulation."[10]

And, in fact, Mill's argument for freedom of expression, in the chapter devoted to that subject, is that it is socially useful. He understands the principle of free expression as having "no application to any state of things anterior to the time when mankind have become capable of being improved by free and equal discussion."[11] Once men have reached that state, however, Mill contends that whether opinions are true, false, or partially true and partially false, their uninhibited expression is always a contribution to the advancement of truth and mankind is always the loser by their suppression. Only complete freedom of expression can maintain those conditions in which opinions will be constantly refined by criticism, men's mental powers will be developed by controversy, the grains of truth will gradually be sifted out from the chaff of error, and true beliefs will be held, not as dead dogmas but as living convictions.

Admittedly, Mill maintains that "*absolute* certainty" is not available to men, and hence we cannot be sure but that the opinion we suppress may be true. "All silencing of discussion is an assumption of infallibility," he says in a famous phrase—and the assumption, he declares, is unwarranted.[12] But to say this is not to found freedom on agnosticism, and it does not bar us from "presuming an opinion to be true because with every opportunity for contesting it, it has not been refuted."[13] If the opportunity for contestation is preserved, progress in the discovery of truth will be made. "As mankind improve the number of doctrines which are no longer disputed or doubted will constantly be on the increase," and there will be "a consolidation ... of true opinions" and a "gradual narrowing of the bounds of diversity of opinion."[14]

Kendall is right, but only up to a point, when he asserts that the inescapable implication of Mill's position is that "a society can ... have no orthodoxy, no public truth, no standard, upon whose validity it is entitled to insist."[15] It would be more accurate, if less complimentary, to say that Mill wants to eat his cake and have it, too. In his society there would indeed be no orthodoxy, that is to say, no truth which, because public, would be immune from criticism, attack or outright denial. Yet there would eventually be a consensus among all or almost all thinking men, and it would consist of those "doctrines which are no longer disputed or doubted." This consensus would of course guide men in their social as well as individual decisions, and would perform the function of a public philosophy. But it would leave them, in Rousseau's phrase, as free as they were before, because they would individually assent to it as a set of convictions which, through discussion and debate, they had come to see as true. How Mill understood "truth" is a matter of considerable dispute among scholars, but there is no doubt that he believed that truth is attainable and that movement toward it is the essence of social progress.

Because Mill believed in truth, the liberty for which he contends throughout chapter 2 is the freedom to express *opinions*. It includes "the fullest liberty of professing and discussing, as a matter of ethical conviction, any doctrine, however immoral it may be considered."[16] But it is still a doctrine that is professed, i.e., a proposition which is put forward as true, is held as a matter of ethical conviction, and is to be both defended and attacked with rational arguments.

Mill is not concerned in this chapter with expressions that do not expound opinions. Utterances and publications which are mere expressions of emotion or mere appeals to the senses, the imagination and the passions are outside the scope of his argument. He is well aware that controversy heightens and exacerbates sectarian feelings. Yet the most impassioned exchange that he has in mind is "the violent conflict between parts of the truth,"[17] and therefore does not include forms of expression that do not fit into the framework of rational discourse. He does hold that it is undesirable to try to put restraints on "what is commonly meant by intemperate discussion, namely invective, sarcasm, personality, and the like."[18] It may be doubted, however, whether he is thinking of or means to defend a mode of discourse which consists principally in accusing one's adversary of engaging in unmentionable activities with his mother.

The point is that Mill's argument proves no more than it set out to prove. All forms of liberty, as John M. Robson says, "are connected not loosely but intimately in Mill's thought with his desire that the truth should make men happy."[19] Mill's contention was that "in an imperfect state of the human mind the interests of truth require a diversity of opinions."[20] From this premise he argued to the conclusion that complete freedom of expressing opinions and beliefs should prevail in society. He was not trying to prove that everything that can be classified as "expression" rather than as "action" must be free and unrestrained. Mill is open to Kendall's charge that he regarded society at large as "*a debating club* devoted above all to the pursuit of truth."[21] But there is no evidence in his plea for liberty of discussion that he looked upon society as a Los Angeles nightclub featuring nude dancing on the bar.

If one wants to search for an argument for unrestrained freedom of expression in *On Liberty*, then, one must look for it, not in chapter 2, but in the following chapters. These chapters are concerned with freedom of action rather than of expression, and Mill admits at the beginning of chapter 3: "No one pretends that actions should be as free as opinions."[22] Nonetheless it is here, if anywhere, that Mill approaches the position that the individual should be free to express what is in him merely because it is in him.

The argument of these chapters, as of the entire essay, is controlled by the premise which Mill states in his introductory chapter in the following terms.

> I forgo any advantage which could be derived to my argument from the idea of abstract right as a thing independent of utility. I regard utility as the ultimate appeal on all ethical questions; but it must be utility in the largest sense, grounded on the permanent interests of man as a progressive being. Those interests, I contend, authorize the subjection of individual spontaneity to external control only in respect to those actions of each which concern the interest of other people.[23]

Mill will argue, therefore, for the broadest possible scope for "individual spontaneity," particularly in chapter 3 on individuality as one of the elements of well-being. He will not do so, however, on the basis of the individual's "abstract right," but solely on utilitarian grounds. But in chapter 3 the concept of utility, if it does not change substantially, at least becomes considerably broader than in chapter 2.

The chapter begins with a parallelism between the freedom to express one's opinions and the freedom to act on those opinions. Public opinion and the force of law may restrain actions "which without justifiable cause do harm to others," and "even opinions lose their immunity when the circumstances in which they are expressed are such as to constitute their expression a positive instigation to some mischievous act." But the individual should be completely free to act "according to his own inclination and judgment in things which concern himself" and "without molestation, to carry his opinions into practice at his own cost."[24]

The freedom of action that Mill advocates is freedom to act on one's opinions or beliefs about how one should live one's own life. It supposes previous deliberation and choice; it is not freedom to act on mere impulse; and it is based on "the same reasons" as the freedom to express opinions. He explains:

> As it is useful that while mankind are imperfect there should be different opinions, so it is that there should be different experiments of living; that free scope should be given to varieties of character, short of injury to others; and that the worth of different modes of life should be proved practically, when anyone thinks fit to try them. It is desirable, in short, that in things which do not primarily concern others individuality should assert itself.[25]

But, in explaining why individuality should assert itself, Mill raises the argument to a new plane and shifts attention from "the appreciation of means toward an acknowledged end" to "the end itself."[26] He quotes with approval a passage from Wilhelm von Humboldt's *The Sphere and Duties of Government,* in which the latter says that "the end of man ... is the highest and most harmonious development of his powers to a complete and consistent whole." The object of men's efforts, according to Humboldt, must therefore be "the individuality of power and development." For this there are two requirements: "freedom, and variety of situations." From them result "individual vigor and manifold diversity," which combine themselves in "originality."[27]

It follows that individual freedom is not merely a means to but an essential part of the end of life. Mill (now in his own words) regrets that "individual spontaneity is hardly recognized by the common modes of thinking as having any intrinsic worth, or deserving any regard on its own account."[28] Mill himself obviously believes that individual spontaneity has intrinsic worth and deserves regard on its own account. It is therefore choiceworthy for its own sake; it is an end, not a mere means.

H. J. McCloskey comments: "Had Mill meant by liberty simply freedom from interference, being let alone, the claim that liberty is of intrinsic value could not be sustained.... There is no special value in the liberty enjoyed by the aimless, shiftless drifter or the sadistic hunter; the situation would be better for the latter's actions not being freely chosen." McCloskey would agree, however, that there is "intrinsic value" in liberty as Mill "often seemed" to conceive it, i.e., "as consisting in good exercises of liberty, in one's being self-developing, or pursuing one's good."[29] That is, in fact, the idea of freedom implicit in Mill's praise of spontaneity.

Freedom, as Mill expounds it here, is freedom to develop oneself; freedom to degrade or to destroy oneself is not proposed as a value in itself. This seems clear from Mill's pleas to society to agree "that the free development of individuality is one of the leading essentials of well-being; that it is not only a co-ordinate element with all that is designated by the terms civilization, instruction, education, culture, but is itself a necessary part and condition of all those things."[30] It may safely be assumed that "those things" are "the permanent interests of man as a progressive being," of which "the free development of individuality" is now presented as being "a necessary part and condition."

Mill's notion of freedom is certainly individualistic. As he said in chapter 1, "the only freedom which deserves the name is that of pursuing our own good in our own way."[31] On the other hand, he is not so subjectivist that he advocates acting on whatever desires we happen to find in ourselves. In his most ardent advocacy of individual freedom, he cannot refrain from emphasizing that the individual needs freedom in order to develop his "higher nature." The mere fact "that people have diversities of taste," he says, would be "reason enough for not attempting to shape them all after one model." But the stronger and more cogent reason is that "different persons also require different conditions for their spiritual development; ... The same things which are helps to one person toward the cultivation of his higher nature are hindrances to another."[32]

Freedom, then, is for the sake of development, understood as the cultivation of the individual's higher nature. Now, to speak of a higher nature is to imply a lower nature which ought not to be developed. One might infer from this that the development of an individual's lower nature is a process which other persons might interfere with without real loss to the individual or to society. The individual must indeed be free to pursue his own good in his own way, but not what is genuinely bad for him, as some things must be if the distinction between the higher and the lower natures has any meaning.

But this is not an inference that Mill will accept. He wants to maintain that, when the individual does what affects only himself, whether for good or ill, "his independence is, of right, absolute. Over himself, over his own body and mind, the individual is sovereign."[33] Mill therefore seeks to block the inference by making freedom identical with development. Freedom is the exercise of individuality, and Mill insists "that the individuality is the same thing with development, and that it is only the cultivation of individuality which produces, or can produce, well-developed human beings."[34]

It is true, of course, that there is no development without the exercise of individual freedom. It does not follow, however, that every exercise of freedom is, merely as such, development. Mill knows this but, as Sir Isaiah Berlin remarks, he

> confuses two distinct notions. One is that all coercion is, in so far as it frustrates human desires, bad as such, although it may have to be applied to prevent other, greater evils; while non-interference, which is the opposite of coercion, is good as such, although it is not the only good. This is the "negative" conception of liberty in its classical form. The other is that men should seek to discover the truth, or to develop a certain type of character of which Mill approved—fearless, original, imaginative, independent to the point of eccentricity, and so on—and that truth can be found, and such character can be bred, only in conditions of freedom. Both are liberal views, but they are not identical, and the connexion between them is, at best, empirical.[35]

We shall return to this point later. For the moment, let us only note that Mill's confusion of the two notions of liberty enables him to identify the individual's freedom from interference with his exercise of individuality, which in turn produces development. The cultivation of individuality, he continues, perfects not only the individual but society as a whole. "In proportion to the development of his individuality, each person becomes more valuable to himself, and is, therefore, capable of being more valuable to others."[36] Freedom, then, as the exercise and expression of individuality, is not only the means to but the condition and substance of the development of the human race. Thus is consummated the marriage of liberalism and utilitarianism.

The indissoluble union between liberty and utility becomes even more apparent if we consider, no longer the average run of men, but the minority of exceptional persons who are needed "not only to discover new truths and point out when what were once truths are true no longer, but also to commence new practices and set the example of more enlightened conduct and better taste and sense in human life." Such people of "originality" and "genius," who can elevate society by their "experiments," deserve and require freedom above all others. They "should be encouraged in acting differently from the mass," even to the point of eccentricity.[37] For eccentricity is the necessary byproduct of liberty, and "the only unfailing and permanent source of improvement is liberty, since by it there are as many possible independent centers of improvement as there are individuals."[38]

The theory of freedom that Mill expounds in chapter 3 is concerned with freedom of action rather than of expression. Yet one could base an extension of his case for freedom of expression on it. What people are free to do in fact as "experiments of living," they must surely be free to treat of in fiction, whether in writing, on the stage or screen, or in any of the other arts. Mill's mind had a pronounced bias toward abstract thought and reasoned argument, and this dominates his discussion of freedom of expression in chapter 2. But the theory of individual freedom that he elaborates in chapter 3 would seem to justify a range of free artistic expression as broad as the range of experiments of living. This extension of Mill's argument is all the more justified because Mill himself so clearly regards experiments of living as a contribution, in action rather than in words, to social discussion of the best manner of living.

On the other hand, just as not everything a human being may choose to do can honestly be called an "experiment of living," so not every representation of what human beings do merits the title of "art" or can be taken as a fictional experiment of living. Many experiments of living will produce bad results and will have to be accounted as failures. But Mill evidently presumed that the experiments for whose freedom he contended in chapter 3 would at least be serious ones and would tend on the whole to "set the example of more enlightened conduct and better taste and sense in human life." The same presumption must be made about artistic expression, if we are to infer its freedom from Mill's arguments for the liberty to engage in experiments of living.

We have therefore not yet answered the question whether Mill's theory of freedom can be extended to "expressions" that pander to what society calls vices and Mill describes as "the self-regarding faults ... which are not properly immoralities" because they do not "involve a breach of duty to others."[39] Mill gives some reason for believing so.

When he comes, in chapters 4 and 5, to the practical application of his theory, he insists that liberty includes the right to engage in practices which perceptibly harm only the persons who indulge in them, e.g., drunkenness, gambling, extravagance, sexual incontinence, idleness. There is an obvious objection to this position and Mill, to his credit, states it clearly and strongly: since these practices do harm, and not good, there is no reason why law and public opinion should not operate against them.

> There is no question here (it may be said) about restricting individuality, or impeding the trial of new and original experiments in living. The only things it is sought to prevent are things which have been tried and condemned from the beginning of the world until now—things which experience has shown not to be useful or suitable to any person's individuality. There must be some length of time and amount of experience after which a moral or prudential truth may be regarded as established; and it is merely desired to prevent generation after generation from falling over the same precipice which has been fatal to their predecessors.[40]

Mill's answer to this is that society may punish the evil acts to which such vices lead, insofar as they do assignable harm to others, e.g., a man's failure to pay his debts or to support his family as a result of his intemperance or extravagance. But society may not punish or restrain the vices themselves. They are immune from social control because they are in the class of self-regarding actions. The freedom that is guaranteed in practice, then, is not the freedom to develop oneself but the freedom to perform self-regarding actions, good or bad. This freedom is nonetheless related to the goal of development by the premise that "for none of these [actions] is anyone accountable to his fellow-creatures, because for none of them is it for the good of mankind that he should be held accountable to them."[41]

Mill's answer to the objection deserves careful attention as much for what he admits as for what he denies. He admits, in fact, the whole substance of the objection and denies only the conclusion drawn from it. He does not pretend that the vices named are experiments in living or that they contribute to the development of individuality. He does not deny that after some length of time and amount of experience we may take a moral or prudential truth as established. Indeed, believing as he did in intellectual and moral progress—for what is *On Liberty* but a promise of progress?—he would have to agree that making progress includes arriving at some conclusions from age-long experience. If we cannot arrive at them, then progress never takes place and is a meaningless term. Not all moral questions are forever open questions, and Mill does not say that they are.

He simply asserts that society must keep its hands off these self-regarding vices "for the sake of the greater good of human freedom."[42] "It is easy," he says, "for anyone to imagine an ideal public which leaves the freedom and choice of individuals in all uncertain matters undisturbed and only requires them to abstain from modes of conduct which universal experience has condemned."[43] But there is no such ideal public; the real public always goes too far and tries to repress conduct that it merely finds offensive. We must therefore build an impregnable wall of separation between self-regarding and other-regarding actions. The reason, however, is not that we can never be sure whether self-regarding actions are harmful and prevent development. It is rather that on balance it is better to protect all self-regarding actions than to trust an unenlightened public to regulate any of them.

Mill therefore denies the public any right to make moral or prudential judgments in regard to the self-regarding conduct of the individual. Lest the public interfere too much, it must not be permitted to interfere at all, because the harm done by its intervention would outweigh the good that would be accomplished by the regulation or prohibition of obvious and undeniable vices. It is on this premise that Mill's case for absolute noninterference with the individual's personal conduct stands or falls.

The premise may be a valid one, but it takes something like an act of faith to accept it. As Berlin remarked, the connection between liberty as noninterference and liberty as development is at best an empirical one: we can affirm it only to the extent that we see that in practice it exists. But the empirical evidence for the connection, in the universal terms in which Mill asserts it, is hardly overwhelming. What historical experience has taught us that the most vigorous and progressive nations are the ones that have drawn the line where Mill draws it between the public and the private spheres of life? Mill's position is at most a prudential judgment and a prediction of consequences, no more capable of being demonstrated than the judgments he rejects.

Nor is it any answer to assert that the only alternative to Mill's liberalism is an all-pervading puritanism that admits no distinction between private and socially-controlled conduct. One could instead approach the question from a different angle, as one of Mill's early critics, Sir James Fitzjames Stephen, did by relying "upon considerations drawn from the nature of law, civil and criminal."[44] That is to say, there is much that society could without injustice prohibit by law but wisely chooses to leave alone, out of an awareness that "[c]riminal law is an extremely rough engine, and must be worked with great caution."[45] Law, and even public opinion, must tolerate many evils for the sake of greater good. This is scarcely a new idea in the history of Western thought,[46] but it does not depend on Mill's premise that over his self-regarding conduct the individual is, of right, absolutely sovereign or on his conviction that the public always goes too far.

So far we have been concerned only with the acts of purely personal vices. Does the principle of individual liberty extend to expressions that instigate other persons to indulge in those vices? In most cases, yes. If it is permissible to get drunk, it is permissible to persuade someone else to get drunk, because "whatever it is permitted to do, it must be permitted to advise to do."[47] So also with gambling, sexual seduction and other activities that affect only what today are called consenting adults.

Mill considers the question of instigation to vice doubtful only when the instigator makes a personal profit from promoting what society judges to be an evil, as do pimps and the keepers of gambling houses. Having argued both sides of the question whether such as they must be tolerated, Mill says in the end that he "will not venture to decide."[48]

But the point on which Mill waffles is the practical point at issue in discussing possible limitations on pornography and other kinds of sensation-mongering in literature and the representational arts. If all profit were eliminated from them, there would be little left to regulate. "It is significant," as Lord Devlin says, "that when Mill touched on this problem—the commercialization of vice—his teaching wavered."[49] And Mill only touches on the problem; it is not one with which he feels comfortable. As Anschutz points out, Mill "never mentions" the case for the censorship of pornographic literature.[50] One can only speculate, therefore, about what he would have said had he explicitly considered the question.

F. L. van Holthoon has argued that Mill's principles would justify a regime of uninhibited freedom of expression. He agrees substantially with Maurice Cowling's thesis that *On Liberty* is not so much a plea for individual freedom as an effort to supersede Christianity by a rationalistic utilitarianism called the Religion of Humanity.[51] But, says Holthoon,

> Mill's intention may be anything but libertarian, the formal application of Mill's principle certainly is. No one, according to Mill, needs account to society for acts which only concern himself, even though his behaviour transgresses all bounds of civilized living and even when it is evident to others that he will hurt his own interests. Within the sphere of liberty Mill will even tolerate the drunkard and the pimp, and it is not at

all far-fetched to justify a most liberal policy towards pornography with an appeal to Mill's principle.[52]

If this interpretation of Mill is correct, then his principles could be extended to protect all forms of expression, however devoid of intellectual or moral content, so long as they were not positive instigations to injure others. But on one significant point Holthoon goes too far. He is not quite right in saying: "Mill will even tolerate the drunkard and the pimp." The drunkard and the fornicator, yes; but it was on the question of tolerating the pimp that Mill wavered. Presumably he would have wavered also on a literature that performs a function analogous to that of a pimp.

One may suspect, however, that such a literature was not quite what Mill was thinking of when he pleaded for freedom for individuality to assert itself. Other writers on Mill have remarked that, whatever the conclusions later generations of liberals were to draw from Mill's principles, his own understanding of their application was limited by his social assumptions. This was true even of his conception of political debate, according to Woods, who says:

> Fundamentally, his view of the ideal society was of an extension of the small section of bourgeois radicals in which he lived—where everyone was fairly well off, everyone was reasonable, and no one allowed emotional considerations to cloud a calm and critical judgement of political problems. It was, no doubt, a pleasant and highminded little circle, but how much relevance had it to the deadly antagonisms of class-struggle in the real world?[53]

Lord Devlin makes a similar comment on Mill's liberalism in morals.

> Evidently what Mill visualizes is a number of people doing things he himself would disapprove of, but doing them openly and earnestly and after thought and discussion in an endeavour to find the way of life best suited to them as individuals. This seems to me on the whole an idealistic picture.[54]

The strength of Woods's and Devlin's criticism is that, however libertarian the formal application of Mill's principles, his was a highly moralistic libertarianism. He wanted an inviolable sphere of individual liberty, but he conceived of it as a sphere in which individuals would express serious opinions on serious subjects and would test those opinions in practice through experiments of living. Even the art to which, we may infer, he would give free rein would be a moralizing art. Robson remarks: "As always in Mill's discussions of man, feeling is the horse, but intellect the rider.... As always with him, then, art centers upon humanity and is dedicated to morality."[55]

It is this moralizing propensity that enables Mill to assume that the net result of a regime of free expression will be moral progress, the development of men's higher natures and the elevation of standards of taste and conduct. He advocates an absolute liberty to indulge in merely personal vices because, he feels, that is the price that must be paid for the kind of freedom in which alone he is really interested. The society he envisions is one in which, in Cowling's words, "men are to be reasoning, arguing, scrutinizing, probing, in order to subject their own lives, and the institutions and conventions by which they are bound, to the most searching practical tests the cultivated reason can devise."[56] Mill is able to visualize such a society as resulting from the freedom which he advocates because he does not sufficiently attend to the possibility that freedom may be used systematically to exploit people's weaknesses, not to develop reason but to deprave and suppress it. The problem created by "expressions" that bypass reason to appeal to men's fears, hatreds and assorted lusts is one that Mill largely ignores.

Perhaps he chooses to ignore it. For example, he admits that "offenses against decency," if committed in public, "may rightly be prohibited." But he hastens to add that "it is unnecessary to dwell" on them, "as they are only connected indirectly with our subject."[57] J. D. Rees comments that it is hard to see why Mill says this, but that it may have been because he realized that to allow punishment of such offenses on the ground that they injured other people's interests enlarged the concept of "interest" more than he cared to admit. On the other hand, Mill recognized that pimps and gambling-house keepers were "classes of persons with an interest opposed to what is considered as the public weal, and whose mode of living is grounded on the counteraction of it."[58] This conflict of interests poses a dilemma which Rees states in these terms:

> Are we to interpret interests so narrowly as to exclude the public interest or so widely as to involve consideration of the general interest and social morality? On the former interpretation we should find ourselves unable to prohibit activity we should want to prohibit; on the latter we should be able to prohibit actions that Mill would certainly wish to be left unrestrained.

Mill's principle, as Rees remarks, "can yield no clear directive in questions of this kind."[59]

In other words, the marriage between liberalism and utilitarianism may not be so complete or so stable as Mill would have us believe. The tension in his thought between the claims of individuality and the demands of social utility is, in significant respects, left unresolved. Mill resolves it to his own satisfaction by concentrating his attention on individuals who might use their freedom to act in ways that would shock the bourgeoisie, but who would in fact themselves be high-minded and reasonable members of that same bourgeoisie. What he says of such people in *On Liberty* may possibly be true so far as it goes. But one is left feeling, with Lord Devlin, that Mill "did not really grapple with the fact that along the paths that depart from traditional morals, pimps leading the weak astray outnumber spiritual explorers at the head of the strong."[60]

It is Mill's failure to grapple with reality that makes it difficult to judge how much freedom of expression can be deduced from his principles. Freedom to express opinions, however immoral, he explicitly advocated in the confidence that truth would prevail in the debate they would provoke. Although he does not say so, it is safe to infer that he would defend a range of artistic exploration of ways of life as broad as the range of experiments of living. He also clearly defended the individual's right to indulge in personal vices and to seduce others into doing the same, so long as he does not do so for profit. But to go beyond this is to go beyond the essay *On Liberty*.

When it comes to a "literature" and an "art" that ignore or subvert man's "higher nature" and appeal only to his lower nature, not only does Mill not state his position, but it is not clear what it would have been had he done so. As Berlin points out, "Mill's ideal...is an attempt to fuse rationalism and romanticism: the aim of Goethe and Wilhelm Humboldt; a rich, spontaneous, many-sided, fearless, free, and yet rational, self-directed character."[61] The argument of *On Liberty* implies a teleology: freedom is required because it serves an intellectual and moral purpose; or, if you will, a certain serious-minded moral freedom *is* that purpose —but not every kind of freedom. It would be hard to say with confidence how Mill would have fitted today's conception of "expression" into this teleology, but one may surmise that he would have experienced some difficulty. The arguments for freedom of expression that he does present are too steeped in a moralistic rationalism to allow the conclusions of our contemporary liberals to be drawn from them with any firmness. For there are more things, not only in heaven, but in Piccadilly and Times Square, than are dreamed of in John Stuart Mill's philosophy.

6

The Polity of Discussion and the Discussion of Polity

Bagehot and Laski

Walter Bagehot and Harold Laski, both Englishmen, were lesser lights than John Stuart Mill but nonetheless made noteworthy contributions to the literature of freedom of speech and press. Bagehot, a Victorian liberal, calmly taught his readers that a polity founded on discussion is the apex of civilization. Laski, writing in the first half of the twentieth century, strenuously urged a constant radical discussion of the polity itself with a view to transforming it into a socialist economy. Both men are examples of late rationalism, with its evolutionary conception of truth, yet they still state the case for freedom of expression as a plea for the liberty of reason to pursue truth.

Walter Bagehot

It is commonly agreed that Bagehot was clever; some would maintain that he was more than merely that. He had, says one commentator, "a versatile and prolific mind, but was primarily a journalist and essayist rather than an original scholar."[1] He has been called England's "greatest journalist" of his day, "a journalist in the sense that Walter Lippmann was."[2] Crane Brinton describes him as "a superior person, but not superior to his age,"[3] and that was the age of Queen Victoria. Not surprisingly, "many of his ideas do ring true to his age, and hence a little false to ours."[4] But, though Victorian, Bagehot was hardly dull or stodgy. "The English are extremely fond of clever controversy," as Brinton says, "and Bagehot himself played up to that fondness."[5]

Bagehot accordingly latched his belief in "government by discussion" on to the then newly-popular theory of evolution by natural selection. The first part of his *Physics and Politics* appeared in the *Fortnightly* in

1867—less than a decade after the publication of Darwin's *The Origin of Species*—though the full book did not come out until 1872. The subtitle of the work is *Thoughts on the Application of the Principles of "Natural Selection" and "Inheritance" to Political Society* and, an English critic sarcastically remarks, "it was, of course, Darwin above all on whom he was drawing for his new excitement."[6] Or, as Brinton puts it, *"Physics and Politics*—the title is misleading, for Bagehot is concerned rather with biology than with physics—... marks one of the first attempts of political thought to find a new ally in the young, and, in 1872, lusty science of biology."[7]

Bagehot's theory of political evolution is, God knows, simple enough. In the Preliminary Age those clans, tribes or nations that had the strongest organization, a patriarchial family structure and a rigid code of morals and law conquered—and often killed off—disorganized and therefore weak groups. These were the social factors that by a kind of natural selection led to the dominance of the fittest nations. But the very strength of the customary law and morals that made them powerful also halted their progress and, almost everywhere, made them stationary societies. Only in rare nations did the practice emerge of carrying on the business of government by discussion. As the practice spread to other areas of life and thought, these nations entered the Age of Discussion in which alone continuous progress is possible. So again, by a process of natural selection, these became the fittest nations, the few truly "first-rate" ones.

It was important to Bagehot's evolutionary thesis to insist that the low morals of savages, as they still existed in remote corners of the world with little change from prehistoric times, were not degraded morals. For that term would imply that these tribes had fallen from a previous and higher level of morality that they had once enjoyed. But this is improbable, because the higher morality would have given them a military prowess they would have been reluctant to lose. Bagehot explains:

> There are many savages who can hardly be said to care for human life, who have scarcely the family feelings, who are eager to kill all old people (their own parents included) as soon as they get old and become a burden; who have scarcely the sense of truth, who (probably from a constant tradition of terror) wish to conceal everything, and would (as observers say) "rather lie than not"; whose ideas of marriage are so vague and slight that the idea "communal marriage," in which all the women of the tribe are common to all the men and them alone, has been invented to denote it: now, if we consider how cohesive and how fortifying to human societies are the love of truth and the love of parents and a stable marriage tie, how sure such feelings would be to make a tribe which possessed them wholly and soon victorious over tribes which were destitute of them, we shall begin to comprehend how

unlikely it is that vast masses of tribes throughout the world should have lost all these moral helps to conquest, not to speak of others.[8]

Poor Bagehot; writing in the Victorian age, he could not know that his savages were ahead, not only of their time, but of his. As he read history, however, its lesson was that "a cohesive 'family' is the best germ for a campaigning nation." The Romans "were ready to obey their generals because they were compelled to obey their fathers; they conquered the world in manhood because as children they were bred in homes where the tradition of passionate valor was steadied by the habit of implacable order."[9]

Prehistoric man emerged from savage disorder to the extent that first the family, and then the polity, established the conditions of order. "*Law*," says Bagehot, "—rigid, definite, concise law—is the primary want of early mankind; that which they need above everything else, that which is requisite before they can gain anything else."[10] This was not the narrowly-limited statute law of the modern state, for what early men needed was "a single government—call it 'church' or 'state' as you like—regulating the whole of human life."[11] The object of such a unified society

> is to create what may be called a *cake* of custom. All the actions of life are to be submitted to a single rule for a single object—that gradually created "hereditary drill" which science teaches to be essential, and which the early instinct of men saw to be essential too. That this *régime* forbids free thought is not an evil,—or rather, though an evil, it is the necessary basis for the greatest good; it is necessary for making the mold of civilization and hardening the soft fiber of early man.[12]

Early societies were therefore intolerant. By systematic discrimination against nonconformists, they bred them, so to speak, out of the population,[13] and by discouraging contact with foreigners, they kept their own type or national character pure. For they knew the danger to their existence "when the sudden impact of new thoughts and new examples breaks down the compact despotism of the single consecrated code, and leaves pliant and impressible man—such as he then is—to follow his unpleasant will without distinct guidance by hereditary morality and hereditary religion."[14]

Man such as he *then* was had an "unpleasant will." Civilized man is different now. The "old oligarchies," Bagehot explains, made "the human nature which after times employ."[15] We "reckon as the basis of our culture upon an amount of order, of tacit obedience, of prescriptive governability,"[16] that to us is so obvious that we take it as natural; but in fact it is a historical acquisition. Yet Bagehot seems to feel that, once acquired, it is not lost easily, if at all.

As, in biological evolution, chance variations produce the types best fitted to survive in their environments, so "chance predominance" in society produces a model of man that attracts admiration by its success. It molds men because of their unconscious but nearly invincible urge "to imitate what is before their eyes, and to be what they are expected to be."[17] This national type or character, once formed, becomes so deeply ingrained that it is transmitted from generation to generation not only psychologically but even genetically. It is clear, Bagehot believes, "that there is a tendency, a probability—greater or less according to circumstances, but always considerable—that the descendants of cultivated parents will have, by born nervous organization, a greater aptitude for cultivation than the descendants of such as are not cultivated; and that this tendency augments in some enhanced ratio for many generations."[18]

The men of the French Constituent Assembly in 1789 were wrong, then, when they looked upon the past as

> a complex error to be got rid of as soon as might be. But that error had made themselves; on their very physical organization the hereditary mark of old times was fixed; their brains were hardened and their nerves were steadied by the transmitted results of tedious usages. The ages of monotony had their use, for they trained men for ages when they need not be monotonous.[19]

The time comes, however, when the ages of monotony can and should end. There is a "whole family of arrested civilizations" which seem "to have prepared all the means to advance to something good, and then to have stopped and not advanced." This is true of "almost every sort of Oriental civilization."[20] The discipline of law and morals that raised them from savagery became a tyranny of custom and fixed opinion that "killed out of the whole society the propensities to variation which are the principle of progress."[21] Liberty becomes essential to progress because it allows these propensities to assert themselves.

Yet hard as it was to form the mold of civilization, it is even harder to break it sufficiently to make progress possible. Bagehot knows that regress and civilizational decline are possible, but he is convinced that on the whole progress is the law of history. The great obstacle to it is that "cake of custom" which made civilization in the first place. It is this cake, and not civilization itself, that must be broken.[22] Civilization, in fact, is in no danger, because it has become an ingrained habit and a genetic endowment. No doubt, it is easier to believe that there will always be an England and England will be free, if one is convinced that England has got into the blood. At any rate, Bagehot drew from the perhaps unlikely source of Darwinism the typically liberal confidence that civilized men are now "tame enough to bear discussion."[23]

Not, of course, that it was always so. Government by discussion "from its origin ... is a plant of singular delicacy; at first the chances are much against its living." It is no wonder, then, that "such states are very rare in history."[24] One of the conditions of their survival was that the number of subjects on which discussion was permitted was at first very small and "the area of free argument was enlarged but very slowly."[25] Nevertheless, the nations that have prevailed in the evolutionary struggle are those that "have passed out of the first stage of civilization into the second stage, out of the stage where permanence is most wanted into that where variability is most wanted,"[26] and these are nations that have allowed freedom of discussion.

History tells us "that the change from the age of *status* to the age of choice was first made in states where the government was to a great and a growing extent a government by discussion, and where the subjects of that discussion were in some degree abstract, or as we should say, matters of principle."[27] North American Indians, says Bagehot, are celebrated orators, but their oratory has led to nothing because it is "a discussion not of principles but of undertakings," e.g., shall we plunder village A or village B?[28] It was in "the small republics of Greece and Italy"[29] that the habit began of discussing "the visible and pressing interests of the community; they are political questions of high and urgent import." If a nation is able "to discuss these questions with freedom and to decide them with discretion, to argue much on politics and not to argue ruinously, an enormous advance in other kinds of civilization may confidently be predicted for it."[30]

For discussion, once admitted on any subject, extends itself to others and dissolves "the sacred charm of use and wont." All authoritative beliefs crumble in the crucible of discussion for "once effectually submit a subject to that ordeal, and you can never withdraw it again; you can never again clothe it with mystery or fence it by consecration." The cake of custom is broken and the clogs on "the ordinary springs of progress" are removed. Discussion "gives a premium to intelligence.... Tolerance too is learned in discussion; and as history shows, is only so learned."[31] Even where tolerance is not universal, as in Elizabethan England it was not, the extent to which it exists makes a fruitful originality possible. "Within certain limits vigorous and elevated thought was respected in Elizabeth's time, and therefore vigorous and elevated thinkers were many." To conclude: "In this manner all the great movements of thought in ancient and modern times have been nearly connected in time with government by discussion."[32]

There are three additional benefits of government by discussion to which Bagehot calls attention because they "have not been sufficiently noticed."[33] The first is paraphrased by Norman St. John-Stevas in these words: "Government by discussion had the supreme merit of restraining the meddling zeal of the activists."[34] Bagehot himself explains: "A main and principal excellence in the early times of the human races is the impulse to action."[35] As one might say, in an age in which you had to kill the other man before he killed you, it was useful to be quick on the draw. But this bent toward immediate action does more harm than good in the modern and complicated world, where "our over-activity is a very great evil."[36] Even our philanthropy, while no doubt it does great good, "also does great evil ... and this is entirely because excellent people fancy that they can do much by rapid action."[37] We do not like to take the time to reflect and to consider action from several points of view before deciding on it. It is therefore one of the blessings of "a polity of discussion" that it "is the greatest hindrance to the inherited mistake of human nature,— to the desire to act promptly, which in a simple age is so excellent, but which in a later and complex time leads to so much evil."[38]

Similarly, in early ages the "most successful races, other things being equal, are those which multiply the fastest," because numbers are an important element of military power. But in our "comparatively uncontentious civilization" men are left with a sexual "desire far in excess of what is needed."[39] Yet this "inherited excess of human nature," too, can receive some remedy from government by discussion. "Nothing promotes intellect like intellectual discussion, and nothing promotes intellectual discussion so much as government by discussion." Men and women who live in a "perpetual atmosphere of intellectual inquiry" will tend to direct their energies into intellectual rather than sexual pursuits. "There is only a certain *quantum* of power in each of our race; if it goes in one way it is spent, and cannot go in another."[40] This proposition may not be received with enthusiasm in intellectual circles today, but all may at least agree that Bagehot did not include a booming pornography industry among the elements of the regime of free discussion.

"Lastly," he says, "a polity of discussion not only tends to diminish our inherited defects, but also, in one case at least to augment a heritable excellence." This is "a subtle quality or combination of qualities singularly useful in practical life," which he calls "*animated moderation.*" It is just the right balance between thought and action, between impulse and judgment, the balance that enables practical men to go far enough without going too far. It is in this quality that the English "excel all other nations" and it accounts for their success in the world.[41] They can thank government by popular discussion for it, because such a government "tends to produce this quality: a strongly idiosyncratic mind, violently disposed to extremes of opinion, is soon weeded out of political life; and a bodiless thinker, an ineffectual scholar, cannot even live there for a day."[42] Bagehot's intellectual ideal is not the philosopher,[43] but the intelligent man of practice: the scientist, the businessman or the statesman.

This appears clearly in his final chapter, in which he argues that "verifiable progress" is not to be judged by advances in "art, morals, or religion"—superior though they doubtless are—where there is endless dispute about what progress is and how we should measure it. We can, however, verify progress in that on which 99 per cent of mankind will agree.[44] That is the application of "the laws of plain comfort and simple present happiness" and the discovery of "new things 'serviceable to man's life and conducive to man's estate' "[45]—the dream of Bacon and Descartes. This admittedly is progress "in the narrowest sense," but we can all agree on what it is and we can be brought to see that government by discussion is its indispensable prerequisite.[46]

Two years after *Physics and Politics*, in 1874, Bagehot read a paper to the Metaphysical Society entitled *The Metaphysical Basis of Toleration*, in which he stated how much and what kind of freedom of discussion he favored. Toleration, as he used it here, he explained, meant (1) "toleration by law," not by society and public opinion; (2) "toleration in the public expression of opinions," not "toleration of acts and practices"; and (3) toleration of "the discussion of impersonal doctrines," not of "accusations of living persons" which would come under the law of libel.[47]

Bagehot does not mention John Stuart Mill by name, but it seems clear that he is careful at the outset to distinguish his position from the one taken in *On Liberty*. Later in his paper he explicitly says that his "argument that the law should not impose a penalty on the expression of any opinion" does *not* "equally prove that society should not in many cases apply a penalty to that expression." Unlike Mill, Bagehot judges the moral coercion of public opinion sometimes useful. Similarly, while he agrees with Mill that the human mind "learns by freely hearing all arguments," he distances himself from Mill by adding, "but in no case does it learn by trying freely all practices." Bagehot's thesis, therefore, does not cover experiments of living.[48] Finally, he is at least clearer than Mill in stating that what he advocates is the free discussion of "impersonal doctrines." He explicitly distinguishes these only from "accusations of living persons." But it would seem that he limits the scope of freedom to the discussion of propositions that can be argued for and against, and does not include "utterances" that form part of no argument and do not bear upon the truth or falsity of such propositions.

Bagehot is talking, then, about the freedom to express opinions. He finds the zeal to persecute for opinion easy to understand. "Persons of strong opinions wish above all to propagate those opinions," he says. "They find close at hand what seems an immense engine for that propagation,—they find the state."[49] But they err in using this engine, for while coercion "extirpates error," it is doubtful whether it "creates belief."[50]

In fact, Bagehot is sure that it cannot create belief. As Jefferson thought that some persons are natural-born Tories and others naturally Whigs, so Bagehot believes that at least some men are "predisposed by nature" in favor of one religion rather than another. There are "minds prone to be Protestant," while other minds are "naturally Catholic." Persecution may prevent such minds from believing the religion that is "congenial" to them, but it cannot make them believe the one that is uncongenial. It can only make them "more or less conscious skeptics." Underlying this view is Bagehot's own persuasion that there are "ultimate truths of morals and religion which more or less vary for each mind," as "principles of taste" do.[51]

The first principles of taste, he explains, are not arrived at by discussion. Nor are they indemonstrable but universally known truths like the first principles of reasoning, e.g., "that a thing cannot *both* be and not be."[52] Neither are they the kind of conclusions, which "are not the result of discussion," that a man arrives at through long and constant experience, e.g., his "opinion ... as to the character of his friends."[53] The principles of taste are rooted in individual temperaments; through the influence of superior individuals they become common to an age and an area; but they are of necessity variable. Yet that is no reason for excluding them from discussion. For there is an "extrication of truth by such discussions," an elimination of extreme and eccentric views, and a gradual elevation of standards of taste.[54]

The same holds true of the ultimate truths of morals and religion:

> some sort of standard and some kind of agreement can only be arrived at in the very same way. The same comparison of one mind with another is necessary; the same discussion; the same use of criticizing minds, the same use of original ones. The mode of arriving at truth is the same, and also the mode of stopping it [i.e., persecution].[55]

This is pretty vague, one must admit, and leaves Bagehot somewhere between scepticism and dogmatism, in a kind of moral and religious relativism which is yet not totally relativistic. It is, in fact, an evolutionary notion of truth. Whatever one may think of it, however, it is clear —because he explicitly says so—that for Bagehot truth is the goal and discussion is the mode of arriving at it.

His main argument for freedom to express beliefs is the one that Locke had expounded in his letters on toleration, and it is pegged to the idea of truth.

> I say that the state power should not be used to arrest discussion, because the state power may be used equally for truth or error, for Mohammedanism or Christianity, for belief or no-belief; but in discussion, truth has an advantage. Arguments always tell for truth as such, and against error as such: if you let the human mind alone, it has a

preference for good argument over bad; it oftener takes truth than not. But if you do not let it alone, you give truth no advantage at all; you substitute a game of force where all doctrines are equal, for a game of logic where the truer have the better chance.[56]

Toleration, then, means freedom to discuss, and discussion is for the sake of truth. The "only limitations" on discussion that Bagehot will admit are two: "that men's minds shall in the particular society be mature enough to bear the discussion and that the discussion shall not destroy the society."[57] The first limitation has been fully explained in our analysis of *Physics and Politics* but the second needs some further explanation. "No government," says Bagehot, "is bound to permit a controversy which will annihilate itself: it is a trustee for many duties, and if possible it must retain the power to perform those duties. The controversies which may ruin it are very different in different countries: the government of the day must determine in each case what those questions are."[58]

This determination is a delicate one and giving government the power to make it obviously involves some risk. But the risk must be taken and, while the determination cannot be made by the simple application of an abstract rule, it can be made by the exercise of practical, prudential judgment. The question is to be answered in the same way as the preliminary question whether a people is mature enough for a regime of free discussion. About this question Bagehot says:

> There are already in inevitable jurisprudence many lines of vital importance just as difficult to draw: the line between sanity and insanity has necessarily to be drawn, and it is as nice as anything can be. The competency of people to bear discussion is not intrinsically more difficult than their competency to manage their own affairs.[59]

Bagehot is a liberal: he wants a "polity of discussion" whenever it is possible. But he is not doctrinaire; he does not insist that we are constantly faced with an "either-or" choice between total freedom and total repression. "We must not assume that the liberty of discussion has no case of exception," he says. "In each instance, let the people decide whether the particular discussion shall go on or not. Very likely, in some cases, they may decide wrong; but it is better that they should so decide than that we should venture to anticipate all experience, and to make sure that they cannot possibly be right."[60]

This statement alone distinguishes Bagehot sharply from our contemporary First Amendment absolutists, and it also sets him apart from Mill with his "one very simple principle." Bagehot's liberalism was less ideological than Mill's and considerably more moderate and sophisticated. Yet in the basic respect he was not far distant from Mill. As David

Easton says, "A true son of the liberal enlightenment and a follower of the Comtean tradition, Bagehot considers progress essentially a mental process, the creation of new ideas which are transmitted to the minds of successive generations."[61] This process he saw as carried on, not by a whole population, but by an educated minority—in the England of his day, the upper middle class. In his best known work, *The English Constitution* (1867), he says: "We have in a great community like England crowds of people scarcely more civilized than the majority of two thousand years ago; we have others, even more numerous, such as the best people were a thousand years since. The lower orders, the middle orders, are still, when tried by what is the standard of the educated 'ten thousand,' narrow-minded, unintelligent, incurious."[62]

"Knowledge spreads from the top down" in Bagehot's theory of social evolution, says David Easton, "from select individuals or groups to the whole community, and accounts for the advance of one nation over another."[63] The select individuals present the original insights and arguments, and the rest of the educated class constitute what Bagehot calls the "court of inquisition" that is "sitting perpetually, investigating —informally and silently, but not ineffectually—what, on all great subjects of human interest, are truth and error."[64] Heirs to the discipline of the ages and civilized to the bone, they are the people who can "bear discussion."[65] As Bagehot points out, one of the "mental conditions" that a nation must have to be capable of parliamentary government is "'rationality'; by which I do not mean reasoning power, but rather the power of hearing the reasons of others, of comparing them quietly with one's own reasons, and then being guided by the result."[66]

Having acquired the distinctly "modern idea" that "the bad religion of A cannot impair here or hereafter the welfare of B,"[67] people so endowed with rationality are prepared to discuss everything. Their discussion will be, as we say today, "open-ended" because "the mere putting up of a subject to discussion, is a clear admission that that subject is in no degree settled by established rule, and that men are free to choose in it."[68]

Brinton well states Bagehot's view. "Not only is it clear that what we may attain of truth must be arrived at by a process of trial and error, but truth itself is not a fixed attainable summit."[69] Still, truth is the goal and, though there will ever remain another peak to scale, it is through discussion that we climb toward it. Whether the history of the twentieth century confirms this confidence in the steady ascent of the mind, everyone may judge for himself. But it can hardly be disputed that Bagehot advocated no other freedom of expression than the freedom of the mind to pursue truth through discussion.

Harold Laski

Harold Joseph Laski (like John Stuart Mill) was "an extraordinarily precocious child,"[70] and in some ways he remained one all his life. He rose to be the professor of political science in the University of London; he became the friend and correspondent of U.S. Supreme Court justices, British Prime Ministers and President Franklin D. Roosevelt; and he was for many years a member of the Executive Committee of the British Labour Party and the Committee's chairman when the Party came to power in 1945. According to his friend and biographer, Kingsley Martin, he was or at least aspired to be the Party's *éminence grise.*[71] Yet he retained throughout a youthful confidence in his own views and eagerness to convince others of them. As Martin says, "Harold was ablaze with the truth that he believed he must convey."[72]

Laski, the exponent of "rationalist European radicalism,"[73] was in fact a man of passionate faith. At the age of seventeen he openly repudiated the Orthodox Judaism in which he had been raised, and wrote in later life: "I cannot even remember a period in which either ritual or dogma had meaning for me."[74] Though his qualifications as a theologian are somewhat obscure,[75] he was convinced that "scientific theology" had destroyed the credibility of revealed religion.[76] But this meant only that he had replaced one faith with another. Not long after his break with his parents' religion he wrote a lengthy essay in which he argued, as Kingsley Martin summarizes it, that Judaism "should welcome the gospel of Darwin and Marx and, renouncing its exclusiveness, recognize that truth can be found only in an atmosphere of freedom and that a universal philosophy of humanism must now take the place of exclusive creeds and rituals."[77] Laski's Jewish heritage inspired "his constant passion for justice for all men"[78] but was translated into an activist secular humanism.

This faith furnished the dynamism of his political thought through all its permutations. "At successive stages of his career," says Herbert A. Deane, "he was an ardent proponent of pluralism, Fabianism, and, finally, Marxist socialism."[79] But each of these stages was the working out in turn of the same basic convictions. "Eclectic" and "uncritical" he may have been, as Deane calls him,[80] but the passion for justice remained constant and the demands of justice, as he came successively to understand them, were asserted with the same confidence at every stage.

It is unnecessary to analyze the whole of his political thought or to trace its development, since we are concerned here only with his views in the two works proposed to us as major sources in the development of the theory of freedom of expression. They are *Authority in the Modern State* which appeared in 1919 during Laski's "pluralist" phase and *Liberty in the*

Modern State, published in 1930 when he was "veering towards the Marxist conception of the state as the instrument of the dominant capitalist class," but had "not yet arrived at a completely Marxist position."[81]

These are works, then, of Laski's pre-Marxist phase. Yet even after he avowedly espoused Marxism, says Kingsley Martin, Laski was always "a Marxist with a difference" and "could never go the whole Marxist hog, because he believed fundamentally in individual liberty."[82] According to R. H. Soltau, "one could describe his philosophy as a restatement of liberalism to meet the conditions of an industrial age after the impact of the socialist challenge.... It was Benthamism with a strong admixture of Marxism, and one wondered at times which element predominated; anyway, the blending was by no means perfect."[83]

Even when he became a Marxist, he remained at heart an individualist. L. Zerby says:

> Laski repeatedly defends three basic ideals: the Kantian ideal of treating man always as an end in himself and never as a means to an end, the traditional utilitarian ideal of the greatest happiness of the greatest number, and the liberal ideals of equality and liberty. The philosophical basis offered for all of these is a rather uncritical individualism.[84]

Laski's ultimate Marxism flows from the conviction that liberty requires and depends on economic equality. But his individualism is the basic element of his thought. In Soltau's words, "the principle that became the starting point of his thinking" was "his profound belief in the final value of the ordinary man as a moral personality."[85]

Authority in the Modern State makes this belief the basis of an attack on the sovereignty of the state or, indeed, of any other institution.[86] The state, Laski insists, is not identical with society. It is "only one among many forms of human association" in which men unite for the promotion of common interests, and it has no overriding claim on their allegiance.[87] The state today, says Laski, "to its members is essentially a great public service corporation," and while it is "helpful to be told that the object of the state is to secure the good life,"[88] its claim on the public's obedience, both as a matter of fact and a matter of right, consists only in the success it actually has in achieving that object. Men may feel that some other association—the church, for example or what in Laski's mind takes the place of the church, the trade union[89]—more effectively delivers the goods they want and so has a higher claim on their loyalty.

Government wields the power of the state, but it cannot command and it will not get obedience merely on the ground that it is endowed with "sovereignty." Men have a right to, and in practice will, judge of the obedience they owe the state in the light of what they perceive the state as doing. If the state in fact consistently acted in accordance with its theoretical purpose of securing the good life of society's members, it would deserve and get their obedience. But the "truth is that in the processes of politics what, broadly speaking, gets registered is not a will that is at each moment in accord with the state-purpose, but the will of those who in fact operate the machine of government."[90] Their will, however, is the will of the owners of the means of production, for "political power is the handmaid of economic power."[91] Therefore, since "the social order of the modern state is not a labour order but a capitalist, ... it must follow that the main power is capitalist also."[92]

Deane comments that Laski's "fundamental objection is to the capitalist state, and not the sovereign state,"[93] and quotes Laski's own statement in this book: "No one would object to a strong state if guarantees could be had that its strength would be used for the fulfillment of its theoretic purposes."[94] This interpretation of Laski, says Deane, "enables us to link his early pluralistic writings with the radically different views he later advocated. For ... if the social order could be transformed from a capitalist to a labor order, there would be no hindrance to the fulfillment by the state of its theoretic purposes and, consequently, no reason for objecting to a strong, or even a sovereign state."[95]

Deane's comment does throw light on the development of Laski's thought. The object of his attack was always the capitalist state, whether he was denying its sovereignty or, later, hoping to take it over for the workers through a "revolution by consent."[96] But there also ran throughout his thought a strain of radical individualism that probably could be reconciled with his ideal of social equality only in the Marxist vision of a classless society in which the state would wither away.

In *Authority in the Modern State* it is the individual, "each one of us," who judges what the good life is and whether the state is serving it.[97] Men "are individuals who are interested passionately in themselves as an end, and no social philosophy can be adequate which neglects that egocentric element." Moreover, "they are bundles of conflicting aims." There is, therefore, no "permanent and external canon" to which we may refer to determine whether "the purposes of men" are being achieved. We can look only to "the consequences of action in the elucidation and enrichment of life."[98] By those consequences, as men judge them, the state is justified or found wanting.

Democracy, therefore, is necessary:

> The will of man is an individual will; and it sweeps into the general will only to the point where the degree of fusion makes possible a social existence. But even while it accepts it questions and by its doubts it dissolves. So that, in any final analysis, democratic government is the only practical government because it is only in a democracy that an individual will can safeguard its reserves.[99]

On the other hand, Laski does not want to take the individual out of social life. Quite the contrary, he envisions a vigorous social life in which individuals participate freely and as equals. "When we insist," he says, "that, in the last analysis, only the individual is sovereign over himself, we make it possible for him to contribute his best to the sum of social life."[100] But to say this implies that there are norms by which the individual's best and the sum of social life may be judged. Laski maintains that there are such norms and that they are to be found in "the modern revival of natural law."[101] He thereby aims to combine the sovereignty of the individual with an objective social good while avoiding recognition of transcendent moral standards and of any moral authority superior to the democratic process.

The members of a modern state, he says, rightly "think that there are certain principles by which its life must be regulated." But "moral ideas cannot escape the categories of evolution."[102] We must not "take the fatal step of arguing that an ideal to be true must be unchanging."[103] Once we understand the evolutionary nature of truth, "[p]olitical good refuses the swaddling clothes of finality and becomes a shifting conception."[104] We recognize then that "every political ideal" is "adequate only for the moment when it is formulated, insofar as it is a system which claims a practical application."[105]

But we must also recognize the truth contained in natural-law theories, namely, "that one of the great mainsprings of human effort is the realisation of a good greater than that which is actually existent." We can retain what there is of value in these theories "if, with Stammler, we regard the idea of natural law as continually changing in content."[106] This evolving content will be furnished by our developing recognition of "the human needs the satisfaction of which history has demonstrated to be essential" and which are "what we mean today by natural rights."[107] A right

> is natural in the sense that the given conditions of society at the particular time require its recognition. It is not justified on grounds of history. It is not justified on grounds of any abstract or absolute ethic. It is simply insisted that if, in a given condition of society, power is so exerted as to refuse the recognition of that right, resistance is bound to be encountered.[108]

We do not regard a right as natural because it has been established for a long time or because it is derived from a transcendental and absolute ethic. But we will recognize it as "natural" if people regard it as so essential to their happiness that they will resist any exercise of power that deprives them of it. Where do people get their ideas of what is essential? From experience, and from that alone. We thus arrive at norms that we may regard as basic and therefore above the daily political battle, while not subjecting ourselves to rules imposed from outside of and above ourselves.

Laski explains the process in these terms:

> What we do is to deposit hypotheses that have come to us from the facts of life; we declare that their application will enrich the content of the social life. These hypotheses are not the mere whims of chance opinion. We cannot, at least in politics, where decision is necessary, take refuge in a scepticism which, logically followed, makes conduct impossible. We urge that the argument for one principle can in fact be better than another.[109]

There will be argument and debate, therefore, about the lessons of experience, because we can learn from experience. So, for example, we have learned that legal regulation of working conditions in factories is better than *laissez-faire*. "When the hypothesis that sums up such a general experience becomes generally enough accepted it gets written into the code of principles that we in general regard as beyond the realm of ordinary discussion." This is how good law develops. The development of natural law with a changing content is the same: "The general rule of conduct is in nowise different save that its substance is perhaps more fundamental."[110]

Government must not be conceded the power to "traverse" those "notions that we have termed rights," i.e., "the fundamental notions of each age." When there is conflict between government and other groups in society, this theory of authority "refers back each action on which judgment is to be passed to the conscience of the individual. It insists that the supreme arbiter of the event is the totality of such consciences."[111] Conscience, then, is the ultimate judge of the state's authority. "Actual law and ideal law may never coincide; but where they come in conflict there can hardly be doubt as to where the ultimate allegiance is due ... the claim of the state upon us ... depends, for its validity, upon the moral appeal it makes to our conscience."[112]

Laski's thesis may be, as Deane says, "political Protestantism with a vengeance."[113] It is in any case the foundation of the theory of freedom of expression that he presents in this book. The totality of individual consciences, which is to judge and limit the activity of the state, cannot form and express itself without complete liberty of thought, utterance and association. The goal of the state is to satisfy the desires of its members, and the "right of free expression ... is obviously essential if desires are to be made known." But Laski does not conceive of the state as a milch cow or of the individual as a calf entitled to its turn at the teats. For him, the state's goal is a moral goal and so "there is cast upon the individual member of the state the duty of scrutinizing its policy; for if he ought ultimately at least to protest, and perhaps to disobey, where his conscience is involved, an active interest in politics is the most indispensable condition of citizenship."[114]

The state can be kept faithful to its moral goal—the welfare of the whole community—only if every member of the state contributes the lessons of his life and experience to the formulation of that goal. If nothing else, he will strive to make sure that his good is not left out of the conception of the common good. But Laski evidently expects more than such self-serving advocacy from the individual. "The greatest contribution that a citizen can make to the state," he says, "is certainly this, that he should allow his mind freely to exercise itself upon its problems."[115] "We ask, in fact from each the best thought he can offer to the interpretation of life."[116] Only by allowing and encouraging him to offer it can the state "truly prosper," because only so can the state govern by the consent of the governed.[117] All of this is on the "assumption ... that every individual is above all a moral being and that the greatest contribution he can make to the state is the effort of his moral faculties."[118]

The freedom of expression for which Laski argues is, then, freedom for men to discuss the great concerns of life without hindrance by the institutions of state or church. The "only real security for social well-being is the free exercise of men's minds,"[119] and "the first lesson of our experience of power is the need of its limitation by the instructed judgments of free minds."[120] But minds that form instructed judgments are not only free and moral, they are also rational. True, the best we can do is "to apply what standards time has painfully evolved,"[121] and we cannot "postulate an unchanging content of goodness." Nonetheless, our idea of what is right has a "certain objectivity, to be established by argument and experience." That requires the exercise of rational minds: "The one thing in which we can have confidence as a means of progress is the logic of reason." That is why we insist "that the mind of each man ... pass judgment upon the state; and we ask for his condemnation of its policy where he feels it in conflict with the right."[122]

Liberty in the Modern State develops this theory of freedom of expression in the direction of a greater subjectivism. Natural law, even with a changing content, disappears from it. Human personality lies even more emphatically in "that uniqueness of individuality, that sense that each of us is ultimately different from our fellows that is the ultimate fact of human experience."[123] Laski, an heir of the Nominalists, raises the uniqueness of the individual to the level of metaphysical statement. "Ours," he says, "is not a universe in which the principles of a unified experience are unfolded. It is a multiverse embodying an ultimate variety of experiences, never identical, and always differently interpreted."[124]

Human nature, then is essentially individual:

> Man is a one among many obstinately refusing reduction to unity. His separateness, his isolation, are indefeasible; indeed, they are so ultimate that they are the basis out of which his civic obligations are builded. He cannot abandon the consequences of his isolation which are, broadly speaking, that his experience is private and the will built out of that experience personal to himself. If he surrenders it to others, he surrenders his personality.[125]

The essence of human personality is will, and will is the desire for a good learned from uniquely personal experience. "Each of us," says Laski, "desires the good as he sees it; and each of us sees a good derived from an individual and separate experience into which no other person can fully enter."[126] Out of these experiences emerge the individual's moral certainties, his convictions about those things that are essential to his happiness; and these convictions are his conscience. Some command issued by external authority, for example, "seems to him a wanton invasion of that happiness. He may be right or wrong in so thinking; the point of fact is that he has no alternative but to go by his own moral certainties." It follows that the "conditions of freedom are ... those which assure the absence of such invasion."[127]

Laski grants that "for most of us, conscience is a poor guide.... But perverse, foolish, ignorant [though it is], it is the only guide we have ... and our freedom comes from acting on its demands."[128] "Law, therefore," he holds, "as coercion is always an invasion of personality, an abridgement of the moral stature of those whom it invades." We cannot do without it but we "must reduce the imperative element to a minimum."[129]

Laski, of course, always thinks of man as living and working with other men in society. But he lays it down that "[t]he ultimate isolation of the individual personality is the basis from which any adequate theory of politics must start." Individuality is basic and society, for all its undeniable necessity, is derivative. "Our connection with others is, at best, partial and interstitial. Our pooling of experiences to make a common purpose is in no case other than fragmentary."[130] Common goals, therefore, are ultimately subordinate to individual desires:

> There is enough similarity of view to enable us, if we have patience and goodwill, to make enough of unity to achieve order and peace. But that similarity is not identity. It does not entitle us to affirm that one's experience can be taken as the representation of another's. It does not justify the inference that I shall find what I most truly desire in the desire of another.[131]

Laski, it should be noted, is not concerned solely with safeguarding the liberty of the individual against the state. Rather, he insists, "we must not think of freedom as involving only an individual set over against the community; it involves also the freedom of groups, racial, ecclesiastical, vocational, set over against the community and the state."[132] That said, it remains true that the individual self is the origin and goal of the state. "The purpose for which authority is exercised is the maximum satisfaction of desire."[133] The desires to be satisfied are ultimately those of individuals; they must therefore be regularly consulted through an open and democratic system of government that maintains an adequate "system of liberties."[134]

In addition to legal freedoms, liberty requires a social atmosphere in which we may feel confident "that in the things we deem significant there is the opportunity of continuous initiative, ... that we can, so to speak, experiment with ourselves, think differently or act differently, from our neighbours without danger to our happiness being involved therein [and] can form our plan of conduct to suit our own character without social penalties."[135] All of this sounds like, and very probably is, a repetition of John Stuart Mill's thesis in *On Liberty*. So, too, is the theory of freedom of expression that Laski expounds while going in certain respects beyond Mill.

He repeats his own argument in *Authority in the Modern State* that, if the authorities are to govern in accordance with the desires of the governed, they must guarantee them complete freedom to express those desires, singly or in association.[136] He restates (without acknowledgment) Mill's argument that mankind is always the gainer from the expression of opinion, whether the opinion be true, partly true, or false.[137] Like Mill, he assumes that the issue involved in suppressing utterance or publication can be reduced to the question of who is "wise enough or good enough to control the intellectual nutrition of the human mind."[138]

For to Laski it is always a question of intellectual nutrition, of "views" or "opinions." Even obscene publications—which, unlike Mill, Laski explicitly deals with—should be free from restraint because they expound unorthodox but useful views. Radclyffe Hall's *Well of Loneliness*, for example, is a "dull and sincere pamphlet" on sexual perversion but treats of "a theme of high importance to society in a sober and high-minded way." D. H. Lawrence's *Lady Chatterley's Lover* has been praised by "eminent American critics ... as the finest example of a novel seeking the truth about the sexual relations of men and women that an Englishman has published in the twentieth century." We need this kind of discussion, Laski contends, if "we are to create a healthy social attitude to the problems of sex," and we must allow writers to deal with them "from a new point of view, and with a frankness that admits the experimental nature of our contemporary solutions." We cannot face "in a scientific fashion" questions "like those of birth-control, extra-marital love, companionate marriage, sexual perversion ... by applying to them the standards of a nomadic Eastern people which drew up its rules more than two thousand years ago."[139]

The opposition to this scientific discussion comes from "fussy and pedantic moralists" who have an unlimited desire to regulate the conduct of other persons. "If they stop the sale of alcohol, they become ardent for the limitation of the right to tobacco." These are the people who want to ban Voltaire's *Candide*, Shaw's *Mrs. Warren's Profession* and the works of Darwin and Gorky. Even worse: "They are horrified by the nude in art."[140] Laski perhaps overlooks the fact to which Pope Pius XII alluded when he remarked: "What interests the masses in this regard is not the beauty of the nude, but the nudity of the beauty."[141] Entrepreneurs have grown rich by not overlooking it, but to Laski all that is at issue is "interference" with "the climate of mental freedom."[142]

On similar grounds he rejects laws against blasphemy or banning from the schools "textbooks which are offensive to a particular denomination."[143] Summarizing the position he has reached so far, he says that "such freedom of expression as I have discussed means freedom to express one's ideas on general subjects, on themes of public importance, rather than on the character of particular persons."[144] Laski would relax the English law of libel somewhat "in all political or quasi-political cases"; still, he admits that libellous statements are not protected by freedom of expression.[145] But he contemplates no kinds of expression other than discussion and libel. One is either expressing "ideas on general subjects, on themes of public importance," or one is attacking someone's character. Laski is as doggedly highminded as John Stuart Mill.

His chief interest is in "the political aspect of freedom of expression which is, of course, the pith of the whole problem."[146] Bagehot had advocated a polity of discussion limited by the proviso that no government is bound to permit a controversy which will annihilate it. Laski argues for continuous radical discussion of the polity itself. "There is," he maintains, "never any such certitude in matters of social constitution as to justify us in saying that any exposition of principles must be suppressed."[147]

The one permissible exception to this rule is that when "it is in fact demonstrable that the speech made had a direct tendency to incite immediate disorder, the punishment of the accused is justified."[148] But no opinion, simply as an opinion, can justly be regarded as endangering the state. On the contrary, it is dangerous to allow government to suppress opinions as dangerous, because government will certainly abuse its power. In so doing, it will deprive itself of the knowledge of people's desires, which it exists to satisfy, and of their grievances, which it ought to redress.[149] It is government's duty and interest always to allow the free expression of opinion, even when it is addressed to the armed forces[150] or in time of war.[151] It was, Laski points out, precisely the wartime censorship that made possible the disastrous Peace of Versailles. Censorship "acted like a miasma to blot out the only atmosphere in which the truth could be manifest,"[152] and prevented the formation of the informed and intelligent public opinion that could have consented to a moderate and rational peace settlement.

Associations ought to enjoy the same freedom of expression as individuals. Laski grants that "the state has a right to protect itself from attack," and to "demand that changes in its organization be the outcome of peaceful persuasion and not the consequence of violent assault." It may therefore rightfully "interfere" when and if groups like the Communists or the Ulster Volunteers make active preparations to use force against it. But he denies that a government is "entitled to suppress associations the beliefs of which alone are subversive of the established order."[153]

Laski says nothing in this book about Adolph Hitler and his National Socialist movement. That is a pity but it is not surprising. The book was published in 1930, so Laski must have finished writing it, at the latest, in 1929 when Hitler was but a cloud on the horizon. When Hitler came to power, Laski denounced him with a severity that he could never bring himself to use toward Stalin and the Soviet regime. But the test of his principles would have been what he said about Hitler *before* he came to power. Laski could consistently have approved suppressing Hitler's private army. But, in consistency, he would also have had to say that *Mein Kampf* and the movement it inspired were the expression of a social grievance to which the Weimar Republic should respond with attentive concern.

Laski seems to say as much in a piece written in 1932, in which he explains that the capitalist order, both economic and political, is in crisis. Resistance is developing everywhere "to the normal technique by which capitalism adjusts itself to a falling market. The growth of socialism in Great Britain, the dissatisfaction with the historic parties in the United States, the rise of Hitlerism in Germany, the profound and growing interest, all over the world, in the Russian experiment, are all of them, in their various ways, the expression of that resistance."[154] But the thesis of the article is that the future belongs to communism unless the capitalist states carry out egalitarian reforms so radical that they will cease to be capitalist.

In a book written in the same year, Laski makes it plain that he does not regard National Socialism as such a reform. "Let us remember," he says, "that Hitlerism is, above all, the expression of emotional indignation against the disturbance of a wonted routine." The routine referred to is that of the "vested interests, traditions, emotions" that accumulate around the profit motive and the capitalist system built on it.[155] Furthermore, Hitlerism is simply irrational. "The attitude of Hitler's supporters to the Jews of Germany is unspeakably vile; but if the Jews trusted to reason only for the defence of their lives their chance of survival would be relatively small. For the temper in which they are attacked is inherently unamenable to rational discussion."[156]

The above are the only references to Hitlerism in these two writings composed in the year before Hitler came to power. They indicate that, for Laski, social criticism of the kind that is amenable to rational discussion is to be expected only from the Left. "We cannot, in fact," he says, "get agreement to maintain the conditions of freedom until we get agreement about its objects. If the state is at all costs to preserve a capitalist society, it will have to suppress those who are resolved upon its transformation; and freedom to suppress is not freedom for the persons suppressed."[157] Hitler's movement evidently figured in Laski's mind only as an emotional and irrational reaction to the transformation of the capitalist order. Its ideology was not a criticism of the social order to be debated with but an aspect of the crisis of capitalism, to which socialism was the only adequate answer. Laski therefore felt no need seriously to address the Hitler phenomenon in his theory of freedom of expression.

It is in this light that we should understand Laski's plea, in *Liberty in the Modern State,* for tolerance of radical criticism of the state. "We must not," he says, "allow ourselves to fall into the error of believing that opinion which is antagonistic to the state-purpose is unworthy to survive." The polity itself is a legitimate subject of discussion, since the constitution of the state and the structure of society may be regarded as grievances, and perhaps rightly so. Men therefore have the right to form associations to propagate their ideas about them. Even if their ideas are wrong, they nonetheless express a resentment against what these men perceive as social injustice. The Communist Party, for example, is an "announcement" that some lives at least are marred by the capitalist regime. To that announcement, suppression is not the proper answer. "Force is never a reply to argument; and until argument itself seeks force as the expression of its principle, it is only by argument that it can justifiably be countered."[158]

In Laski's lexicon, argument is the expression of experience, and this in turn is experience of the satisfaction or frustration of desire. He constantly uses both terms, "experience" and "desire," without qualifications or distinctions, as though all desires and experience were on the same level. But he clearly is not thinking of trivial experience or transient desire when he speaks of each man's "ultimately unique" experience, the significance of which "he alone can fully appreciate," and which reveals "what he cannot help taking to be the lesson of his life."[159] This must be experience which shows a man what he deeply and truly wants, and constitutes for him the fundamental moral truth. And perhaps this is the point to which an evolutionary view of truth is bound to come.

The difficulty in building a social and political order on this view of truth is that all these uniquely individual experiences will inevitably clash with one another. Yet men do and must live together in society, and "the conflict of experience means the imposition of certain ways of behaviour upon all of us lest conflict destroy peace." We must therefore endeavor "to extract from the experience of society certain principles of action by which, in their own interest, men ought to be bound."[160] In this effort we must rely on reason in order to arrive at justice.

"Governing principles emerge," says Laski, "but they emerge through the wills of individual minds."[161] Each citizen owes society "the contribution of his instructed judgment to the public good." Such judgment "is considered and not impulsive." It results from "an attempt to penetrate behind the superficial appearance to what is truth-seeming," and is arrived at "after evidence has been collected and weighed, distortion allowed for, prejudice discounted."[162]

To get citizens who can form such judgments, we must educate men to love truth and to approach it with an open mind.[163] We must also give them access to a steady flow of factual information free from "the control of news by special interests,"[164] which "do not want the general reporting of experience, but only of that experience which favours themselves."[165] But this consideration leads to a more general proposition which is the conclusion of Laski's theory of liberty: that reason can prevail, and justice be done, and freedom be universally enjoyed only in a society based on economic equality.

"For," he says, "the real meaning of democratic government is the equal weighing of individual claims to happiness by social institutions. A society built upon economic inequality cannot attempt that sort of measure."[166] But this is not only the real meaning of democratic government, it is the dictate of reason. Men, indeed, may "be persuaded by reason that one vision of desire is better than another vision," but "the experience commended to them must persuade and not enforce, if they are to accept its implications with a sense of contentment."[167] This can only mean that men may be induced by explanation and argument to see that some interpretation of their experience, other than the one they have arrived at by themselves, better answers that experience. On the social level, it means that they may be led through discussion to see that a certain policy better satisfies their desires than the one they themselves originally favored. But if this process of discussion is to result in a sense of contentment, it must be one which all the participants enter on equal terms. Reason therefore requires democratic equality.

And it must be complete equality. The possession of shares of wealth, power and privilege greater than those of the mass of men engenders in the *beati possidentes* a passion to keep what they have, and "and in the presence of passion people become blind to truth."[168] From such people we cannot expect publication of the truth or openminded and rational discussion of public policy. They will, to be sure, "allow freedom in inessentials; but when the path of freedom is an attack upon their monopoly they will define it as sedition or blasphemy."[169] The privileged "are afraid of reason, for this involves an examination into their own prerogative and, as at least probable, a denunciation of the title by which it is preserved."[170]

Laski does not explain what reason is or how it operates. But throughout the last two chapters of this book he asserts repeatedly and emphatically that reason, given full rein and free expression, inexorably leads to the demand for equality, as when he says, for example, that "the rule of reason in a community means that a special interest must always give way before the principles it discovers."[171] Reason proceeds from the radical subjectivity of desire, and therefore of truth, but it arrives at the objective necessity of political and economic equality.

Zerby comments that Laski's theory in this work is "based upon a specific and questionable interpretation of self."[172] Certainly it is an interpretation that relativizes truth and makes reason instrumental to desire. Laski, however, is able to screen his theory from the disintegrating effects of this conception of reason by the same highminded moralism that protected Mill. People will be reasonable and decent and tolerant if we free them to express their desires on equal terms. In this sense Laski can profess an enormous faith in reason and base his whole theory of freedom of expression on it. One cannot put it better than he does himself in the words with which he closes *Liberty in the Modern State:*

> it has been claimed that truth can be established by reason alone; that departure from the way of reason as a method of securing conviction is an indication always of a desire to protect injustice. Where there is respect for reason, there, also, is respect for freedom. And only respect for freedom can give final beauty to men's lives.[173]

7

The American Way

Chafee and Meiklejohn

One of the reasons for the failure of the United States ever to produce a major political theorist is that we live under a written Constitution that is actively and continuously interpreted by a Supreme Court. Theoretical issues in politics tend therefore to be reduced to the categories of constitutional law. Our discussion of freedom of expression has for this reason been an unending argument over the meaning of "the freedom of speech, or of the press" that is guaranteed by the First Amendment. Our theorizing on the subject has in consequence a distinctly legalistic cast.

Probably no writer has had a greater influence on the thinking of the Supreme Court and of the informed public about the meaning of this clause of the First Amendment than Zechariah Chafee, Jr. A professor of law, and of old New England stock, he produced a typically American theory of freedom of speech and press. The other writer considered here, Alexander Meiklejohn, was born in England of Scottish parentage, though educated from childhood in America. Not because of his foreign birth, however, but because he was a philosopher rather than a lawyer, he developed a theory of the First Amendment that has not commended itself to the Supreme Court. Nonetheless it deserves attention because of the clarity with which it addresses the basic issue of why this or any other nation should protect a defined freedom to speak and publish.

Zechariah Chafee, Jr.

In the summer of 1919 Harold Laski, then teaching at Harvard, invited Zechariah Chafee, Jr., to tea to meet Justice Oliver Wendell Holmes, Jr., of the U.S. Supreme Court. The occasion for this meeting was an article that Chafee had published in the June number of the *Harvard Law Review*.[1] In it Chafee praised Holmes for formulating the clear and present danger test for deciding freedom of speech and press cases under the First Amendment in *Schenck v. U.S.* (249 U.S. 47) but criticized him for giving the test a restrictive rather than an expansive application. What effect the meeting had on Holmes is not directly known, but it has been remarked that by November of the same year, in his dissenting opinion in *Abrams v. U.S.* (250 U.S. 616), Holmes adopted Chafee's position and began to use the clear and present danger formula "as a positive rule to defend free speech."[2]

Chafee's entry into the field of civil rights, and of freedom of speech in particular, was "almost accidental."[3] Yet, though he did not know it, when he began to publish on the subject, he "had found his life's work."[4] He had joined the faculty of the Harvard Law School at the age of 30 in 1916. As the new boy on the faculty, he inherited a third-year equity course which the previous teacher, Roscoe Pound, had tried to liven up by introducing the question of injunctions for libel. The need to deal with this question led Chafee to read all the existing cases on the limits of the constitutional right to freedom of speech and, as a result, to realize how incomplete and unsatisfactory the state of constitutional law on the subject was. Then came the World War I espionage and sedition laws and scores of new cases,[5] and Chafee was propelled into becoming an authority on a subject in which prior to 1916 he had not shown "even the slightest curiosity."[6]

It was Chafee's newfound interest in freedom of speech that inspired Laski to suggest to Herbert Croly, editor of *The New Republic*, that he ask Chafee for an article dealing with court decisions under the Espionage Act.[7] Chafee wrote the article, which appeared in that journal's November 16, 1918 number, and continued and expanded it in his *Harvard Law Review* article the following year. "Throughout the next forty years," says J. Prude, "in books, articles, pamphlets, and occasionally in speeches, he would repeatedly return to the problem of determining the true limits of freedom of expression."[8] He was still doing so in *The Blessings of Liberty* which appeared less than a year before his death in 1957.

Chafee's reflections on the effect of World War I and its aftermath on civil liberty were summed up in his *Freedom of Speech*. Published in 1920, it has been described as "the seminal twentieth-century treatise on the subject."[9] We shall, however, analyze his thought in two later works. *Free Speech in the United States*[10] was written at the request of the Harvard University Press as a replacement for the long out of print *Freedom of Speech* and is, as Chafee explains, an effort "to fuse together ... all my ideas past and present on freedom of speech."[11] *The Blessings of Liberty*,[12] he tells us, is not intended to bring *Free Speech in the United States* "down to date" but is a thorough remolding of a number of his written and spoken discussions of Bill of Rights problems in the post-World War II period and "gives my reflections at the close of 1955."[13] There is, in fact, no significant change of view between the books, and we may agree with Prude that throughout his writings Chafee's "formulation of the legal questions remained essentially unaltered."[14]

Chafee was a professor of law and wrote on freedom of speech within the American constitutional system. The greater part of these two works consequently is devoted to the discussion of particular federal and state laws and of cases that had arisen under those laws. But we may prescind from these particulars and try to abstract the basic premises on which he advocated and interpreted freedom of speech and press.

As a lawyer, Chafee took the decisions of the U.S. Supreme Court as final: if the Court said that something was constitutional, then it was. But he always insisted that the wisdom of legislation was more important than its constitutionality, and that the First Amendment was something more than that degree of restraint on governmental action that could and would be enforced by the courts. It is also, he says, "an exhortation and a guide for the action of Congress" and "a declaration of national policy in favor of the public discussion of all public questions." The amendment therefore should make Congress "reluctant and careful" about enacting restrictions on utterance, "even though the courts will not refuse to enforce them as unconstitutional."[15] Ultimately, he says, freedom of speech must depend on public opinion: "In the long run the public gets just as much freedom of speech as it really wants."[16] Chafee's argument, therefore, like Mill's, is intended to persuade the public of the wisdom of a regime of free and open discussion.

As Prude says, Chafee did not defend free speech because it was in keeping with the Constitution or because it was an absolute or natural right.

> Rather, drawing on Holmes' "legal realism," which insisted that principles governing human conduct could be evaluated solely by their ability to meet real and pressing social needs, and on the general utilitarian outlook of John Stuart Mill, whose essay "On Liberty" he frequently cited, Chafee consistently, almost stubbornly, defended free speech simply because it was "wise," because the practical consequences of free discussion would be beneficial.[17]

Chafee, for example, denied that the First Amendment "left the common law as to seditious libel in force."[18] Auerbach points out that, as Leonard Levy later showed in his *Legacy of Suppression*, on this matter "Chafee probably was in error." But he was shrewd enough "to cover his bet on the intention of the framers" and to argue that, whatever it was, it did not forever crystallize the meaning of the amendment.[19] To elucidate that meaning, Chafee would draw on constitutional history and judicial interpretation, but it seems clear that his final appeal was to "the purpose free speech serves in social and political life."[20]

"The true meaning of freedom of speech," then, is derived from its purpose. "One of the most important purposes of society and government is the discovery and spread of truth on subjects of general concern. This is possible only through absolutely unlimited discussion."[21] The policy behind the First Amendment "is the attainment and spread of truth, not merely as an abstraction, but as the basis of political and social progress."[22] The Constitution thus fosters "the interest of the community in the discovery and dissemination of truth."[23] Even the "normal criminal law" presumes "that truth will prevail over falsehood if both are given a fair field, and that argument and counter-argument are the best method which man has devised for ascertaining the right course of action for individuals or a nation."[24]

Public discussion involves both those who speak and those who hear, and the "real value of freedom of speech is not to the minority that wants to talk, but to the majority that does not want to listen."[25] Two interests, in fact, are protected by the constitutional guarantee of freedom of speech. "There is an individual interest, the need of many men to express their opinions on matters vital to them if life is to be worth living, and a social interest in the attainment of truth, so the country may not only adopt the wisest course of action but carry it out in the wisest way."[26] From the viewpoint of both interests, freedom of speech is for the sake of discussion, and discussion is for the sake of truth and wisdom.

Since freedom of speech serves a purpose, it is not an end in itself, to be pursued without limit. Chafee lays it down at the beginning of *Free Speech in the United States* that his book "is an inquiry into the proper limitations upon freedom of speech, and is in no way an argument that any one should be allowed to say whatever he wants anywhere and at any time."[27] Nor is the purpose of freedom of speech the only one to be kept in view. Having said, as we have seen, that "the discovery and spread of truth ... is possible only through absolutely unlimited discussion," Chafee adds:

> Nevertheless, there are other purposes of government, such as order, the training of the young, protection against external aggression. Unlimited discussion sometimes interferes with these purposes, which must then be balanced against freedom of speech, but freedom of speech ought to weigh very heavily in the scale.[28]

As appears clearly and repeatedly throughout the two works we are considering here, freedom of speech does indeed weigh heavily in Chafee's scale. "No free speech problem can be satisfactorily solved by men who think only of the risk from open discussion," he says. "It is indispensable to balance against those risks the deeply felt realization that one of the most important purposes of society and government is the discovery and spread of true facts and sound judgments on subjects of general concern."[29] Nevertheless, freedom of speech has to be balanced against other social interests and purposes of government.

Furthermore, not all kinds of speech are of equal value in relation to the attainment of truth; some, in fact, are of no value. Chafee does not deal at length with such kinds of speech, since his overriding concern is to defend the freedom to express opinions, but he does mention them. We can all agree, he says, that the First Amendment does not "wipe out the common law as to obscenity, profanity, and defamation of individuals."[30] The reason for this is that

> profanity and indecent talk and pictures, which do not form an essential part of any exposition of ideas, have a very slight social value as a step toward truth, which is clearly outweighed by the social interests in order, morality, the training of the young, and the peace of mind of those who hear and see.[31] Words of this type offer little opportunity for the usual process of counter-argument. The harm is done as soon as they are communicated, or is liable to follow almost immediately in the form of retaliatory violence. The only sound explanation of the punishment of obscenity and profanity is that the words are criminal, not because of the ideas they communicate, but like acts because of their immediate consequences to the five senses. The man who swears in a street car is as much a nuisance as the man who smokes there. Insults are punished like a threatening gesture, since they are liable to provoke a fight. Adulterated candy is no more poisonous to children than some books. Grossly unpatriotic language may be punished for the same reasons. The man who talks scurrilously about the flag commits a crime, not because the implications of his ideas tend to weaken the Federal Government, but because the effect resembles that of an injurious act such as trampling on the flag, which would be a public nuisance and a breach of the peace.[32]

Chafee reveals here his pronounced tendency to assume that speech is unprotected when and insofar as it is virtually an action or at least an incitement to immediate action. Yet his argument would seem to cover forms of expression that do not demonstrably incite to any immediate action but which, far from forming an essential part of any exposition of ideas, are a systematic appeal to sick appetites. The speech he thinks it necessary to protect is the kind that offers "opportunity for the usual process of counter-argument." It is clear that, in his mind, this category does not include all kinds of "expression."

If a meeting held in a public street "is going to cause trouble, not just because of the unpopularity of its views but because it expresses them in offensive ways, it may be unlawful *per se.*"[33] "Nobody can quarrel with the legislation banning filthy publications" from the mails,[34] and if "films are clearly filthy," those who produce and show them "can readily be punished by state and federal prosecutions."[35] The "post office has performed a valuable service in stamping out the commercialized exploitation of the young by vicious advertisements" (though "beyond this its powers over speech are very questionable").[36] More generally, "the law must draw some line between decency and indecency, a line between permitted art and art that can be punished or suppressed."[37] (One may ask: Are all of the above "expressions" unprotected because they are direct incitements to action?) There is also a line between legitimate criticism of an individual and defamation of his character. English juries, Chafee remarks, are more ready than American ones to award substantial damages in defamation suits, "and this greater sensitiveness to the value of reputation may be the indication of a more civilized community."[38] Chafee therefore rejects as "extreme" the belief that "the First Amendment renders unconstitutional any Act of Congress [or of a state legislature, he would add after 1925] without exception 'abridging the freedom of speech, or of the press,' that all speech is free, and only action can be restrained and punished."[39]

Nevertheless, he wrote to expand rather than to contract the area in which speech was to be free. Having explained why some kinds of words are not protected by the First Amendment, he adds that "all these crimes of injurious words must be kept within very narrow limits if they are not to give excessive opportunities for outlawing heterodox ideas."[40] The line between protected and unprotected speech coincides with the line between speech that advocates ideas (however heterodox or wrong) and speech that does not. Nor, as the historical background of the First Amendment shows, are the ideas advocated to be confined to political ones. "It is true that untrammeled speaking and printing about candidates and issues had come to be regarded before our Revolution as an essential part of the process of self-government, but the men who strove to establish liberty of the press also cared greatly about science, art, drama, and poetry." When they wrote the First Amendment, they used the phrase, "the freedom of speech, or of the press ... to embrace the whole realm of thought."[41]

Chafee's objection to the vagueness of "obscenity" as a legal norm is that it has led to "many decisions" that "have utterly failed to distinguish nasty talk or the sale of unsuitable books to the young from the serious discussion of topics of great social significance." Prosecution for obscene or blasphemous utterances may be "simply a roundabout modern method to make heterodoxy in sex matters and even in religion a crime."[42] This consideration does not persuade Chafee that indecency should not be a reason for legal restraint on utterance; it leads him, rather, to the "conclusion, both as to plays and books, ... that decisions on the issue of indecency should be made by the citizens themselves through qualified juries."[43] But his reason for wanting a distinction to be made between the indecent book, play or film,[44] and the one that merely shocks because it conflicts with prevailing beliefs, is that "[f]reedom of speech covers much more than political ideas. It embraces all discussion which enriches human life and helps it to be more wisely led."[45]

The discussion that wins by far the greater part of Chafee's attention, however, is political discussion, and the greatest threat he sees to political discussion is sedition laws. His attack on all such laws therefore takes up the greater part of the two books under consideration here. This attack, and his energetic defense of the right of Communists and other radicals to express their views—including the belief that the government ought to be overthrown by force—led many persons to accuse him of sympathy with their objectives. But this was to misunderstand Zechariah Chafee.

He was, after all, a ninth-generation New Englander who "enjoyed a background comfortable in family and social position, some independent means, and excellent opportunities, first in business and then in private practice before he came to teach at the law school in 1916."[46] The law school, moreover, was Harvard's. Chafee had no serious quarrel with the order of society of which he was a beneficiary. But he could see why the disinherited had one, and he felt that preventing them from stating it was contrary to the Anglo-Saxon spirit of fair play.[47]

There was also another and deeper reason for letting radicals talk. It was not that Chafee thought they had anything valuable to say. "The real problem with stifling radical voices," as Prude puts it, "was that the process of repression would silence others as well."[48] In Chafee's own words,

> my contention is that the pertinacious orators and writers who get hauled up [before the courts] are merely extremist spokesmen for a mass of more thoughtful and more retiring men and women who share in varying degrees the same critical attitude toward prevailing policies and institutions. When you put the hotheads in jail, these cooler people do not get arrested—they just keep quiet. And so we lose things they could tell us, which would be very advantageous for the future course of the nation. Once the prosecutions begin, then the hush-hush begins too. Discussion becomes one-sided and artificial. Questions that need to be threshed out do not get threshed out.[49]

The expression of the most radical economic and political views must therefore be tolerated and protected for the sake of discussion. "There should," says Chafee, "be no legislation against sedition and anarchy. We must legislate and enforce the laws against the use of force, but protect ourselves against bad thinking and speaking by the strength of argument and a confidence in American common sense and American institutions."[50] This means that "the boundary line of free speech ... is fixed close to the point where words will give rise to unlawful acts."[51] In Chafee's view, "under the First Amendment, lawless acts are the main thing. Speech is not punishable for its own sake, but only because of its connection with those lawless acts, whether they occur or not."[52]

As a legal test to determine the point where words will give rise to unlawful acts, Chafee prefers the phrase used by Judge Learned Hand, "direct incitement to violent resistance." Still, he feels, Holmes' clear and present danger formula has the merit of having won the unanimous agreement of the Supreme Court and will serve well enough to maintain in practice the principle that "the First Amendment entitles most speech to be let alone."[53]

If we do not make the close connection of words with lawless acts the decisive factor in finding utterances criminal and constitutionally unprotected, we are thrown back on "bad tendency" as the test.[54] "The real issue in every free speech controversy," says Chafee, "is this: whether the state can punish all words which have some tendency, however remote, to bring about acts in violation of law, or only words which directly incite to acts in violation of law."[55] If we accept bad tendency as the test, the result in practice is the persecution of dissidents and the suppression of unpopular views.[56] Yet the public thereby harms itself more than the dissidents, for "it is only by absence of penalties for such utterances that a self-governing people can learn and disseminate the truth on public affairs."[57] Bad tendency as the test of criminality is "wholly inconsistent with freedom of speech and any genuine discussion of public affairs."[58]

It does not matter that, under Chafee's norm, the speech that is protected may be frankly and overtly revolutionary. "If there was one thing which the First Amendment was meant by our ancestors to protect," he says, "it was criticism of the existing form of government and advocacy of change." Nor does it matter that those who criticize the existing order often do so in strong and intemperate language, "for the greater the need of change, the greater the likelihood that agitators will lose their temper over the present situation."[59]

Besides, the risks taken in allowing the free expression of revolutionary views are small. A "survey of past English and American efforts to end sedition by severe penalties" shows that the "persons punished were for the most part unimportant and comparatively harmless."[60] In peacetime, "those who love disorder for its own sake are so few that a revolution is improbable unless there are very strong reasons for discontent."[61] "History, " indeed, "shows that sedition is often the symptom and not the cause of serious unrest."[62] We can go farther and say: "The prime cause of all dangerous political agitation is discontent."[63]

Where men in threatening numbers feel intensely dissatisfied, the intelligent response is to try to "understand the causes of their discontent, studying with open minds all the existing information, and then take constructive steps to end that discontent and substitute positive ideals for those we want to drive out."[64]

Chafee is confident that if we try, we shall succeed. "Whatever the cause of their calling themselves Communists, there is always, I feel very strongly, a good chance of reconciling them to American ways," he says.[65] "A savings bank account, a steady job, and plenty of good-humored toleration and friendly help and encouragement, will bring into harmony with our ideals all but a few heated theorists, who are not likely to be such a menace to our national safety that we cannot counteract them by sound reasoning."[66] "The only possibility of Communistic control of this country," he wrote in 1955, "would come from quite another source than our tolerance of revolutionary propaganda."

> Imagine a prolonged period of enormous unemployment; the dollar buying what a dime buys now, and perhaps worth a nickel next week, who knows; ever-mounting taxes; the national revenue heavily mortgaged for decades by unwise commitments to groups of the aged at the expense of active men and women and their children; voters hating and despising the men they themselves have put in office because they had nobody better to choose from. That is when communism might grow by leaps and bounds, not because of what 70,000 Communists say but because of what the hopeless facts say. Maggots live in rotten meat.[67]

Nor does the experience of other countries afford any lessons to the contrary. "We need not be frightened by the experiences of European governments, at least those which like France and the Weimar Republic were riddled from top to bottom with disloyalty and economic conflicts so that it seems unlikely that the most rigorous suppression of public meetings could have prolonged their lives. Maggots live in rotten meat."[68]

If, then, we are intelligent enough to keep the meat from going rotten, we may trust reason to prevail in the open discussion on which the health of the polity depends. Milton and John Stuart Mill, living in a simpler age, thought it would be enough to remove the legal obstacles to the free expression of ideas, and fruitful discussion would ensue. We are now aware, however, that "truth does not seem to emerge from a controversy in the automatic way their logic would lead us to expect." But that only means that we must make positive efforts to cut through the fog of misrepresentation and propaganda, and actively promote rational discussion "by wise improvements in technique." "Reason," Chafee admits, "is more imperfect than we used to believe. Yet it still remains the best guide we have; better than our emotions, better than patriotism, better than any single human guide, however exalted his position."[69]

The twentieth century's waning faith in reason evidently disturbed
Chafee, because in *The Blessings of Liberty* he returned to the question and
devoted a whole chapter to it under the heading, "Does Freedom of
Speech Really Tend to Produce Truth?"[70] Skeptical critics, he says there,
now maintain that what emerges from the clash of ideas, instead of
truth, is simply nothing at all. According to the University of Chicago
economist, Frank Knight, whom Chafee quotes at length, there is little
need to suppress discussion, because so few people want to engage in it,
and what takes place under the name of discussion is a game in which (as
Vincent T. Lombardi was later to instruct us), winning is the only thing.
Knight asserts that even "specialized professional intellectuals have
shown little enough capacity to maintain the spirit of discussion." One
can expect even less from the general public when their vital concerns
are at stake. "In the field of morals and politics—to say nothing of
religion—it is questionable whether the net result has been progress
toward consensus or the multiplication of controversy."[71]

Knight raises a valid issue. If the promises of earlier advocates of
complete freedom of expression are to be believed (one thinks especially
of John Stuart Mill), we should by now have arrived, if not at truth, at
least at a growing consensus on what we believe to be truth. The trend,
however, seems to be in the other direction. The more fully we have
accepted the free expression of all ideas, the more we have multiplied, not
agreement, but division of opinions. As a recent writer has put it,
"Disintegration is the defining experience of the culture of modernism."[72]

Chafee does not address himself to the question whether freedom of
discussion has produced the promised results, beyond admitting that,
after reading Knight, he "can no longer think of open discussion as
operating like an electric mixer, which is the impression left by Milton
and Jefferson—run it a little while and truth will rise to the top with the
dregs of error going down to the bottom."[73] Instead, he gives reasons for
continuing to believe that discussion will produce the desired results.
Reason, he says, as he did before, "remains the best guide we have,"[74]
and, if we pay careful attention to the societal process of discussion, we
can observe how, slowly and subtly, it purifies our opinions and leads us
toward truth.

Truth may refer to our beliefs about "the highest matters"—God, the
universe and our reasons for living. At this level of truth, Chafee offers
only a pious hope: "Let us trust that the search for truth in our
understanding of the highest matters will continue to be untrammeled."[75]
But the truth with which he is most concerned is that of the judgments
of fact and value involved in framing public policy. Here, he believes, we
can see "what goes on while the conflicting statements of individuals are
getting transformed into a satisfactory basis for public action." The free

flow of information and the conflicting interpretations of it may grad-ually force us to modify our view of the facts; the clash of proposals leads us to change our minds on the wisdom of policies; sometimes we are compelled to confront issues about which we have previously cared and thought little. "All this shaping and reshaping takes time, and a good deal of it is not deliberate reasoning like solving an algebraic equation. What matters greatly is a willingness to receive impressions from many differ-ent sources and the opportunity for such impressions to reach us."[76]

Chafee does not advert to the distinction between theoretical and practical truth—and perhaps was unaware that there is such a distinction —but what he has just described is the process by which practical reason arrives at practical truth. "Now," he says, "if into this delicate process the government injects threats of penalties and perhaps actual suppression, the disastrous consequences are easily recognized."[77] It is not necessary to detail them, since they all come down to one: government will prevent the pursuit of truth through rational discussion.

Chafee's defense of the freedom of speech and press is dominated from beginning to end by the notion that freedom of expression is the necessary means by which reason may pursue truth. So much is this so that, in a brief commemorative piece written shortly after Chafee's death, Ernest Angell expressed some slight dismay over his insistence that "sedition laws and the like seriously hinder the attainment of truth. One might wish," says Angell, "that he had more boldly stated the case for the partial character of truth—the argument that modern societies function best, if haltingly, in a pluralism of choices, no one of which offers any guarantee of attaining immunity from error."[78] But Angell's criticism only emphasizes the conclusion that, liberal though Chafee's views undoubtedly were on the limits of freedom of expression, he did not propose expression as an end in itself, detached from the rational and moral purposes it served. Expression, to him, was for the sake of discussion, and discussion was for the rational pursuit of truth. Further-more, truth was only one—though a most important one—of society's goals, and other social purposes could be balanced against it. Chafee strove to strike the balance close to the point where words become actions. But he recognized that there are different kinds of "words," and it is by no means evident that, even on his premises, the balance must be struck at that point with regard to all of them. In any case, his thesis is simple and plain: "'Freedom of speech and of the press' is to be unabridged because it is the only means of testing out the truth."[79] It is told of an American tourist that while travelling around Ireland, he lost his way and stopped to ask a farmer how to get to Galway. "Well, now," said the farmer after a moment's thought, "if I wanted to get to Galway, I wouldn't start from here." If one wanted to get to a theory of uninhibited freedom of expression, one probably wouldn't start with Chafee's conception of freedom of speech as a means to truth.

Alexander Meiklejohn

The same can be said of Alexander Meiklejohn's theory of the freedom of speech and press. It differs significantly from Chafee's and is in one important respect an absolutist theory. But those who wish to advocate a policy of unrestrained freedom of expression will be well advised not to start from Meiklejohn's principles.

Willmoore Kendall sees Meiklejohn as "the first writer to urge upon us ... in their specific application to constitutional problems in the United States" libertarian predilections for "a society in which there is no legal or governmental barrier to unrestricted liberty of choice by the citizens among all conceivable alternatives in religion, politics, morals, and indeed in all areas of possible controversy." Meiklejohn, says Kendall, "more I think than any writer including Zechariah Chafee, Jr., is responsible for their current regnancy among American intellectuals."[80] Meiklejohn, it must be admitted, is as open as was John Stuart Mill to Kendall's charge that he regarded society at large as a debating club in which men sought the truth about serious matters. But that is still a far cry from a society in which anything goes so long as it is merely expressed.

Meiklejohn had this in common with Mill: he was an intellectual's intellectual. His career was entirely an academic one, devoted to teaching philosophy from 1897 to his retirement in 1938, and occasionally thereafter. Even during his years as President of Amherst College, 1912-1924, he taught a sophomore course in logic. Both as administrator and as professor he propounded an exalted view of the function of the human mind and a perhaps exaggerated faith in the power of emancipated reason.

According to a former student and admirer, Meiklejohn's creed as President of Amherst was that "it is wrong to define the aims of liberal education in terms of character, or good citizenship, or religious faith, or anything other than the goals of honest inquiry." It was not that he considered the other goals as unimportant, but he felt that "we must make sure that they come under the control of intelligence." Therefore, "in college we concentrate on the role of critical thought."[81]

Meiklejohn, it appears, made the usual liberal Protestant odyssey (emulated by Catholics only in later decades), in which "an inquiring mind" leaves the "authoritarian and literalistic elements in the older creed" and heads toward the Ithaca of "a rational, liberal faith."[82] As a friend of his said in a memorial article written after his death in 1964, Meiklejohn's "integrity quite forbade any facile or evasive solution of the conflict between his early faith and the new findings of science. ... The answers might be found in philosophy."[83] Philosophy thus played an important role in human life, the performance of which depended on the exercise of critical intelligence.

His doctrine on freedom of speech and press, however, was not intended exclusively or even primarily to protect the freedom of philosophical inquiry. It was, rather, a political doctrine arising out of political needs and designed to maintain the freedom of political inquiry and discussion. But his philosophical and his political beliefs both sprang from the same faith in reason.

His book on the freedom of speech and press is entitled *Political Freedom: the Constitutional Powers of the People*.[84] It consists of two parts. Part One is, "with a minor change, the text of the book *Free Speech and Its Relation to Self-Government*, published in 1948." Part Two "is a collection of papers, written between 1948 and 1958."[85] In this work Meiklejohn asserts that the true meaning of "the freedom of speech" protected by the First Amendment to the U. S. Constitution is "the unqualified freedom of public speech." This, he says, is a political freedom, "valid only in and for a society which is self-governing. It has no political justification where men are governed without their consent."[86]

Meiklejohn, in fact, while citing the Declaration of Independence as the voluntary compact by which Americans made themselves a political society, quietly abandons the Declaration's appeal to Nature and Nature's God. He says:

> So far as we can see, the non-human universe has no moral principles. It neither knows nor cares about human dignity, nor about anything else. And further, we may agree that respect for human dignity is not a *human* ultimate. That attitude of mutual regard is created and justified only insofar as groups of men have succeeded in binding themselves together into a fellowship which, by explicit or implicit compact, maintains a "way of life."[87]

Human dignity therefore is factitious; men must create it for themselves. But when they have brought it into being, it constitutes the supreme law of the society they have made. The Declaration of Independence "expresses a voluntary compact among political equals."[88] The compact is reaffirmed in the Preamble to the Constitution, in whose words

> it is agreed, and with every passing moment it is reagreed, that the people of the United States shall be self-governed. To that fundamental enactment all other provisions of the Constitution, all statutes, all administrative decrees, are subsidiary and dependent. All other pur-

poses, whether individual or social, can find their legitimate scope and meaning only as they conform to the one basic purpose that the citizens of this nation shall make and shall obey their own laws, shall be at once their own subjects and their own masters.[89]

This is more than a legally binding agreement. It is "the moral compact on which our plan of self-government rests." It is the source of our dignity as citizens and of the respect that we owe our fellow citizens, for "men are not recognizable as men unless, in any given situation, they are using their minds to give direction to their behavior."[90] By it, "we are pledged together to create a society in which men shall have the status of governors of themselves. They must move, not with bayonets behind, but with purposes ahead."[91] The purposes that the American people hold in common and which constitute their public interest are the ones stated in general terms in the Preamble to the Constitution.[92]

It is the freedom of the citizens of such a society to participate in the process of governing themselves that the First Amendment protects. Through the Constitution, it is true, they have delegated authority to the three branches of the national government, but they have not delegated all their authority. "By establishing themselves as an active and responsible 'electorate' they have become a Fourth Branch of the government. By virtue of that establishment they have 'reserved' a freedom for their electoral activities with which the other branches are forbidden to interfere."[93]

Free men, who govern themselves, must not be protected from any idea on the ground that it is unwise, or unfair, or dangerous, because it is they "who must pass judgment upon unwisdom and unfairness and danger." To deny them "acquaintance with information or opinion or doubt or disbelief or criticism" that is relevant to any issue they must decide is to distort their communal judgment. *"It is that mutilation of the thinking process of the community against which the First Amendment to the Constitution is directed."* The freedom of speech that it guarantees is not a Law of Nature or a principle of abstract Reason, but "a deduction from the basic American agreement that public issues shall be decided by universal suffrage."[94]

The First Amendment, then, protects public speech about public matters. "It was written to clear the way for thinking which serves the general welfare." It contemplates the speech of "men who plan and advocate and incite toward corporate action for the common good." From their public discourse no "plan of action" or "relevant idea" may be excluded, even if it should be the idea of a man who opposes a war in which the nation is engaged, or who attacks democracy or advocates communism. "So long as his active words are those of participation in public discussion and public decision of matters of public policy, the freedom of those words may not be abridged."[95] "Any such suppression of ideas about the common good," Meiklejohn declares, "the First Amendment condemns with its absolute disapproval. The freedom of ideas shall not be abridged."[96]

The amendment's protection, so far as it extends, is absolute because it serves an absolute public need. "Free men need the truth as they need nothing else. In the last resort it is only the search for and the dissemination of truth that can keep our country safe."[97] But "the only truth which we self-governing men can rely on is that which we win for ourselves in the give and take of public discussion and decision. What we think together at any time is, for us, our truth at that time."[98] Thinking together requires "that whatever truth may become available shall be placed at the disposal of all the citizens of the community." Winning new truth is, of course, "very important." But the First Amendment is primarily "a device for the sharing of whatever truth has been won." It is this need, "our deepest need," for the full and free sharing of truth by all citizens participating in the process of self-government that makes the First Amendment's protection of public speech and discussion absolute.[99]

The freedom of speech guaranteed by the amendment is thus both absolute and limited, and the absoluteness and the limitation derive alike from the public need for truth. "The guarantee given by the First Amendment ... is assured only to speech which bears, directly or indirectly, upon issues with which voters have to deal—only, therefore, to the consideration of matters of public interest."[100] It follows that the amendment *"does not forbid the abridging of speech.* But at the same time, *it does forbid the abridging of the freedom of speech."*[101] The freedom of speech which may not be abridged is not "unregulated talkativeness," or every individual's right to "talk as he pleases, when he pleases, about what he pleases, about whom he pleases, to whom he pleases." It is "freedom of discussion for those minds" that have come together "to decide matters of public policy."[102] The First Amendment's language is indeed absolute, but its meaning is this: "In the field of common action, of public discussion, the freedom of speech shall not be abridged."[103]

Large areas of speech and publication thus remain outside the amendment's guarantee but are not left, in Meiklejohn's theory, wholly without constitutional protection. His thesis is that "under the Constitution, there are two different freedoms of speech, and, hence, two different guarantees of freedom rather than only one."[104] The first freedom is that of the public discussion of "the common needs of all the members of the body politic," and it "has a constitutional status which no pursuit of an individual purpose can ever claim."[105] It alone, therefore, is guaranteed by the First Amendment. The other freedom of speech covers all other kinds of utterance. This freedom of speech is a private right and an individual possession. As such it is protected, like life and property, by the Due Process Clause of the Fifth Amendment but, like life and property, it is protected "not from regulation, but from undue regulation." This freedom of speech, then, is not an absolute but a relative constitutional right that may be abridged for sufficient public reason.[106]

Meiklejohn's constitutional theory on this point is unique. At least so far as this writer is aware, no one else has adopted it. Certainly the U.S. Supreme Court has never recurred to the Fifth Amendment's guarantee against deprivation of "liberty" without due process of law for the protection of freedom of speech. It is true, as Meiklejohn points out, that the Court has found freedom of speech to be included in the "liberty" protected against action by the several states by the Due Process Clause of the Fourteenth Amendment.[107] One could argue, with Meiklejohn, that therefore the "liberty" protected by the parallel (and original) Due Process Clause in the Fifth Amendment must also include a guarantee of freedom of speech distinct from and less absolute than the First Amendment's guarantee. But the Court has, in fact, not so much as glanced in that direction.

On the contrary, the Court has set its gaze in the opposite direction. Individual members of the Court—Justices Jackson, Frankfurter, Harlan and Rehnquist—have argued over the years that freedom of speech, when invoked against action by the states, should be interpreted less strictly and rigidly than when the federal government is involved, because it is protected only by the requirements of due process of law. But the Court has not heeded even that argument. So far as it is concerned, freedom of speech has only one meaning at both the national and state levels, and that is the meaning found in the First Amendment. Meiklejohn knows this but regrets it, because he believes that including all protected speech under the First Amendment dilutes the absolute freedom of public speech and leaves it "safe only from *undue* abridgment."[108] "Public discussion," he says, "has thus been reduced to the same legal status as private discussion."[109]

Even though he be but a voice crying in the wilderness with his distinction between First Amendent and Fifth Amendment guarantees of freedom of speech, Meiklejohn makes a point which is independent of the distinction. There are different kinds of expression that serve different purposes and deserve different levels of constitutional protection. If we cannot recognize this by distinguishing between First Amendment and Fifth Amendment guarantees, then we must do so by distinguishing among different kinds of speech in relation to the First Amendment alone. Insisting that "expression" is "expression," and that all expressions are equal leads inexorably either to absolutizing the protection of them all or, what is more likely, to relativizing that protection for all of them and, what is more, relativizing it in exactly the same way and in the same degree for all expressions.

But to return to Meiklejohn. "There are," he says, "in the theory of the Constitution, two radically different kinds of utterances. The constitutional status of a merchant advertising his wares, of a paid lobbyist fighting for the advantage of his client, is utterly different from that of a citizen who is planning for the general welfare."[110] Zechariah Chafee, Jr., therefore is simply wrong when he says that, in addition to "a social interest in the attainment of truth," the First Amendment also protects "an individual interest, the need of many men to express their opinions on matters vital to them."[111] According to Meiklejohn, the protection of the latter interest belongs to the Fifth Amendment, which "gives assurance that a private need to speak will get the impartial consideration to which it is entitled."[112] But it also makes the private right to speak "liable to such abridgments as the general welfare may require."[113]

As he says himself, Meiklejohn's position on this point

> has sharp and, at times, decisive implications for many issues of civil liberty now in dispute among us. It would be a fascinating and important task to follow those implications as they bear upon the rights to freedom which are claimed, for example, by lobbyists for special interests, by advertisers in press or radio, by picketing labor unions, by Jehovah's Witnesses, by the distributors of handbills on city streets, by preachers of racial intolerance, and many others. In all these cases the crucial task is that of separating public and private claims. But such discussion would go far beyond the limits of the present inquiry.[114]

He is even willing to consider the possibility "that the freedom of the 'pursuit of truth'" by research scholars "must ... be abridged" when the research is in areas of atomic and bacteriological knowledge that can be put to military uses.[115]

The courts, Meiklejohn points out, have already recognized many kinds of speech as subject to legal regulation or outright prohibition. "Thus libels, blasphemies, attacks upon public morals or private reputation have been held punishable." So also the obvious abuses of speech like falsely shouting fire in a crowded theatre, counselling murder and incitement to riot. "And this listing of legitimate legislative abridgments of speech could be continued indefinitely. Their number is legion."[116]

Meiklejohn takes a dyspeptic view of those great fora of the inquiring mind, the media of mass communication. "The radio, as we now have it," he wrote in 1948, "is not cultivating those qualities of taste, of reasoned judgment, of integrity, of loyalty, of mutual understanding upon which the enterprise of self-government depends. On the contrary, it is a mighty force for breaking them down." This should teach us the danger of a "merely formalistic" acceptance of the First Amendment principle of freedom of speech. "Misguided by that formalism," we have used the principle "for the protection of private, possessive interests with which it has no concern. It is misinterpretations such as this which, in our use of the radio, the moving picture, the newspaper and other forms of publication, are giving the name 'freedoms' to the most flagrant enslavements of our minds and wills."[117] In 1958 he added that "privately sponsored television has proved to be even more deadly."[118]

Meiklejohn's doctrine on freedom of expression is thus a nuanced one. To use a term he would surely have rejected, one could even call it balanced. It was shaped by an overriding purpose, the maximum availability of truth in the public discussion of public affairs. In regard to such speech his position was absolutist. He quoted with approval Justice Holmes' famous dissenting dictum in *Gitlow v. New York*: "If, in the long run, the beliefs expressed in proletarian dictatorship are destined to be accepted by the dominant forces of the community, the only meaning of free speech is that they should be given their chance and have their way."[119] One might be tempted to reply to Holmes with the remark that a French military observer in the Crimea made when he saw the charge of the Light Brigade: *"C'est magnifique, mais ce n'est pas la guerre."* But Meiklejohn's comment on Holmes' words is: "That is Americanism."[120] Meiklejohn, of course, was confident that the beliefs expressed in proletarian dictatorship would not be accepted because "whenever, in the field of ideas, the advocates of freedom and the advocates of suppression meet in fair and unabridged discussion, freedom will win."[121] Nevertheless, absolute though his claim for the freedom of public speech was, it was still only for public speech that he claimed the protection of the First Amendment.

For the rest, he recognized that "there are many 'forms of speech' about whose freedom the amendment has no concern. To fix our attention, as we commonly do, upon an individual 'right to speak' is to lose sight of the essential issue."[122] It is also a mistake to conceive of speech as immune from regulation simply because it is speech. "Speech," says Meiklejohn, "as a form of human action, is subject to regulation in exactly the same way as is walking, or lighting a fire, or shooting a gun. To interpret the First Amendment as forbidding such regulation is to so misconceive its meaning as to reduce it to nonsense."[123] The First Amendment admits of no exception, according to Meiklejohn, because there is so much in the way of speech and publication that it was never meant to cover.

Although Meiklejohn strenuously rejects the notion of a "balancing test" as applied to speech protected by the First Amendment,[124] it is obvious that he accepts such a test as applicable to all other speech. It is also clear that, for him, the freedom of expression is closely related to the freedom of the rational mind. His concept of truth seems to have been a relativist one—"What we think together at any time is, for us, our truth at that time"[125]—but there is no hint that he thought that all expressions, however removed from reason, contributed to the pursuit of truth. On the contrary, his judgment was severe on the exploitation of the media of communication by private interests: "It corrupts both our morals and our intelligence."[126] On Meiklejohn's scale of values, expression merely as expression ranked low and its justification, when it had one, was the service that it rendered to purposes above and beyond itself.

8

A Pearl in the Garbage
Conclusion

The foregoing review of major sources in the development of the theory of freedom of expression shows that these sources argued almost exclusively in terms of reason, truth, and moral and political development. They were, of course, arguing for freedom of speech and press, not against it. The case they made therefore emphasized the benefits that society would derive from allowing men freely to speak their minds and express their thoughts; they did not dwell on the limits they would put on that expression. But their understandable failure to do so is relatively unimportant. What matters here is that the freedom they contended for was the freedom of reason to pursue the true and the good through discussion and debate. This is a broad freedom, but not a simply amorphous one. Having a goal, it does have limits, and there is much in the way of expression that it does not cover or covers only lightly.

The thrust of these men's argument was certainly against the idea of an "orthodoxy," that is, of an established public truth which, because established, was to be held immune from criticism. They did not agree with Edmund Burke that it is the misfortune, and not the glory, of this age, that everything is to be discussed. They believed, in varying degrees, that everything should be discussed, but not because nothing is true. Rather, it was because they saw discussion as the method by which the human mind acquires a fuller and sounder knowledge of truth.

Whether the freedom of expression that the latter half of the twentieth century has achieved represents the fulfillment of their ideal may be open to question. Some observers, at least, have doubted it. Bertrand de Jouvenel, for instance, says: "The founders of democracy always believed that the free expression of opinions would secure, by a sort of natural selection, the survival and triumph of the most rational opinions. Experience has not verified this hypothesis."[1] But the soundness of Jouvenel's criticism is a question beyond the purview of this book. It is enough to have shown that the modern tradition of freedom of speech and press rests upon the relationships among expression, reason and truth.

The writers whose works constitute this tradition have their own limitations, as one would expect. None of them was a truly great writer, except John Milton. None of them was a first-rate philosopher, with the possible exception of Spinoza. John Locke was a major figure in the history of Western philosophy because of the influence he had on later generations and has to this day. But it is hard, for this commentator at least, to take him with full seriousness as a philosopher. John Stuart Mill would probably be known today only to specialists were it not for the enduring popularity of *On Liberty*. The other writers whose thought we have analyzed were articulate intellectuals who abode their destined hour and went their way. As time goes by, it proves to be their fate, as it is of almost all of us who write for publication, that the world has little noted nor long remembered what they said here.

Still, these men were all of them, even Milton in his way, rationalists. Milton, the only artist among them, was the only one to plead for the reading of "bad books" as a necessary exposure of virtue to the entice-ments of vice. The rest of them, when they adverted at all to "bad books," defended them for their intellectual content, the unorthodox but possibly true ideas that they conveyed. The case that could be made for the freedom of artistic expression in the service of beauty is hardly touched on in their writings. Their case was pitched rather in terms of truth, which they assumed would also make people good.

Their rationalism, it must be admitted, was a fairly thin one and became thinner as the generations succeeded one another. With Laski it almost peters out. What they meant by truth is often obscure and those of them who attempted to explain it, as Locke did, helped perhaps as much to weaken as to foster men's confidence in the power of reason to attain it. Yet they always argued from some conception of reason and of truth. Even an evolutionary view of truth still assumes truth to be a goal towards which we move and implicitly asserts that we can measure movement in that direction. The whole idea of intellectual progress, and the consequent advance of civilization, on which these men based their demand for freedom of thought and expression, would collapse if truth were simply unattainable.

The core of their argument was, in Spinoza's words, that "human wits are too blunt to get to the heart of all problems immediately; but they are sharpened by the give and take of discussion and debate, and by exploring every possible course men eventually discover the measures they wish, measures which all approve and which no one would have thought of before the discussion."[2] As Meiklejohn saw, it is at least problematical to what extent this argument supports "the rights to freedom which are claimed, for example, by lobbyists for special interests, by advertisers in press and radio, by picketing labor unions, by Jehovah's Witnesses, by the distributors of handbills on city streets, by preachers of racial intolerance, and many others."[3] Laski recognized in 1932 that, confronted with Hitler's propaganda, "if the Jews trusted to reason only for the defence of their lives their chance of survival would be relatively small. For the temper in which they are attacked is inherently unamenable to rational discussion."[4] So intent was Laski on claiming freedom for radical leftwing propaganda that he did not pause to ask why freedom should also be guaranteed to these other expressions that threatened people's lives and were inherently unamenable to rational discussion. But in the light of the tradition of which we take Laski as a part, it is a valid and necessary question. For the tradition stands for nothing if not for rational discussion as an avenue to truth.

Yet to assert that truth is beyond the reach of reason is the constant temptation of contemporary liberals. In order to protect its central value, individual freedom, the liberal mind is impelled (and often yields to the impulse) to deny that there are any standards of truth, goodness or beauty, or even of common decency, on which a limitation of expression could be based. This is more than a denial that any person, any institution and, above all, any church, has a full and final grasp of truth. That much would be compatible with a belief in a collective process of discussion and argument aimed at truth. The liberal temptation is a deeper one: to lapse into radical skepticism and moral relativism in order to leave the individual free to set his course by whatever standards he chooses.

But this is to leave him in midocean without a compass, because in order to assure his freedom, we have postulated that there are no rationally-grounded standards that he can choose. This guarantees to be sure, that no one else has a ground for imposing a standard upon him. It also makes it impossible for him to impose one on himself on any principle that can be validated by reason. Furthermore, and not merely incidentally, it destroys any rational basis for attaching importance to freedom of expression.

If expression need serve no goals beyond itself, if all expressions are on the same level because they are all identical in the only essential respect, that of being expressions, then to say that they are all equally valuable is tantamount to saying that they are equally valueless. Freedom to speak and publish was originally advocated for the services it would render to reason in the pursuit of truth. Now it is defended on the ground that, not only is there no definitive standard by which we may judge what is true, there is not even any standard by which we can distinguish reason in pursuit of truth from passion in the pursuit of pleasure, or greed in quest of gain, or the *libido dominandi* in its drive for power. But to take this position is to undermine the whole case for the freedom of the mind and its expression in speech and publication.

Justice Brennan strongly believed in "the transcendent value of speech" and often asserted it. But speech has no transcendent value in and of itself. Much speech, in fact, has no value at all. The value of "expression" is the value of that which is expressed, nothing more. Expression is valuable because it is the expression of a mind making some effort to grasp reality. Yet even this is not a transcendent value because the product of any particular mind may be shallow or distorted.

The only transcendent values are the truth, goodness and beauty that inhere in the real, and it is basic to any effective defense of freedom of expression to maintain that the human mind can at least approach them through the exercise of its intellectual powers. False ideas have their value, as Mill contended, and so, too, do even silly or dangerous ideas in the process of discussion. But their value consists in the service they eventually render to true ideas. This is the lesson taught by the whole tradition we have considered here: freedom of expression is desirable because (and therefore to the extent that) it is necessary for human minds, through communication with each other, to pursue the truth, above all the truth they need for the guidance of their social and individual lives.

It is also the substance of the thesis argued in this book. In order to frame a rationally defensible theory of freedom of expression, we need to shift the focus of attention from expression in itself to the purposes that expression serves. If we do this, we shall find that we must make distinctions among kinds, modes and media of expression. We shall also find that we cannot treat all kinds and manners of expression as if they all stood on the same level and were equally deserving of protection.

Much of this may be granted by libertarians who are prepared to make a strategic retreat and fall back to the next line of defense. All expressions, they will argue, however mindless and pernicious they may appear to the unsophisticated to be, really do perform an intellectual and socially useful function; all therefore deserve full protection. Donald Thomas, for example, tells us that "the pornographer's effect is to subvert the prevailing moral values of society"—yet we need him. Says Thomas:

> In literary terms, pornography is destructive of moral aspirations, as satire may be, and yet, depending on one's view of the human race and its predicament, pornography may be as necessary as satire. The fiction of DeSade or the satire of Swift can only aim to mock human nature as it is, not to transform it into anything better. It is a recognition of

something more than the darker side of human nature that while the propagandist of the new order prophesies that the heavens shall declare the glory of man, he hears at his shoulder a derisive chuckle.[5]

As Thomas sees it, pornography is a kind of satire and a useful antidote to Marxist dreams of Utopia. But the current social reality in the United States is that pornography is big business, said to gross at least four billion dollars a year and to be increasingly controlled by organized crime.[6] So great is its success that *Time* has casually referred to "the U.S., where hard-core pornography can be bought openly in Mom-and-Pop candy stores."[7] This business has little to do with the kind of literary efforts that Thomas seems to have in mind.

The hardheaded gentlemen who run the pornography industry know that they make money by giving the customer what he wants, and it is doubtful if the average patron of X-rated films is looking for derisive chuckles. Nor is he greatly interested in commentary on the human predicament, though he may have to put up with some of it if the filmmaker still thinks he has to show the courts that his product has some redeeming social value. Profitmaking pornography, however, to the extent that it dares, ignores these distractions and goes (to put it delicately) straight for the jugular.

What the customers want is male sexual fantasy, divorced from any human reality. In real life, prostitutes (about whom, etymologically, pornography is written) have other purposes in living than satisfying male sexual desire. Even the legendary prostitute with a heart of gold, who is entirely happy in her work, has some joys and sorrows not simply reducible to that work, if she is a real human being. But the women in commercialized pornography have no other function; they are mere creatures of fantasy, abstractions from reality that retain only those qualities which make them pleasure-giving objects. Of course there have been writers who used obscenity for satirical purposes. But such writers do not furnish the staple diet of the patrons of mass pornography. To paraphrase the poet, the readers of this "literature" look not for mind in women. It is precisely this mindless appeal to raw appetite that furnishes the dominant theme of the material taken as a whole in pornographic writings, films and other productions.

This material is therefore undeserving of protection as an exercise of freedom of expression. It is urged, however—and whoever said it first, it is now a commonplace—that we should be willing to wade through an ocean of garbage because there might be a pearl in it. To this remarkable argument it is a sufficient answer that we know that it is an ocean of garbage, but we do not know if there is a pearl in it. Nor do we know whether, even if there is a pearl, it is of such value that it is worth wading through an ocean of garbage to get it. Still less do we know that wading through this ocean is the only way to find this pearl. It might, after all, be an insight that has also occurred to someone else who was capable of expressing it without burying it in an ocean of garbage.

Both of the above arguments are attempts to show that one can find some content in every expression, however depraved, that justifies its publication. So one can, too, but only if one is determined beforehand to find some justification for every expression. This kind of argument is really a reversion to the position that expression is an end in itself regardless of its content. The argument collapses once we look at the content of certain expressions and ask what contribution they make to the purposes of a civilized society.

Pornography is only the extreme example of expression of no or very dubious worth. Advertising, too, is a big business, certainly a legitimate one, but few would defend it for its contributions to the quest for meaning in human life. When it threatens something that we take seriously, like health, we are willing to ban it, as we banned cigarette advertising from the airwaves.[8] The number of other expressions which, if they deserve protection at all, deserve something less than absolute protection, as Meiklejohn said, is legion. Even political speech, which it is the primary purpose of the First Amendment to protect, and which Meiklejohn would protect absolutely, at some point becomes so irrelevant to the purposes of a constitutional democracy that it loses its claim to immunity.

Justice Holmes' much admired dictum that "the only meaning of free speech" is that "the beliefs expressed in proletarian dictatorship ... should be given their chance and have their way" is in reality a piece of political doctrinairism. It was an irresponsible statement, or rather, it would have been one if Holmes had really meant it. The chances are, however, that he did not and only meant that we could safely let totalitarians talk because we could be sure that not many people in this country would agree with them. If that is all he meant, he was right in his practical judgment. But that is not what he said, and what he said was silly.

We know nothing about human beings that leads us to believe that they are willing to sacrifice their property, their religion, their control over the education of their children, and possibly their very lives to a proletarian dictatorship because they have been assured from the bench that that is the only meaning of free speech. Men have been known to pledge their lives, their fortunes and their sacred honor on the outcome of a war. They do not stake them on the outcome of an election to the results of which they propose tamely to submit. Nor are they likely to wait peacefully to see how a political contest comes out when it threatens to prevent any subsequent election from being held. One of the essential conditions for the successful operation of a constitutional democracy is that the political stakes must not be too high. To ignore that elementary truth is to make the First Amendment a charter for civil war.

But Holmes was willing to make his reading of social reality—revolutions don't happen in this country—the meaning of the First Amendment, even though he professed to be keenly aware of how changeable social reality is. His dictum was at best a prudential judgment about a set of social facts and their probable consequences. All brave statements about the right to advocate and to associate for the violent overthrow of the government rest on such prudential judgments. They always include either the unexpressed qualifying clause, "when the Supreme Court judges that no undue risks are involved," or the indemonstrable prediction that undue risks will never be involved.

To say that the limits are set even on political speech by prudential judgments is not to say that such judgments must always or usually be in favor of political repression. It is only to say that they are prudential judgments. Such judgments may and, for sound reasons, generally will be in favor of letting people talk even though what they say, if acted upon by a sufficient number of hearers, would lead to the end of constitutional government. Whether courts of law are the organs of government best qualified to make the judgment in this matter is another question. Suffice it to say here that courts are certainly not required by the First Amendment to lay it down that prudential judgments may never be made in the area of expression.

The final argument on which defenders of an unlimited freedom of expression are forced back is that the risks in allowing any limitation on expression are always greater than the risks in giving expression free rein, at least in the long run. This was, as we have seen, John Stuart Mill's ultimate reason for insisting on the degree of individual freedom that he advocated: the public always goes too far. This argument reveals the doctrinaire mind's fear of prudential judgments and especially its fear of allowing the public to make them. The public is unenlightened and prone to "hysteria," a disease to which intellectuals are notoriously immune. The public therefore must not be trusted to have a part in deciding First Amendment cases.

It was "an accepted article of faith" among eighteenth-century advocates of freedom of speech and press that juries should be allowed to decide, not only the fact of publication, but also the question whether a publication was criminal and subject to legal penalty. Juries, it was felt, were the natural protectors of popular liberties from the tyranny of royal judges. The desired reform was accomplished in Great Britain by Charles James Fox's Libel Act of 1792 and was brought to the United States, curiously enough, by the infamous Sedition Act of 1798. (The juries promptly disappointed the reformers by the verdicts they brought in.)[9] But in the present century the U.S. Supreme Court went far toward repealing this reform by taking unto itself a flood of First Amendment cases.

Judgment in matters involving the freedom of speech and press was removed from juries, local governments and state legislatures, and was transferred to the Supreme Court Building in Washington. So we had for a period of years what Justice Black called the "absurd spectacle" of Supreme Court justices "sifting through books and magazines" and trooping to the basement of their building to see an unending series of really or allegedly obscene films in order to determine whether they had "redeeming social value."[10] For all the justices knew, there might be a pearl in all that garbage. But, pearl or no pearl, the Court's liberal wing were determined that no one in the United States except themselves could find anything obscene, and they were seldom willing to do so. Justice Black's only complaint was that he was never willing and therefore saw no reason for wasting time on such material.

With the passing of the Warren Court and the dwindling in numbers of the liberal wing, the Court has become more ready to grant states and localities some discretion in judging when freedom of expression is being abused. But the liberal objection remains the same: the public always goes too far, therefore the public must never be allowed to judge. This in effect is to hold that common sense and the judgment of ordinary men and women, of the kind who sit on juries, have nothing to do with questions involving the limits of expression.

Underlying this distrust of popular judgment is the centuries-old liberal quest for abstract, utterly impersonal rules of law, that have only to be applied to cases as they arise, without the necessity of any personal judgment at all. Categories such as "obscenity," "defamation," or "advocacy of violent overthrow" must be rejected because they cannot be precisely defined. If they are allowed to remain part of the law, it becomes necessary for juries and trial courts to decide what they mean in their application to particular cases. Given that much leeway, juries will surely throw out the pearls with the garbage.

Yet this difficulty can be exaggerated. Chief Justice Warren himself once pointed out: "In other areas of the law, terms like 'negligence,' although in common use for centuries, have been difficult to define except in the most general manner. Yet the courts have been able to function in such areas with a reasonable degree of efficiency." He felt obliged, it must be granted, to add, "The obscenity problem, however, is aggravated by the fact that it involves the area of public expression, an area in which a broad range of freedom is vital to our society and is constitutionally protected."[11] But to say that a problem is aggravated is not to say that it is rendered insoluble. Juries, applying general legal definitions and instructed by trial judges, are capable of passing judgment on obscenity and other abuses of freedom of expression. They are often more capable of doing so than civil-liberties lawyers and literary critics who have a vested interest in not recognizing the obvious. When juries err by clear excess, they are subject to correction by appellate courts which will themselves pass prudential judgments on the matter —sound ones, we may hope.

For there is no escaping the personal judgments of human minds in the application of law to concrete decisions. Personal judgment is unavoidable, in fact, even in the hardest of "hard sciences." Some human minds must judge what constitutes evidence and when the evidence proves a conclusion. There is no set of facts "out there" that talks to men and tells them what is true. All the more so in the area of practical judgment which guides human action, an area that includes the domain of law. Judgment here necessarily requires evaluation of the facts, estimation of the relative weight and force of a multitude of factors and an effort rationally to predict consequences. Practical judgment is not a blind shot in the dark, but neither is it the mathematical demonstration of an ineluctable conclusion.

This conception of the practical function of reason, however, is intolerable to the doctrinaire mind. Such a mind deals only in logical extremes. The needle on the gauge must point either to zero degrees or to 180 degrees, because there is no fully demonstrable reason for its coming to rest at any one of the 179 other degrees in between. So we must have either uninhibited freedom of expression or total repression. We are always confronted with the choice between Fanny Hill and Torquemada because, logically, there is no other choice.

Yet the claim that in the long run the risks involved in allowing any limitation on freedom of expression are always greater than those involved in removing all limitations, is itself a prudential judgment and a prediction of consequences. There is no way of proving it. There is not even much reason for believing it. Consider the names of Shakespeare, Molière, Cervantes and Dostoievski. Add Dante and Goethe, if you wish. Not one of them lived in a liberal democracy. Yet critics have compared their writings favorably with the best work of Ernest Hemingway and Norman Mailer. One would be hard put to it, in fact, to come up with the name of a single author of the same stature as these great writers, who lived under a regime of complete freedom of expression or even, for that matter, in a modern liberal democracy.

Neither, of course, did any of the men named above live in Stalin's Russia or under an equally repressive tyranny. Writers need freedom, as do scientists, scholars, teachers and voters. But the question is how much and what kind of freedom? That question can be answered only by addressing oneself to the further question, what do they need freedom for? The purposes of freedom must define its nature and its limits. Inquiry into those purposes will yield a more intelligent theory of freedom of expression than groping for a pearl in the garbage or dreading the loss of a pearl if any garbage at all is thrown out.

There is another argument that deserves brief mention before we close. It is that the thesis argued in these pages, while it may compel admiration for its eloquence or for its jesuitical cleverness, is unfortunately useless. It defines no rules of law and it does not tell courts how to decide cases. It may therefore have some place among what Justice Powell called "the theoretical abstractions of a political science seminar,"[12] but lawyers cannot use it.

To this there are two answers. The first is that, while the Constitution must be interpreted and applied by courts of law, it was not written for the convenience of lawyers and courts. It provides basic norms for the government of a nation, which nation is not well served by reducing its constitution to the kind of rules that courts find it easiest to apply. As Chief Justice Burger put it for the Supreme Court, "no amount of 'fatigue' should lead us to adopt a convenient 'institutional' rationale —an absolutist, 'anything goes' view of the First Amendment—because it will lighten our burdens."[13]

The second and more important answer is that the interpretation of a constitution, especially of one that contains broad and sweeping phrases like "the freedom of speech, or of the press," "due process of law," or "the equal protection of the laws," necessarily requires criteria of interpretation and therefore some conception of the purposes understood by and implied in the clauses being interpreted. In short, it needs a theory of constitutional ends and means. An absolutist or quasi-absolutist theory of the freedom of speech and press is, after all, no more than that—a theory. The only way to counter it is with another and possibly better theory. The alternative theory may do nothing more than shift the perspective in which we look at constitutional rights and so furnish a different starting point for the detailed legal thinking. Yet even this much, little though it be, is worth doing, for the end is in the beginning.

Notes

Notes to the Introduction

1. Miss Lovelace's own later comment on *Deep Throat* was: "Every time someone watches that movie, they are watching me being raped." *New York Times*, December 18, 1983, p. 44, col. 1.

2. "The Outrageously Immoral Fact," in Clor, Harry M., ed., *Censorship and Freedom of Expression* (Chicago: Rand McNally, 1971), 43.

3. 421 U.S. 151 (1973).

4. New York: Vintage Books, 1967.

5. Ibid., viii, 115.

6. New York: Vintage Books, 1970.

7. Ibid., 8.

8. Ibid., 17.

9. 314 U.S. 252, 263, 265 (1941). It occurred earlier, however, as "liberty of expression" in *Schneider v. State*, 308 U.S. 147, 163 (1939).

10. *General Theory*, 7; *System of Freedom*, 8.

11. 383 U.S. 463, 489 (1966).

12. 409 U.S. 109, 123 (1972).

13. *General Theory*, 3, n. 1. The publication data have been omitted since they will be supplied when these works are discussed at length.

Notes to Chapter One

1. Announcing the judgment of the Court, *Curtis Publishing v. Butts*, 388 U.S. 130, 148, 149.

2. For the Court, *Dennis v. U.S.*, 341 U.S. 494, 503 (1951).

3. A number of the statements quoted will refer to freedom of association but, as the Court has said, "while the freedom of association is not explicitly set out in the [First] Amendment, it has long been held to be implicit in the freedoms of speech, assembly, and petition." *Healy v. James*, 408 U.S. 169, 181 (1972).

4. "Congress shall make no law ... abridging the freedom of speech, or of the press." First Amendment to the Constitution of the United States. To which add: "It is no longer open to doubt that the liberty of the press, and of speech, is within the liberty safeguarded by the due process clause of the Fourteenth Amendment from invasion by State action." Hughes, C. J., for the Court, *Near v. Minnesota*, 283 U.S. 697, 707 (1931). Note also: "It is, of course, a commonplace that the constitutional guarantee of free speech is a guarantee only against abridgment by government, federal or state." Stewart, J., for the Court, *Hudgens v. NLRB*, 424 U.S. 507, 513 (1976).

5. Roberts, J., dissenting, *Thomas v. Collins*, 323 U.S. 516, 548 (1945).

6. Murphy, J., for the Court, *Thornhill v. Alabama*, 310 U.S. 88, 95 (1940).

7. Brennan, J., for the Court, *Speiser v. Randall*, 357 U.S. 513, 521 (1958).

8. *Palko v. Connecticut*, 302 U.S. 319, 327 (1937).

9. *Time v. Hill*, 385 U.S. 374, 389 (1967).

10. *Palko v. Connecticut*, supra, at 325.

11. *Pickering v. Board of Education* 391 U.S. 563, 573 (1968).

12. 376 U.S. 254, 296–297 (1964).

13. Vinson, C. J., for the Court, *Dennis v. U.S.*, 341 U.S. 494, 503 (1951).

14. 2 Cooley's *Constitutional Limitations*, 8th ed., p. 886, quoted with approval by Sutherland, J., for the Court, *Grosjean v. American Press Co.*, 297 U.S. 233, 249–250 (1936).

15. For the Court, *Mills v. Alabama*, 384 U.S. 214, 218 (1966).

16. For the Court, *Stromberg v. California*, 283 U.S. 359, 369 (1931).

17. Concurring, *Thomas v. Collins*, 323 U.S. 516, 545 (1945).

18. Dissenting, *Terminiello v. Chicago*, 337 U.S. 1, 32 (1949).

19. *Cantwell v. Connecticut*, 310 U.S. 296, 310 (1940).

20. *Associated Press v. U.S.*, 326 U.S. 1, 20 (1945).

21. *Grosjean v. American Press Co.*, 297 U.S. 233, 250 (1936).

22. Dissenting, *Bridges v. California*, 314 U.S. 252, 291, 293 (1941).

23. Douglas, J., joined by Black, J., dissenting, *Adler v. Board of Education*, 342 U.S. 485, 511 (1952).

24. *Red Lion Broadcasting Co. v. FCC*, 395 U.S. 367, 390 (1969).

25. Dissenting, *Columbia Broadcasting Co. v. Democratic Committee*, 412 U.S. 94, 189 (1973).

26. Holmes, J., dissenting, *Abrams v. U.S.*, 250 U.S. 616, 630 (1919).

27. Concurring in part, *Dennis v. U.S.*, 341 U.S. 494, 550 (1951).

28. Concurring, *Thomas v. Collins*, 323 U.S. 516, 545 (1945).

29. *NAACP v. Button*, 371 U.S. 415, 444–445 (1963).

30. *Gertz v. Welch*, 418 U.S. 323, 339–340 (1974).

31. Brennan, J., for the Court, *New York Times v. Sullivan*, 376 U.S. 254, 270 (1964), quoting Brandeis, J., concurring, *Whitney v. California*, 274 U.S. 357, 375 (1927).

32. Frankfurter, J., for the Court, *Drivers Union v. Meadowmoor Co.*, 312 U.S. 287, 293 (1941).

33. *Thomas v. Collins*, 323 U.S. 516, 537 (1945).

34. *NAACP v. Button*, 371 U.S. 415, 429 (1963).

35. 376 U.S. 254, 270.

36. *Stanley v. Georgia*, 394 U.S. 557, 564.

37. Brennan, J., for the Court, *Time v. Hill*, 385 U.S. 374, 388 (1967).

38. Harlan, J., announcing judgment of Court, *Curtis Publishing Co. v. Butts*, 388 U.S. 130, 149 (1967).

39. Concurring in part, *Dennis v. U.S.*, 341 U.S. 494, 550 (1951).

40. *Curtis Publishing Co. v. Butts*, supra, at 147. The interior quotation is from the Letter to the Inhabitants of Quebec, 1 *Journals of the Continental Congress*, 108, and has often been cited by the Justices of the Court.

41. Brennan, J. for the Court, *Keyishian v. Board of Regents*, 385 U.S. 589, 603 (1967).

42. *Winters v. New York*, 333 U.S. 507, 510 (1948).

43. 310 U.S. 296, 310 (1940).

44. For the Court, *Hannegan v. Esquire, Inc.*, 327 U.S. 146, 158 (1946).

45. See his dissenting opinion, joined by Black, J., *Roth v. U.S.*, 354 U.S. 476, 508 (1957).

46. Dissenting, *Byrne v. Karalexis*, 396 U.S. 976, 979 (1969).

47. Dissenting, *Paris Adult Theatre I v. Slaton*, 413 U.S. 49, 70 (1973).

48. Dissenting, *Dyson v. Stein*, 401 U.S. 200, 211–215 (1971). Cf. his dissenting opinion in *Miller v. California*, 413 U.S. 15, 37–47 (1973).

49. Dissenting, *U.S. v. 12 200-Ft. Reels*, 413 U.S. 123, 137 (1973).

50. Dissenting, *Paris Adult Theatre I v. Slaton*, 413 U.S. 49, 71–72 (1973).

51. This is an inference from the fact that he joined Justice Reed in a dissenting opinion in which the latter said that he accepted "the constitutional power of a state to pass group libel laws to protect the public peace." 343 U.S. 250, 283 (1952). In his own dissenting opinion in the same case, Justice Douglas said that it would be constitutional to proscribe a conspiracy of the Nazi type "which was aimed at destroying a race by exposing it to

contempt, derision, and obloquy.... For such a project would be more than the exercise of free speech. Like picketing, it would be free speech plus." Ibid., at 284.

52. Concurring, *Rosenblatt v. Baer*, 383 U.S. 75, 90 (1966). Cf. his dissenting opinion in *Gertz v. Welch*, 418 U.S. 323, 356–359 (1974).

53. See separate opinion of Black, J., in *Rosenblatt v. Baer*, supra, at 95. It sometimes appears that the sweeping denial of the constitutionality of libel laws means only that "the First Amendment guarantees to each person in this country the unconditional right to print what he pleases about *public* affairs." Black, J., joined by Douglas, J., dissenting, *Ginzburg v. Goldwater*, 396 U.S. 1049, 1050 (1970) (emphasis added). On the other hand, after Justice Black's retirement, Douglas dissented from a decision in favor of the plaintiff in an invasion of privacy suit against the *Cleveland Plain Dealer* for publishing known false statements about a private family, and began one sentence with the words, "Whatever might be the ultimate reach of the doctrine Mr. Justice Black and I have embraced [on the unconstitutionality of libel laws]...." He thus indicated that, while he might not know how far he was willing to extend the right to publish libels, he did not confine it to statements about public figures. *Cantrell v. Forest City Publishing Co.*, 419 U.S. 245, 255 (1974).

54. Concurring, *Rosenbloom v. Metromedia*, 403 U.S. 29, 57 (1971).

55. Dissenting, *Gertz v. Welch*, 418 U.S. 323, 355–356 (1974).

56. E.g., Black, J., for the Court, *Bridges v. California*, 314 U.S. 252, 263 (1941); Douglas, J., dissenting, *Dennis v. U.S.*, 341 U.S. 494, 584–585 (1951), and *Beauharnais v. Illinois*, 343 U.S. 250, 284–285 (1952).

57. Douglas, J., concurring, *Brandenburg v. Ohio*, 395 U.S. 444, 454 (1969). Black, J., concurring, ibid., at 449, stated his explicit agreement with this view.

58. Joined by Black, J., concurring, *Garrison v. Louisiana*, 379 U.S. 64, 82 (1964).

59. Joined by Black, J., concurring, *New York Times v. U.S.*, 403 U.S. 713, 720 (1971).

60. Dissenting, *Mishkin v. New York*, 383 U.S. 502, 518 (1966).

61. Joined by Douglas, J., concurring in part, *Yates v. U.S.*, 354 U.S. 298, 343–344 (1957).

62. Joined by Warren, C. J., and Black, J., dissenting, *Times Film Corp. v. Chicago*, 365 U.S. 43, 84 (1961).

63. Concurring, *Memoirs v. Massachusetts*, 383 U.S. 413, 433 (1966).

64. Dissenting, *Hamling v. U.S.*, 418 U.S. 87, 140–141 (1974).

65. "Two members of the Court have consistently adhered to the view that a State is utterly without power to suppress, control, or punish the distribution of any writings or pictures upon the ground of their 'obscenity.'" Per curiam, *Redrup v. New York*, 386 U.S. 767, 770 (1967), where the reference is obviously to Black and Douglas, JJ.

66. See, e.g., their opinions in *Dennis v. U.S.*, 341 U.S. 494, 579–580, 584–585 (1951); *Yates v. U.S.*, 354 U.S. 298, 343–344 (1957); *Speiser v. Randall*, 357 U.S. 513, 536 (1958); *Communist Party v. S.A.C. Board*, 367 U.S. 1, 147 (1961); *Scales v. U.S.*, 367 U.S. 203, 260, 265, 269–270 (1961); *Du Bois Clubs v. Clark*, 389 U.S. 309, 314 (1967); and the opinion of Douglas, J., dissenting, *Cole v. Richardson*, 405 U.S. 676, 689 (1972).

67. Joined by Black, J., dissenting, *Roth v. U.S.*, 354 U.S. 476, 514 (1957). But see his later opinions in *Ginzburg v. U.S.*, 383 U.S. 463, 491–492 (1966), and *Ginsberg v. New York*, 390 U.S. 629, 655–656 (1968), where it appears that the distinction between the noxious and its opposite has vanished.

68. Dissenting, *Dyson v. Stein*, 401 U.S. 200, 209 (1971).

69. Dissenting, *Konigsberg v. State Bar of California*, 366 U.S. 36, 78 (1961).

70. Dissenting, *Communist Party v. S.A.C. Board*, 367 U.S. 1, 147 (1961). He was, of course, echoing Holmes, J., dissenting, *Gitlow v. New York*, 268 U.S. 652, 673 (1925). For a similar statement of faith in education as the remedy, see Douglas, J., dissenting, *Dyson v. Stein*, 401 U.S. 200, 208 (1971).

71. Douglas, J., joined by Black, J., dissenting, *Roth v. U.S.*, 354 U.S. 476, 509 (1957).

72. Concurring, *Memoirs v. Massachusetts*, 383 U.S. 413, 426 (1966). "Advocacy which is in no way brigaded with action should always be protected by the First Amendment." Douglas, J., joined by Black, J., concurring, *Speiser v. Randall*, 357 U.S. 513, 536 (1958).

73. Concurring, *Brandenburg v. Ohio*, 395 U.S. 444, 456–457 (1969).

74. Dissenting, *Pittsburgh Press v. Human Relations Commission*, 413 U.S. 376, 399 (1973).

75. Dissenting, *Tinker v. School District*, 393 U.S. 503, 524 (1969).

76. Dissenting, *Brown v. Louisiana*, 383 U.S. 131, 162 (1966).

77. It is interesting, however, that when a young man named Cohen was convicted for wearing a jacket that carried the words, "F--- the Draft," on its back in the Los Angeles County Courthouse, Justice Black voted to uphold his conviction and joined a separate opinion in which Justice Blackmun said: "Cohen's absurd and immature antic, in my view, was mainly conduct and little speech." *Cohen v. California*, 403 U.S. 15, 27 (1971). This seems a bit facile.

78. See, e.g., his opinions in *Konigsberg v. State Bar of California*, 366 U.S. 36, 61–62 (1961); *In re Anastaplo* 366 U.S. 82, 110–112 (1961); *Scales v. U.S.*, 367 U.S. 203, 261–261 (1961); *Time v. Hill*, 385 U.S. 374, 399–400 (1967); and the opinions of Douglas, J., in *Scales v. U.S.*, supra, at 270–271, and *Garrison v. Louisiana*, 379 U.S. 64, 80–83 (1964).

79. For the Court, *Marsh v. Alabama*, 326 U.S. 501, 509 (1946).

80. Concurring, *Smith v. California*, 361 U.S. 147, 157–159 (1959).

81. Joined by Warren, C. J., and Douglas, J., dissenting, *Konigsberg v. State Bar of California*, 366 U.S. 36, 61 (1961).

82. Joined by Douglas, J., concurring, *Time v. Hill*, 385 U.S. 374, 399–400 (1967).

83. Dissenting, *Branzburg v. Hayes*, 408 U.S. 665, 713 (1972); cf. ibid., at 716.

84. For the Court, *Ginzburg v. U.S.*, 383 U.S. 463, 470 (1966).

85. For the Court, *Near v. Minnesota*, 283 U.S. 697, 708 (1931).

86. *Konigsberg v. State Bar of California*, 366 U.S. 36, 49–51.

87. Ibid., at 49, n. 10.

88. For the Court, *Chaplinsky v. New Hampshire*, 315 U.S. 568, 571–572. Interestingly, this opinion was joined by Justices Black and Douglas—a youthful indiscretion which they outgrew.

89. For the Court, 354 U.S. 476, 481, 484 (1957).

90. For the Court, *Herbert v. Lando*, 441 U.S. 153, 158 (1979).

91. For the Court, *Drivers Union v. Meadowmoor Co.*, 312 U.S. 287, 293 (1941).

92. For the Court, *Cantwell v. Connecticut*, 310 U.S. 296, 309–310 (1940).

93. 376 U.S. 254, 279 (1964).

94. *Garrison v. Louisiana*, 379 U.S. 64, 75 (1964).

95. *Time v. Hill*, 385 U.S. 374, 390 (1967).

96. *St. Amant v. Thompson*, 390 U.S. 727, 732 (1968).

97. For the Court, *American Communicatons Assn. v. Douds*, 339 U.S. 382, 394 (1950).

98. For the Court, 249 U.S. 47, 52.

99. Dissenting, 250 U.S. 616, 628 (1919).

100. For the Court, 341 U.S. 494, 505.

101. *Brandenburg v. Ohio*, 395 U.S. 444, 447. But note the earlier statement of the Court that *Dennis v. U.S.*, supra, and *Yates v. U.S.*, 354 U.S. 298 (1957) "have definitely laid at rest any doubt that present advocacy of *future* action for violent overthrow satisfies statutory and constitutional requirements equally with advocacy of *immediate* action to that end." *Scales v. U.S.*, 367 U.S. 203, 251 (1961). See *Yates v. U.S.*, supra, at 321, for a precise definition of the kind of advocacy intended.

102. *Ginsberg v. New York*, 390 U.S. 629, 641 (1968).

103. For the Court, 341 U.S. 494, 508 (1951). The Chief Justice added: "Overthrow of the Government by force and violence is certainly a substantial enough interest for the Government to limit speech."

104. Concurring, *Whitney v. California*, 274 U.S. 357, 377 (1927).

105. For the Court, 391 U.S. 367, 376–377.

106. *Food Employees v. Logan Valley Plaza*, 391 U.S. 308, 323 (1968).

107. *Cox v. Louisiana*, 379 U.S. 536, 555 (1965).

108. *U.S. v. O'Brien*, 391 U.S. 367, 376 (1968).

109. *Tinker v. School District*, 393 U.S. 503, 505–506 (1969).

110. Concurring and dissenting, *Smith v. California*, 361 U.S. 147, 170 (1959).

111. 341 U.S. 494, 542, 544 (1951).

112. 339 U.S. 382, 399 (1950).

113. For the Court, 341 U.S. 494, 503 (1951).

114. Cf., e.g., his separate opinions in *Bridges v. California*, 314 U.S. 252, 293 (1941) and *Kovacs v. Cooper*, 336 U.S. 77, 95 (1949).

115. *Pickering v. Board of Education*, 391 U.S. 563, 568. Mr. Pickering, to be sure, won his case against the Board, but that only means that the Court struck the balance in his favor.

116. Brennan, J., for the Court, *Speiser v. Randall*, 357 U.S. 513, 526 (1958).

117. Ibid., at 525.

118. Brennan, J., for the Court, *NAACP v. Button*, 371 U.S. 415, 433 (1963). "Narrow specificity" was another constitutional doctrine that was to have a long life ahead of it and to be frequently restated by at least some justices. See also *Dombrowski v. Pfister*, 380 U.S. 479, 487 (1965), where the need for "breathing space" issued in the doctrine that enforcement of a law might be unconstitutional because it had a "chilling effect" on the exercise of First Amendment freedoms.

119. For the Court, 354 U.S. 476, 481, 488 (1957).

120. For the Court, *Bantam Books v. Sullivan*, 372 U.S. 58, 66 (1963).

121. For the Court, *Carroll v. Commissioners of Princess Anne*, 393 U.S. 175, 183 (1968).

122. Brennan, J., for the Court, *NAACP v. Button*, 371 U.S. 415, 438 (1963).

123. Brennan, J., for the Court, *Gooding v. Wilson*, 405 U.S. 518, 521 (1972).

124. Brennan, J., joined by Marshall, J., dissenting, *FCC v. Pacifica Foundation*, 438 U.S. 726, 773 (1978).

125. Joined by Marshall, J., concurring in part, *Hynes v. Mayor of Oradell*, 425 U.S. 610, 628 (1976).

126. Announcing judgment of Court, *Elrod v. Burns*, 427 U.S. 347, 360 (1976).

127. *Nixon v. Administrator*, 433 U.S. 425, 467–468 (1977).

128. Stewart, J., joined by Brennan and Marshall, JJ., dissenting, *Branzburg v. Hayes*, 408 U.S. 665, 725 (1972).

129. Brennan, J., joined by Stewart and Marshall, JJ., concurring in judgment, *Nebraska Press Ass'n. v. Stuart*, 427 U.S. 539, 572 (1976).

130. Brennan and Marshall, JJ., joined the dissenting opinions of other justices in *Saxbe v. Washington Post*, 417 U.S. 843 (1974), and Brennan, J., joined Stevens, J., dissenting, in *Houchins v. KQED*, 438 U.S. 1 (1978), a case in which Marshall, J., did not participate.

131. Marshall, J., joined by Brennan, J., dissenting, *Jones v. North Carolina Prisoners' Union*, 433 U.S. 119, 146 (1977).

132. Joined by Marshall, J., dissenting, *Greer v. Spock*, 424 U.S. 828, 852 (1976).

133. Joined by Marshall, J., concurring in judgment, *McKinney v. Alabama*, 424 U.S. 669, 684 (1976).

134. *California v. La Rue*, 409 U.S. 109, 118 (1972); cf. 111–112.

135. Dissenting, ibid., at 139. Brennan, J., dissented separately.

136. *Gooding v. Wilson*, 405 U.S. 518 (1972); *Lewis v. New Orleans*, 415 U.S. 130 (1974).

137. *Cole v. Richardson*, 405 U.S. 676, 691 (1972).

138. Brennan, J., joined by Stewart and Marshall, JJ., dissenting, *Hamling v. U.S.*, 418 U.S. 87, 142 (1974); *Smith v. U.S.*, 431 U.S. 291, 310 (1977).

139. Brennan, J., joined by Stewart and Marshall, JJ., dissenting, *Roaden v. Kentucky*, 413 U.S. 496 (1973); *Alexander v. Virginia*, 413 U.S. 836 (1973); *Splawn v. California*, 431 U.S. 595 (1977); *Ward v. Illinois*, 431 U.S. 767 (1977).

140. Brennan, J., joined by Stewart and Marshall, JJ., dissenting, *Paris Adult Theatre I v. Slaton*, 413 U.S. 49, 103 (1973).

141. Joined by Douglas and Brennan, JJ., dissenting, *Arnett v. Kennedy*, 416 U.S. 134, 229 (1974).

142. Concurring, *Cole v. Richardson*, 397 U.S. 238, 240 (1970).

143. Dissenting, *Lewis v. New Orleans*, 415 U.S. 130, 136–137 (1974).

144. 438 U.S. 726, 751–755.

145. Ibid., at 766.

146. Ibid., at 774–776.

147. Ibid., at 777.

148. Ibid., at 773.

149. Dissenting in part. *Herbert v. Lando*, 441 U.S. 153, 183, n. 1 (1979).

150. *Healy v. James*, 408 U.S. 169, 171 (1972).

151. *Branzburg v. Hayes*, 408 U.S. 665, 681, 690 (1972).

152. *Pell v. Procunier*, 417 U.S. 817, 822, 824 (1974).

153. *Gertz v. Welch*, 418 U.S. 323, 341 (1974).

154. *Buckley v. Valeo*, 424 U.S. 1, 24–25 (1976).

155. Concurring in part, *Dennis v. U.S.*, 341 U.S. 494, 544–545 (1951). See ibid., at 549, for Frankfurter's recognition that "a public interest is not wanting in granting freedom to speak their minds even to those who advocate the overthrow of the Government by force."

156. 336 U.S. 77, 96 (1949).

157. Dissenting, *Ginsberg v. New York*, 390 U.S. 629, 650 (1968).

158. 343 U.S. 250, 263 (1952).

159. Dissenting, ibid., at 274.

160. Dissenting, *Panhandle Oil Co. v. Knox*, 277 U.S. 218, 223 (1928).

161. Dissenting, *Carey v. Population Services*, 431 U.S. 678, 718 (1977).

162. Dissenting, *Branzburg v. Hayes*, 408 U.S. 665, 745–746 (1972)

163. For the Court, *Kingsley Books v. Brown*, 354 U.S. 436, 441 (1957).

164. *Police Dept. of Chicago v. Mosely*, 408 U.S. 92, 95.

165. Dissenting, *Lehman v. Shaker Heights*, 418 U.S. 298, 316.

166. *Hudgens v. NLRB*, 424 U.S. 507, 520.

167. For the Court, *Young v. American Mini Theatres*, 427 U.S. 50, 65–69.

168. Ibid., at 67.

169. Ibid., at 85.

170. Stevens, J., for the Court, *FCC v. Pacifica Foundation*, 438 U.S. 726, 744–745. It should be noted that what Stevens rejected was "the assumed premise [of *Roth v. U.S.*] that all communications within the protected area are equally immune from governmental restraint, whereas those outside that area are utterly without social value and, hence deserving of no protection." Obscenity, in his view, was "a public nuisance which is entitled to at least a modicum of First Amendment protection." Dissenting, *Smith v. U.S.*, 431 U.S. 291, 318, 312 (1977). "The fact," however, "that a type of communication is entitled to some constitutional protection does not require the conclusion that it is totally immune from regulation." Concurring in part, *Carey v. Population Services*, 431 U.S. 678, 716 (1977). The degree of permissible regulation would depend on the content of the communication.

171. Concurring in part, *FCC v. Pacifica Foundation*, supra, at 761.

172. For the Court, *Ohralik v. Ohio State Bar*, 436 U.S. 447, 455–456 (1978).

173. For the Court, *Virginia Pharmacy Board v. Virginia Consumer Council*, 425 U.S. 748, 771, n. 24 (1976).

174. Concurring, ibid., at 779–780.

175. Dissenting, *Saia v. New York*, 334 U.S. 558, 566 (1948).

176. *Southeastern Promotions v. Conrad*, 420 U.S. 546, 557 (1975).

177. Rehnquist, J., for the Court, *Jones v. North Carolina Prisoners' Union*, 433 U.S. 119, 136 (1977).

178. *Obscenity and Public Morality: Censorship in a Liberal Society* (Chicago and London: University of Chicago Press, 1969), 25.

179. Ibid., 27–28.

180. 354 U.S. 476, 485 (1957).

181. *Kingsley International Pictures v. Regents*, 360 U.S. 684, 688.

182. 333 U.S. 507, 510.

183. *Stanley v. Georgia*, 394 U.S. 557, 566 (1969).

184. Dissenting, supra, at 528.

185. 354 U.S. 476, 489 (1957) (emphasis added).

186. Announcing judgment of Court, *Memoirs v. Massachusetts*, 383 U.S. 413, 419 (1966), where he himself supplied the emphasis.

187. 386 U.S. 767.

188. 413 U.S. 15, 24, 26, 36 (1973).

189. For the Court, *Paris Adult Theatre I v. Slaton*, 413 U.S. 49, 67 (1973).

190. *Miller v. California*, supra, at 34.

191. Dissenting, *FCC v. Pacifica Foundation*, 438 U.S. 726, 773 (1978).

192. Dissenting, *Kunz v. New York*, 340 U.S. 290, 302 (1951).

193. Concurring, *Jacobellis v. Ohio* 378 U.S. 184, 197 (1964).
194. *Smith v. U.S.*, 431 U.S. 291, 305 (1977).
195. New York: Random House, 1970.
196. *Paris Adult Theatre I v. Slaton*, 413 U.S. 49, 63 (1973).
197. Ibid., at 60 ff.
198. Dissenting, *Ginzburg v. U.S.*, 383 U.S. 463, 498 (1966).
199. 403 U.S. 15 (1971); 408 U.S. 901 (1972); 410 U.S. 667 (1973).
200. Powell, J., dissenting, *Rosenfeld v. New Jersey*, 408 U.S. 901, 904 (1972).
201. *The Public Philosophy* (New York: Mentor Books, 1956). 97–98.

Notes to Chapter Two

1. "How to Read Milton's 'Areopagitica,'" *Journal of Politics*, 22 (1960), as reprinted in Kendall, Nellie D., ed., *Willmoore Kendall contra Mundum* (New Rochelle, NY: Arlington House, 1971), 168–169.
2. Sirluck, Ernest, "Introduction," *Complete Prose Works of John Milton*, vol. II, ed. E. Sirluck (New Haven: Yale University Press; London: Oxford University Press, 1959), 163.
3. *Milton and the Puritan Dilemma* (Toronto: University of Toronto Press, 1942), 88.
4. *Complete Prose Works*, ed. Sirluck, II, 797; the complete text of the Order is found in Appendix B, ibid., 797–799.
5. Sirluck takes this as Milton's genuine position. "Introduction," ibid., 163–164.
6. Joseph Anthony Wittreich, Jr., so argues in "Milton's *Areopagitica*: its Isocratic and Ironic Contexts," in Simmonds, James D., ed., *Milton Studies*, 4 (Pittsburgh: University of Pittsburgh Press, 1972), 109 ff.
7. "It is remarkable how generally this view has been accepted, for it is widely at variance with the facts." Sirluck, "Introduction," op. cit., 158.
8. *Areopagitica*, in *Complete Prose Works*, II, ed. Sirluck, 505. All subsequent references to *Areopagitica* will be to this edition.
9. Ibid., 569. Sirluck remarks in a footnote: "There is an ambiguity here. It was a legal offence for books to be published anonymously or without the publisher's imprint, even though they were neither 'mischievous' nor libellous; it was another offence to publish 'mischief' or libel, even though the publication carried the name of author and publisher."
10. Ibid., 565.
11. See, for example, Gilman, Wilbur Elwyn, *Milton's Rhetoric: Studies in His Defense of Liberty* (University of Missouri Studies, 1939), 10; Wolfe, Don Marion, *Milton in the Puritan Revolution* (New York: Thomas Nelson and Sons, 1941), 136; Read, Herbert, *A Coat of Many Colours* (New York: Horizon Press, 1956), 336–337; Laski, Harold, "The *Areopagitica* of Milton after Three Hundred Years," in Ould, Hermon, ed., *Freedom of Expression* (Port Washington, New York, and London: Kennikat Press, 1970), 175.
12. *Legacy of Suppression* (Cambridge, MA: Belknap Press of Harvard University Press, 1960), 95.
13. Op. cit., 169.
14. Ibid., 175–177. For an even more radical assertion of Milton's authoritarianism, see Illo, John, "The Misreading of Milton," *Columbia University Forum*, 8, 2 (Summer 1965), 38–42.
15. "The Philosophical Basis of Toleration," in Ould, ed., op. cit., 78.
16. *Areopagitica*, 528.
17. Ibid., 492.
18. Ibid.
19. Ibid., 513.
20. Ibid., 530–531.
21. Ibid., 532.
22. Ibid., 548.
23. Ibid., 562–563.
24. "The divorce pamphlets, the *Areopagitica* and *Of Education* form a group not only in

time but because each contributes to Milton's definition of Christian liberty, 'domestic or private.'" Op. cit., 118.

25. Ibid., 75.
26. *Areopagitica*, 549–551.
27. "Introduction," op. cit., 180.
28. *Areopagitica*, 561.
29. "Lessons of the Areopagitica," *Contemporary Review*, 166 (1944), 344.
30. *Areopagitica*, 514.
31. Ibid., 514–515.
32. Ibid., 515–516.
33. Ibid., 516–517.
34. Ibid., 512.
35. Ibid., 521.
36. Ibid., 523–526.
37. Ibid., 526.
38. Ibid., 528.
39. Rice, Warner G., "A Note on Areopagitica," *Journal of English and Germanic Philology*, 40 (1941), 476.
40. *Areopagitica*, 532.
41. "Un classique de la liberté: l'Aréopagitique de John Milton," *Critique* 13 (1957), 201.
42. Ibid., 204–205.
43. Ibid., 202. The translation is mine; the original is: *"L'idée que l'on pût lire ou écrire sans avoir présente à l'esprit sa responsabilité ne l'effleurait pas, lui aurait paru vide de sens."*
44. Op. cit., 339.
45. "Milton's Defense of Bawdry," in Patrick, John Max, ed., *SAMLA Studies in Milton* (Gainesville: U. of Florida Press, 1953), 69–71.
46. *Areopagitica*, 514–515.
47. *A Long Time Burning: the History of Literary Censorship in England* (New York and Washington: Frederick A. Praeger, 1969), 16 ff.
48. *Areopagitica*, 528.
49. Ibid., 517, 516. James Holley Hanford describes Milton's moral ideal in these terms: "Deeply sympathetic with the aspirations of men toward freedom of life he yet esteems freedom only as the essential condition for the functioning and self-development of the 'inner check.' Outward freedom and inward control or freedom with discipline is the authentic humanistic formula which Milton applies in all the domains of education, politics, morality, religion, and art.... The Platonic subordination of the lower faculties of man to the higher is the central doctrine of his philosophy of life." *John Milton: Poet and Humanist* (Cleveland: Western Reserve University Press, 1966), 182. Cf. Dowden, Edward, *Puritan and Anglican* (London: Kegan Paul, Trench, Trübner & Co., 1900), 133; Mayoux, op. cit., 196; Woodhouse, A. S. P., "Milton, Puritanism and Liberty," *University of Toronto Quarterly*, 4 (1935), 497–498.
50. *Areopagitica*, 527; emphasis added.

Notes to Chapter Three

1. *Politics and Vision* (Boston and Toronto: Little, Brown & Co., 1969), 293.
2. *The Social Teaching of the Christian Churches*, trans. Olive Wyon, vol. II (New York: Macmillan, 1931), 637.
3. *Legacy of Suppression*, 101.
4. This and the other works of Locke cited here are to be found in *The Works of John Locke*, a new edition, corrected, in 10 volumes (London: Thomas Tegg; et al., 1823, reprinted by Scientia Verlag Aalen, Germany, 1963). The *Essay* on understanding was published in 1690, the first *Letter Concerning Toleration* in 1689, the second letter in 1690, the third in 1692, while the fourth was left unfinished at his death in 1704. *The Reasonableness of Christianity* appeared in 1695.

5. Op. cit., 100.
6. "Faith and Knowledge in Locke's Philosophy," in Yolton, John W., ed., *John Locke: Problems and Perspectives* (Cambridge: Cambridge University Press, 1969), 195.
7. *Essay Concerning Human Understanding*, Book IV, ch. 16, sect. 4; *Works*, vol. III, pp. 104, 103.
8. "Civil Theology of Liberal Democracy: Locke and his Predecessors," *Journal of Politics*, 34 (1972), 16.
9. Ibid., 11.
10. *Natural Right and History* (Chicago and London: University of Chicago Press, 1953), 248.
11. Ibid., 226–230.
12. "John Locke's Philosophy of Religious Toleration," *Personalist*, 46 (1965), 247.
13. "Absolute Democracy or Indefeasible Right: Hobbes versus Locke," *Journal of Politics*, 38 (1975), 755.
14. *Understanding*, IV, 5, 11; III, 7.
15. Ibid., II, 23, 32; II, 30.
16. Locke says this repeatedly, but see for example ibid., II, 31, 6–13; II, 129–135.
17. Ibid., III, 3, 20; II, 185.
18. Ibid., III, 3, 11; II, 172.
19. Ibid., II, 30, 5; II, 124.
20. Ibid., III, 6, 3; II, 208–209.
21. Ibid., III, 10, 17; II, 279. Cf. III, 11, 20; II, 301, and IV, 4, 13–14; II, 392–393.
22. Ibid., III, 4, 2; II, 186.
23. Ibid., II, 32, 11–12; II, 140–141.
24. Ibid., III, 5, 3; II, 196.
25. Ibid., III, 9, 7; II, 254.
26. Ibid., III, 9, 9; II, 256.
27. Ibid., II, 20, 2; I, 231.
28. Ibid., II, 21, 54–55; I, 272–274.
29. Ibid., II, 28, 6; II, 97.
30. Ibid., II, 28, 5; II, 97.
31. Ibid., II, 28, 8; II, 98.
32. Ibid., II, 21, 60; I, 277–278.
33. *Works*, VII, 150.
34. "His whole nature had a tendency towards a Calvinistic sobriety, industry and utilitarian objectivity, and the whole temper of his mind was always characterized by a piety which was as fine and clear as it was warm and earnest." Troeltsch, op. cit., II, 637.
35. *John Locke's Political Philosophy* (Oxford: Clarendon Press, 1973) 10–11. Cf. Ashcraft, op. cit., 214.
36. Op. cit., 25–26.
37. "The State of Nature and the Nature of Man in Locke," in Yolton, ed., op. cit., 100–101.
38. E.g., Leyden, W. von, "John Locke and Natural Law," *Philosophy*, 21 (1956), 23–35, as reprinted in Schochet, Gordon J., *Life, Liberty and Property: Essays on Locke's Political Ideas* (Belmont, CA: Wadsworth Publishing Co., 1971), 16.
39. *Understanding*, IV, 3, 23; II, 374.
40. Ibid., II, 1, 2; I, 83.
41. Ibid., IV, 9, 2 and 3; III, 54.
42. Ibid., IV, 2, 14; II, 327–328.
43. Ibid., IV, 7, 7; III, 26.
44. Ibid., IV, 6, 13; III, 18.
45. Ibid., IV, 1, 2; II, 308.
46. Ibid., IV, 1, 4; II, 309–310.
47. Ibid., IV, 3, 2; II, 329.
48. Ibid., IV, 2, 14; II, 327.
49. Ibid., IV, 2, 7; II, 323.
50. Ibid., IV, 2, 14; II, 327. The qualifying phrase, "at least in all general truths," is

added because of the possibility of doubting whether we know the particular truth of an external object's existence through the senses. But, as we have seen and he explains on the same page, Locke is sure that we do.

51. Ibid., IV, 16, 6; III, 105.
52. Ibid., IV, 3, 29; II, 381.
53. Ibid., IV, 13, 2; III, 92–93.
54. Ibid., IV, 19, 13; III, 155.
55. Ibid., IV, 18, 7; III, 144.
56. Ibid., IV, 18, 5; III, 141.
57. Ibid., IV, 18, 8; III, 144.
58. Ibid., IV, 18, 5; III, 142.
59. Ibid., IV, 19, 14; III, 156.
60. Ibid., Introduction; I, 4.
61. Ibid., Epistle to the Reader, I, lii.
62. Ibid., I, 4, 12; I, 67.
63. Ibid., I, 4, 9; I, 65. John Dunn remarks that Locke "feels it necessary only to demonstrate the existence of a God to feel that he has established the existence of a substantially Christian God." *The Political Thought of John Locke* (Cambridge: Cambridge University Press, 1969), 194.
64. *Understanding*, I, 4, 16; I, 71.
65. Ibid., I, 3, 13; I, 46.
66. Ibid., I, 3, 10; I, 42.
67. Ibid., II, 28, 11; II, 101–103.
68. Ibid., II, 28, 11; II, 102–103.
69. Ibid., II, 28, 10; II, 99.
70. Ibid., IV, 12, 7; III, 83.
71. Ibid., IV, 3, 18; II, 368.
72. Ibid., IV, 12, 8; III, 84.
73. Op. cit., 187.
74. *Understanding*, II, 13, 28; I, 173.
75. Ibid., IV, 3, 20; II, 371.
76. Ibid., III, 9, 23; II, 267.
77. Op. cit., 219.
78. *The Religious Opinions of Milton, Locke and Newton* (New York: Russell & Russell, 1941), 107, 91.
79. *Works*, VII, 132–133.
80. Ibid., VII, 134.
81. Ibid., VII, 135.
82. Ibid., VII, 137.
83. Ibid., VII, 139–140.
84. As Dunn points out, the mass of men are joined in their ignorance of the full law of nature "by every pre-Christian human being, by Plato and Confucius and Zeno, and conceivably by every Christian moral philosopher up to the year 1695. Most notably of all they are joined ... by Locke himself." Op. cit., 234–235.
85. *Reasonableness*, VII, 142–143.
86. Ibid., VII, 144.
87. Ibid., VII, 146.
88. Op. cit., 194–195.
89. *A Letter Concerning Toleration, Works*, VI, 24. This letter will henceforth be cited as *First Letter.*
90. "The Two Democratic Traditions," *Philosophical Review,* 61 (1952), 456–457.
91. *First Letter,* VI, 35.
92. Ibid., VI, 45–47.
93. Ibid., VI, 47.
94. Ibid., VI, 45.
95. *A Third Letter for Toleration, Works,* VI, 418–419.
96. *First Letter,* VI, 12.

97. Ibid., VI, 9–10. Locke's political philosophy and his theory of the goals of civil society are explained at length in his *Second Treatise of Government*, but that work seems to add nothing to the discussion of our topic beyond what is stated here.
98. *First Letter*, VI, 11.
99. Ibid., VI, 40.
100. Ibid., VI, 19.
101. Ibid., VI, 38.
102. Ibid., VI, 6.
103. Ibid., VI, 41.
104. Ibid., VI, 5.
105. Ibid., VI, 18.
106. *Third Letter*, VI, 402.
107. Ibid., VI, 334.
108. Ibid., VI, 419.
109. Ibid., VI, 299.
110. *First Letter*, VI, 19.
111. Ibid., VI, 11.
112. Ibid., VI, 28.
113. Op. cit., 339.
114. *First Letter*, VI, 41.
115. *Third Letter*, VI, 334.
116. Ibid., VI, 420.
117. Ibid., VI, 144.
118. *First Letter*, VI, 41–42.
119. Ibid., VI, 11.
120. Ibid., VI, 20.
121. Ibid., VI, 39.
122. *The Moral and Political Philosophy of John Locke* (New York: Columbia University Press, 1918), 154.
123. All of the above is from Thomas, Donald, *A Long Time Burning*, 28.
124. *Works*, III, 294–300.

Notes to Chapter Four

1. *Spinoza and the Rise of Liberalism* (Boston: Beacon Press, 1958), 101.
2. Ibid., 40.
3. *The Political Philosophy of Spinoza* (New York & London: Columbia University Press, 1968), 7.
4. Spinoza, Benedict de, *The Political Works*, translated and edited by A. G. Wernham (Oxford: Clarendon Press, 1958), 227. All references to the *Tractatus Theologico-Politicus* (henceforth *T T-P*) and the *Tractatus Politicus* (henceforth *T P*) will be to this volume.
5. *T T-P*, ch. 20, 229.
6. Ibid.
7. *The Political Works*, "Introduction," 21.
8. *T T-P*, ch. 16, 129.
9. Ibid., 231.
10. *T P*, ch. 3, 291 (emphasis added).
11. *T T-P*, ch. 20, 233.
12. *T P*, ch. 4, 303.
13. Feuer believes that when Spinoza makes this concession, "the core of the argument for freedom is surrendered." Op. cit., 115.
14. *T T-P*, ch. 20, 243.
15. Ibid., 239.
16. *Spinoza's Political and Ethical Philosophy* (Glasgow: James Maclehose & Sons, 1903), 481.

17. *T T-P*, ch. 20, 239.
18. *T P*, ch. 9, 427.
19. "Benedict Spinoza," in Strauss, Leo, & Cropsey, Joseph, eds., *History of Political Philosophy*, 2d ed. (Chicago: Rand McNally, 1972), 443.
20. Ibid., 449.
21. *La philosophie politique de Spinoza* (Paris: J. Vrin, 1976), 168.
22. *T T-P*, ch. 7, 109.
23. Ibid., ch. 20, 235.
24. Op. cit., 169.
25. Ibid., 170.
26. *T T-P*, ch. 5, 93.
27. Ibid., ch. 16, 135.
28. Ibid., ch. 3, 51.
29. Ibid., ch. 4, 71.
30. *T P*, ch. 3, 299.
31. Ibid., ch. 2, 269.
32. Ibid., 273.
33. Ibid., 271.
34. Ibid., 271–273.
35. Ibid., ch. 4, 303.
36. *T T-P*, ch. 20, 229–231.
37. *T P*, ch. 5, 311.
38. Ibid., ch. 10, 435–437.
39. Ibid., 437.
40. Cf., e.g., Feuer, op. cit., 214, and McShea, op. cit., 50–52.
41. Op. cit., 485.
42. *Spinoza* (London: Penguin, 1953), 182–183.
43. Op. cit., 153.
44. *Jefferson and Civil Liberties: the Darker Side.* (Cambridge, MA: Belknap Press of Harvard University Press, 1963), p. 197, n. 29.
45. Ibid., 51.
46. Reprinted, New York: DaCapo Press, 1970.
47. *Legacy of Suppression*, 283.
48. *Jefferson and Civil Liberties*, 55.
49. Ibid., 56.
50. Ibid., 52.
51. *Legacy of Suppression*, 283.
52. Ibid., 288–289.
53. "Freedom of the Press and the Alien and Sedition Laws: a Reappraisal," *The Supreme Court Review:* 1970, ed. Philip B. Kurland (Chicago and London: University of Chicago Press, 1970), 138.
54. *A Treatise concerning Political Enquiry*, 140.
55. Ibid., 263.
56. Ibid., 23, 28.
57. Ibid., 65.
58. Ibid., 66.
59. Ibid., 96.
60. Ibid., 32.
61. Ibid., 48.
62. Ibid., 49–53.
63. Ibid., 53; cf. 55, 62.
64. Ibid., 14–15.
65. Ibid., 97.
66. Ibid., 54–60.
67. Ibid., 63.
68. Ibid., 198.
69. Ibid., 29.

70. Ibid., 24.
71. Ibid., 118.
72. Ibid., 119.
73. Ibid., 121.
74. Ibid., 119–121.
75. Ibid., 25, 26.
76. Ibid., 26. This theme, that progressive enlightenment is the essential requirement of good government, is restated throughout the volume.
77. Ibid., 137–138.
78. Ibid., 116.
79. Ibid., 45.
80. Ibid., 45–46.
81. Ibid., 130.
82. Ibid., 46.
83. Ibid., 34.
84. Ibid., 122–124.
85. Ibid., 135.
86. Ibid., 54.
87. Ibid., 58.
88. Wortman describes the role of government in these terms: "It is unquestionably necessary that Government should possess sufficient energy for the suppression and coercion of Vice; it is further admitted, that a ferocious and unpolished people should be controuled by powerful institutions: but, then, the energies of Government should be properly directed; its authority should be constantly interposed to prevent violence and crimes, and never exerted to restrain that circulation of knowledge and sentiment which is essential to general improvement." Ibid., 132.
89. Ibid., 39.
90. Ibid., 42–43.
91. Ibid., 46.
92. Ibid., 150.
93. Ibid., 170.
94. Ibid., 169.
95. Ibid., 171.
96. Ibid., 158–159.
97. Ibid., 223.
98. Ibid., 229.
99. *The First Amendment and the Future of American Democracy* (New York: Basic Books, 1976), 113.
100. Ibid., 105.
101. Walter Berns's remark is apropos here: "One looks in vain for a discussion of the problem of vulgar speech or of obscenity in the records of the Constitutional Convention of 1787 or in the *Federalist Papers* or in the debates in the First Congress on the First Amendment, which fact allowed Justice Douglas to jump to the conclusion that censorship of obscenity is a product of latter-day squeamishness, but from which it is more reasonable to conclude that the Founders took it for granted that obscenity was not constitutionally protected speech." Ibid., 195.
102. Op. cit., 247–248.
103. Ibid., 250.

Notes to Chapter Five

1. Review of Levy, Leonard W., *Jefferson and Civil Liberties*, in *The Stanford Law Review*, 16 (1964), as reprinted in Kendall, Nellie D., ed., *Willmoore Kendall contra Mundum*, 291.
2. *On Liberty and Liberalism: the Case of John Stuart Mill* (New York: Knopf, 1974), xxi.

3. Coss, John Jacob, ed., *The Autobiography of John Stuart Mill* (New York: Columbia University Press, 1924), 177.

4. *Poetry and Philosophy: A Study in the Thought of John Stuart Mill* (London: Hutchinson, 1961), 46.

5. *John Stuart Mill* (New York: Dover Publications, 1969), 22.

6. *On Liberty*, ed. Currin V. Shields (Indianapolis and New York: The Library of Liberal Arts, Bobbs-Merrill Co., 1956), 13.

7. Ibid., 99–100.

8. Ibid., 16.

9. Ibid., 21.

10. *The Philosophy of J. S. Mill* (Oxford: Clarendon Press, 1953), 49–50.

11. *On Liberty*, 14.

12. Ibid., 21.

13. Ibid., 24.

14. Ibid., 53.

15. "The Open Society and Its Fallacies," *American Political Science Review*, 54 (1960), 974.

16. *On Liberty*, 20, n. 1.

17. Ibid., 63.

18. Ibid., 65. An example of what Mill's father thought permissible "indecency," directed against a dishonest judge, may be illuminating: "Here, I may cry, is an act for the indignation of mankind! Here is a villain, who invested with the most sacred of trusts, has prostituted it to the vilest of purposes! Why is he not an object of public execration? Why are not the vials of wrath already poured forth upon his odious head?" "Liberty of the Press," in Mill, James, *Essays on Government, Jurisprudence, Liberty of the Press, and Law of Nations* (1825) (New York: Augustus M. Kelley, 1967), 33.

19. *The Improvement of Mankind: the Social and Political Thought of John Stuart Mill* (London: Routledge & Kegan Paul, 1968), 200.

20. *On Liberty*, 62.

21. "The Open Society," 977.

22. *On Liberty*, 67.

23. Ibid., 14.

24. Ibid., 67–68.

25. Ibid., 68.

26. Ibid., 69.

27. Ibid., 69–70. A similar passage from the same work of Humboldt appears on the flyleaf of *On Liberty*.

28. Ibid., 69.

29. *John Stuart Mill: a Critical Study* (London: Macmillan, 1971), 128.

30. *On Liberty*, 69.

31. Ibid., 16.

32. Ibid., 82.

33. Ibid., 13.

34. Ibid., 77.

35. *Four Essays on Liberty* (London, Oxford, New York: Oxford University Press, 1969), 128.

36. *On Liberty*, 76.

37. Ibid., 78–81.

38. Ibid., 86.

39. Ibid., 96.

40. Ibid., 98.

41. Ibid., 96.

42. Ibid., 100.

43. Ibid., 102.

44. *Liberty, Equality, Fraternity* (1873), ed. White, R. J. (Cambridge: Cambridge University Press, 1967), 155, n.

45. Ibid., 140.

46. Cf., e.g., St. Thomas Aquinas, *Summa Theologiae*, I–II, q. 96, a. 2.

47. *On Liberty*, 120.

48. Ibid., 122.

49. *The Enforcement of Morals* (London: Oxford University Press, 1965), 108.

50. Op. cit., 50. Donald Thomas comments that "it is interesting to see that while Mill in the essay *On Liberty* makes a number of references to events of 1857 and 1858 involving freedom of expression, he makes no mention of Lord Campbell's Obscene Publications Act of 1857." *A Long Time Burning*, 215.

51. Cowling, *Mill and Liberalism* (Cambridge: Cambridge University Press, 1963), xiii.

52. *The Road to Utopia: a Study of John Stuart Mill's Social Thought* (Assen: Van Gorcum & Co., 1971), 14.

53. Op. cit., 130.

54. Op. cit., 107.

55. "J. S. Mill's Theory of Poetry," *University of Toronto Quarterly*, 39 (1960), as reprinted in Schneewind, J. B., ed., *Mill* (London: Macmillan, 1969), 273, 278.

56. Op. cit., 48.

57. *On Liberty*, 119.

58. Ibid., 120.

59. "A Re-reading of Mill on Liberty," *Political Studies*, 8 (1969), 129.

60. Op. cit., 108.

61. Op. cit., 199.

Notes to Chapter Six

1. Maxey, Chester C., *Political Philosophies*, rev. ed (New York: Macmillan, 1948), 551.

2. Grant, George, reviewing *The Collected Works of Walter Bagehot*, vols. V–VIII, ed. Norman St. John-Stevas, in *The Globe and Mail*, Toronto, March 1, 1975, p. 31.

3. *English Political Thought in the 19th Century* (New York: Harper & Bros., 1972), 185.

4. Ibid., 181.

5. Ibid., 183.

6. Sisson, C. H., *The Case of Walter Bagehot* (London: Faber and Faber, 1972), 82.

7. Op. cit., 189.

8. *Physics and Politics*, in *The Works of Walter Bagehot* (Hartford, CT: The Travelers Insurance Co., 5 vols, 1889), IV, 511–512. Cf. 525–526. Sisson regards the publication of Bagehot's works by an insurance company as "a mysterious departure from that institution's ordinary line of business." Op. cit., 9–10. But Jacques Barzun explains that Bagehot would have found it "delightful that the first collected edition of his works should have been put together by the president of an American insurance company and issued to the policy holders for their good." Bagehot, *Physics and Politics*, with an introduction by Jacques Barzun (New York: Knopf, 1948), xxiv.

9. *Works*, IV, 517–518.

10. Ibid., IV, 440.

11. Ibid., IV, 444.

12. Ibid., IV, 445.

13. Ibid., IV, 534.

14. Ibid., IV, 454.

15. Ibid., IV, 453.

16. Ibid., IV, 443.

17. Ibid., IV, 451.

18. Ibid., IV, 431.

19. Ibid., IV, 447.

20. Ibid., IV, 465.

21. Ibid., IV, 468.

22. Ibid., IV, 465.

23. The phrase is taken from *The Metaphysical Basis of Toleration, Works*, II, 344, but in the passage where he uses it, Bagehot is only repeating what he had said in *Physics and Politics*.

24. *Physics and Politics, Works,* IV, 559–560.

25. Ibid., IV, 563.

26. Ibid., IV, 471.

27. Ibid., IV, 543.

28. Ibid., IV, 549–550.

29. Ibid., IV, 543.

30. Ibid., IV, 546.

31. Ibid., IV, 546–547.

32. Ibid., IV, 549.

33. Ibid., IV, 563.

34. *Walter Bagehot* (Bloomington: Indiana University Press, 1959), 47.

35. *Works,* IV, 564.

36. Ibid., IV, 565.

37. Ibid., IV, 566.

38. Ibid., IV, 569.

39. Ibid., IV, 571.

40. Ibid., IV, 574.

41. Ibid., IV, 574–575.

42. Ibid., IV, 576.

43. Cf. ibid., IV, 567.

44. Ibid., IV, 579.

45. Ibid., IV, 582.

46. Ibid., IV, 589.

47. *Works,* II, 339–340.

48. Ibid., II, 358.

49. Ibid., II, 340.

50. Ibid., II, 342.

51. Ibid., II, 356–357.

52. Ibid., II, 349.

53. Ibid., II, 351.

54. Ibid., II, 352–356.

55. Ibid., II, 356.

56. Ibid., II, 343.

57. Ibid., II, 357.

58. Ibid., II, 347.

59. Ibid.

60. Ibid., II, 357–358.

61. "Walter Bagehot and Liberal Realism," *American Political Science Review,* 43 (1949), 22.

62. *Works,* IV, 55.

63. Op. cit., 24.

64. *Metaphysical Basis, Works,* II, 343.

65. We may perhaps hope to find such people only in an Anglo-Saxon nation. "Even some very high races, as the French and the Irish," Bagehot remarks, "seem in troubled times hardly to be stable at all, but to be carried everywhere as the passions of the moment and the ideas generated at the hour may determine." *Physics and Politics, Works,* IV, 541.

66. *English Constitution, Works,* IV, 35.

67. *Physics and Politics, Works,* IV, 545.

68. Ibid., IV, 546.

69. Op. cit., 186. Cf. *Works,* IV, 570–571.

70. Deane, Herbert A., *The Political Ideas of Harold J. Laski* (New York: Columbia University Press, 1955), 4.

71. *Harold Laski* (New York: Viking Press, 1953), ix, 92, 207, 248.

72. Ibid., 80.

73. Ibid., 216.

74. Quoted in Deane, op. cit., 53.

75. Something perhaps may be inferred about them from his statement that he "read

Paine's *Age of Reason* with admiration for its cogency of argument, its trenchant style, its fearless appetite for truth." *Liberty in the Modern State* (New York and London: Harper & Bros., 1930), 94.

76. *Authority in the Modern State* (New Haven: Yale University Press, third printing, 1927), 109, 123.
77. Op. cit., 15.
78. Deane, op. cit., 54.
79. Ibid., 3.
80. Ibid., 132; cf. 36–38, 44–45, 83, 107–108, 112, 118, 174, 176, 187.
81. Ibid., 87.
82. Op. cit., 81, 82.
83. "Professor Laski and Political Science," *Political Quarterly,* 21 (1950), 306.
84. "Normative, Descriptive and Ideological Elements in the Writings of Laski," *Philosophy of Science,* 12 (1945), 143.
85. Op. cit., 303.
86. A large part of the book is devoted to an analysis of the views of Catholic writers on the authority of the Church, with the winners of the argument being those who, like Lamennais and Tyrrell, eventually left the Church.
87. *Authority,* 65.
88. Ibid., 31.
89. Laski learned much from J. N. Figgis's theory of the corporate personality of the church, but "he tends to read 'trade union' wherever Figgis wrote 'church.'" Deane, op. cit., 29.
90. *Authority,* 37.
91. Ibid., 38.
92. Ibid., 88.
93. Op. cit., 19.
94. *Authority,* 374.
95. Op. cit., 19–20.
96. The phrase is Laski's, quoted by Kampelman, M. M., "Harold J. Laski: a Current Analysis," *Journal of Politics,* 10 (1948), 151.
97. *Authority,* 30.
98. Ibid., 177.
99. Ibid., 164.
100. Ibid., 318.
101. Ibid., 63.
102. Ibid., 42.
103. Ibid., 124.
104. Ibid., 166.
105. Ibid., 165.
106. Ibid., 64.
107. Ibid., 101–102.
108. Ibid., 43.
109. Ibid., 61.
110. Ibid., 61–62.
111. Ibid., 65.
112. Ibid., 312.
113. Op. cit., 38.
114. *Authority,* 47.
115. Ibid., 56.
116. Ibid., 122.
117. Ibid., 57.
118. Ibid., 59.
119. Ibid., 55.
120. Ibid., 69.
121. Ibid., 107.
122. Ibid., 121–122.

123. *Liberty,* 17.
124. Ibid., 74.
125. Ibid., 24.
126. Ibid., 21.
127. Ibid., 26–27.
128. Ibid., 76.
129. Ibid., 75.
130. Ibid., 21.
131. Ibid., 74.
132. Ibid., 31. Cf. 67–70.
133. Ibid., 60–61.
134. Ibid., 27–28. Cf. 31, 33, 58, 61.
135. Ibid., 29.
136. Ibid., 81–83.
137. Ibid., 86–88.
138. Ibid., 89.
139. Ibid., 90–92.
140. Ibid., 190–191.
141. *Acta Apostolicae Sedis*, 44 (1952), 872.
142. *Liberty,* 192.
143. Ibid., 93–97.
144. Ibid., 99.
145. Ibid., 99–101.
146. Ibid., 102.
147. Ibid., 105.
148. Ibid., 111–112.
149. Ibid., 104–106, 112–113.
150. Ibid., 106–108.
151. Ibid., 113–129.
152. Ibid., 129.
153. Ibid., 166–168.
154. "England Confronts a New World," in Schmalhausen, Samuel D., *Recovery through Revolution* (New York: Covici-Friede-Publishers, 1933), 80–81.
155. *Democracy in Crisis* (Chapel Hill: University of North Carolina Press, 1933), 66.
156. Ibid., 190–191.
157. Ibid., 211.
158. *Liberty,* 172–177.
159. Ibid., 195–196.
160. Ibid., 196.
161. Ibid., 22.
162. Ibid., 198.
163. Ibid., 203–210.
164. Ibid., 203.
165. Ibid., 211.
166. Ibid., 229.
167. Ibid., 280.
168. Ibid., 223.
169. Ibid., 218.
170. Ibid., 253.
171. Ibid., 255.
172. Op cit., 130.
173. *Liberty,* 288.

Notes to Chapter Seven

1. "Freedom of Speech in War Time," 32 (1919), 932–973.

2. Prude, J., "Portrait of a Civil Libertarian: the Faith and Fear of Zechariah Chafee, Jr.," *Journal of American History*, 60 (1973), 640; Ragan, F. D., "Justice Oliver Wendell Holmes, Jr., Zechariah Chafee, Jr., and the Clear and Present Danger Test for Free Speech: the First Year, 1919," *Journal of American History*, 58 (1971), 37, 43–45.

3. Griswold, Erwin N., "Zechariah Chafee, Jr.," *Harvard Law Review*, 70 (1957), 1338.

4. Prude, op. cit., 633–634.

5. Auerbach, J. S., "Patrician as Libertarian: Zechariah Chafee, Jr., and Freedom of Speech," *New England Quarterly*, 42 (1969), 514.

6. Prude, op. cit., 634.

7. Auerbach, op. cit., 515; Ragan, op. cit., 37.

8. Op. cit., 634.

9. Auerbach, op. cit., 531.

10. Cambridge, MA: Harvard University Press, 1941; the third printing, 1947, is used here.

11. *Free Speech*, xi. He says on the same page, concerning *Freedom of Speech*, "I still hold all the views there stated."

12. Philadelphia and New York: J. B. Lippincott Co., 1956.

13. *Blessings*, 37.

14. Op. cit., 639.

15. *Free Speech*, 6; cf. 167, 232, 433; and *Blessings*, 89, 91, 137. It should be noted that Part I of *Free Speech* is simply a revision of *Freedom of Speech* and continues "to speak as of 1920" (ibid., xi), when the First Amendment was still considered to bind Congress but not the states; hence the references to Congress alone.

16. *Free Speech*, 564.

17. Op. cit., 642.

18. *Free Speech*, 20; cf. 149.

19. Op. cit., 522.

20. *Free Speech*, 16.

21. Ibid., 31; cf. 415.

22. Ibid., 137.

23. Ibid., 509.

24. Ibid., 155.

25. Ibid., xiii.

26. Ibid., 33.

27. Ibid., 4.

28. Ibid., 31; cf. 401.

29. *Blessings*, 65.

30. *Free Speech*, 14.

31. The reader will recognize these words as the ones which the U.S. Supreme Court incorporated into its opinion in *Chaplinsky v. New Hampshire*, 315 U. S. 568, 572 (1942).

32. *Free Speech*, 150; cf. *Blessings*, 115.

33. *Free Speech*, 161.

34. Ibid., 300.

35. Ibid., 542.

36. Ibid., 550.

37. Ibid., 529.

38. Ibid., 548.

39. Ibid., 8; cf. 530.

40. Ibid., 152.

41. *Blessings*, 78–79; cf. *Free Speech*, 150, 545.

42. *Free Speech*, 150–151.

43. Ibid., 540. He continues: "The practical problem is to make such jury verdicts more convenient than in the ordinary criminal prosecution, so as to lessen the risk of honest

theater owners, producers, publishers, and booksellers who are anxious to obtain a legal determination before going ahead."

44. Chafee agrees, however, "that a photoplay differs in significant ways from a book or newspaper." Ibid., 315.

45. Ibid., 545.

46. Angell, Ernest, "Zechariah Chafee, Jr.: Individual Freedoms," *Harvard Law Review,* 70 (1957), 1342.

47. Auerbach, op. cit., 522.

48. Op. cit., 643.

49. *Free Speech*, 561; cf. 241.

50. Ibid., 195.

51. Ibid., 35; cf. 139, 152.

52. *Blessings*, 69; cf. 137.

53. Ibid., 69–71; cf. *Free Speech*, 42–46; 157–158.

54. *Free Speech*, 180.

55. Ibid., 23.

56. Ibid., 287.

57. Ibid., 57.

58. Ibid., 85; cf. 121.

59. Ibid., 103; cf. 124, 187.

60. Ibid., 513.

61. Ibid., 158.

62. Ibid., 516.

63. Ibid., 493.

64. Ibid., 194.

65. Ibid., 492.

66. Ibid., 239

67. *Blessings*, 128–129.

68. *Free Speech*, 435.

69. Ibid., 559–561.

70. *Blessings*, 102–115.

71. Ibid., 103–104.

72. Unger, Roberto Mangabeira, *Knowledge and Politics* (New York: Free Press, 1975), 26.

73. *Blessings*, 107.

74. Ibid., 110.

75. Ibid., 105.

76. Ibid., 111; cf. 105–107.

77. Ibid., 111.

78. Op. cit., 1344.

79. *Free Speech*, 137–138.

80. Review of Levy, *Jefferson and Civil Liberties* in *Willmoore Kendall contra Mundum*, op. cit., 291.

81. Bixler, Julius Seelye, "Alexander Meiklejohn: the Making of the Amherst Mind," *New England Quarterly*, 47 (1974), 183.

82. Ibid., 188.

83. Pope, Alexander Upham, "Alexander Meiklejohn," *American Scholar*, 34 (1965), 642.

84. New York: Harper & Bros., 1960.

85. *Political Freedom*, vii.

86. Ibid., 84. Cf. xvi.

87. Ibid., 69.

88. Ibid., 15.

89. Ibid., 18.

90. Ibid., 13.

91. Ibid., 70.

92. Ibid., 81.

93. Ibid., 96.

94. Ibid., 27.
95. Ibid., 42. Cf. 37.
96. Ibid., 28.
97. Ibid., 59.
98. Ibid., 73.
99. Ibid., 75.
100. Ibid., 79. Cf. 122.
101. Ibid., 21.
102. Ibid., 25–26.
103. Ibid., 36. Cf. 60.
104. Ibid., 8.
105. Ibid., 55.
106. Ibid., 37.
107. Ibid., 52–53.
108. Ibid., 54.
109. Ibid., 51.
110. Ibid., 37.
111. *Free Speech*, 33.
112. *Political Freedom*, 54–55.
113. Ibid., 80. Cf. 57.
114. Ibid., 83.
115. Ibid., 88.
116. Ibid., 113.
117. Ibid., 87–88.
118. Ibid., xvi.
119. 268 U. S. 652, 673 (1925).
120. *Political Freedom*, 42–43.
121. Ibid., 140.
122. Ibid., 95.
123. Ibid., 114.
124. Ibid., 56–57.
125. Ibid., 73.
126. Ibid., 87.

Notes to Chapter Eight

1. *Problems of Socialist England*, trans. J.F. Huntington (London: Batchworth Press, 1949), 156.
2. Supra, p. 76.
3. Supra, p. 140.
4. Supra, p. 121.
5. *A Long Time Burning*, 313, 315.
6. *Forbes*, 122, 6 (Sept. 18, 1978), 81, 87. *Time* has referred to "the estimated $5 billion U.S. pornography market" (April 13, 1981, p. 82); cf. Schwartz, Tony, "The TV Pornography Boom," *The New York Times Magazine* (September 13, 1981), 44 ff.
7. June 2, 1980, p. 77.
8. The Supreme Court upheld this legislation without comment and in two words: "Judgment affirmed." *Capital Broadcasting Co. v. Kleindienst*, 405 U.S. 1000 (1972).
9. Levy, *Legacy of Suppression*, 131.
10. Dissenting, *U.S. v. 37 Photographs*, 402 U.S. 363, 380 (1971).
11. Dissenting *Jacobellis v. Ohio*, 378 U.S. 184, 199 (1964).
12. Dissenting, *Elrod v. Burns*, 427 U.S. 347, 382 (1976).
13. *Miller v. California*, 413 U.S. 15, 29 (1973).

Bibliography

This bibliography includes only those works cited in the footnotes. The reference in all citations of opinions of the U.S. Supreme Court is to the *United States Reports*, abbreviated to U.S.

Aarsleff, Hans, "The State of Nature and the Nature of Man in Locke," in Yolton, John W., ed., *John Locke: Problems and Perspectives*. Cambridge: Cambridge University Press, 1969.

Angell, Ernest, "Zechariah Chafee, Jr.: Individual Freedoms," *Harvard Law Review*, 70 (1957), 1341–1344.

Anschutz, R. P., *The Philosophy of J. S. Mill*, Oxford: Clarendon Press, 1953.

Ashcraft, Richard, "Faith and Knowledge in Locke's Philosophy," in Yolton, John W., ed., *John Locke: Problems and Perspectives*. Cambridge: Cambridge University Press, 1969.

Auerbach, J. S., "Patrician as Libertarian: Zechariah Chafee, Jr., and Freedom of Speech," *New England Quarterly*, 42 (1969), 511–531.

Bagehot, Walter, *The Works of Walter Bagehot*. Hartford, CT: Travelers Insurance Company, 5 vols., 1889.

———, *Physics and Politics*. With an introduction by Jacques Barzun. New York: Alfred A. Knopf, 1948.

Barker, Arthur Edward, *Milton and the Puritan Dilemma*. Toronto: University of Toronto Press, 1942.

Berlin, Isaiah, *Four Essays on Liberty*. London, Oxford, New York: Oxford University Press, 1969.

Berns, Walter, "Freedom of the Press and the Alien and Sedition Laws: a Reappraisal," in *The Supreme Court Review: 1970*, ed. Philip B. Kurland. Chicago and London: University of Chicago Press, 1970.

———, *The First Amendment and The Future of American Democracy*. New York: Basic Books, 1976.

Bixler, Julius Seelye, "Alexander Meiklejohn: the Making of the Amherst Mind," *New England Quarterly*, 47 (1974), 179–195.

Brinton, Crane, *English Political Thought in the 19th Century*. New York: Harper & Bros., 1962.

Britton, Karl, *John Stuart Mill*. New York: Dover Publications, 1969.

Byrne, James W., "John Locke's Philosophy of Religious Toleration," *The Personalist*, 46 (1965), 245–252.

Chafee, Zechariah, Jr., "Freedom of Speech in War Time," *Harvard Law Review*, 32 (1919), 932–973.

———, *Free Speech in the United States.* Cambridge, MA: Harvard University Press, 1941, 3rd printing, 1946.

———, *The Blessings of Liberty.* Philadelphia and New York: J. B. Lippincott Co., 1956.

Clor, Harry M., *Obscenity and Public Morality: Censorship in a Liberal Society.* Chicago and London: University of Chicago Press, 1969.

———, ed., *Censorship and Freedom of Expression: Essays on Obscenity and the Law.* Chicago: Rand McNally, 1971.

Cowling, Maurice, *Mill and Liberalism.* Cambridge: Cambridge University Press, 1963.

Deane, Herbert A., *The Political Ideas of Harold J. Laski.* New York: Columbia University Press, 1955.

Devine, F. E., "Absolute Democracy or Indefeasible Right: Hobbes versus Locke," *Journal of Politics*, 37 (1975), 736–768.

Devlin, P., *The Enforcement of Morals.* London: Oxford University Press, 1965.

Dowden, Edward, *Puritan and Anglican.* London: Kegan Paul, Trench, Trubner & Co., 1900.

Duff, Robert A., *Spinoza's Political and Ethical Philosophy.* Glasgow: James Maclehose & Sons, 1903.

Dunn, John, *The Political Thought of John Locke.* Cambridge: Cambridge University Press, 1969.

Easton, D., "Walter Bagehot and Liberal Realism," *American Political Science Review*, 43 (1949), 17–37.

Emerson, Thomas I., *Toward a General Theory of the First Amendment.* New York: Vintage Books, 1967.

———, *The System of Freedom of Expression.* New York: Vintage Books, 1970.

Evans, B. Ifor, "The Lesson of the *Areopagitica*," *Contemporary Review*, 166 (1944), 342–346.

Feuer, Lewis S., *Spinoza and the Rise of Liberalism.* Boston: Beacon Press, 1958.

Gilman, Wilbur Elwyn, *Milton's Rhetoric: Studies in His Defense of Liberty.* University of Missouri Studies, 14 (1939).

Gilbert, Allen H., "Milton's Defense of Bawdry," in Patrick, John Max, ed., *SAMLA Studies in Milton.* Gainesville: University of Florida Press, 1953.

Gough, J. W., *John Locke's Political Philosophy.* Oxford: Clarendon Press, 2nd ed., 1973.

Grant, George, review of *The Collected Works of Walter Bagehot*, vols. V–VIII, ed. St. John-Stevas, Norman, in *The Globe and Mail*, Toronto, March 1, 1975.

Griswold, Erwin N., "Zechariah Chafee, Jr.," *Harvard Law Review*, 70 (1957), 1337–1340.

Hampshire, Stuart, *Spinoza.* London: Penguin, 1953.

Hanford, James Holly, *John Milton: Poet and Humanist.* Cleveland: Western Reserve University Press, 1966.

Himmelfarb, Gertrude, *On Liberty and Liberalism: The Case of John Stuart Mill.* New York: Alfred A. Knopf, 1974.

Holthoon, F. L. van, *The Road to Utopia: A Study of John Stuart Mill's Social Thought.* Assen: Van Gorcum & Co., 1971.

Illo, John, "The Misreading of Milton," *Columbia University Forum,* 8 (1965), 38–42.

Jouvenel, Bertrand de, *Problems of Socialist England,* trans. J. F. Huntington. London: Batchworth Press, 1949.

Kampelman, M. M., "Harold J. Laski: a Current Analysis," *Journal of Politics,* 10 (1948), 131–154.

Kendall, Wilmoore, "The Open Society and Its Fallacies," *American Political Science Review,* 54 (1960), 972–979.

———, *Willmoore Kendall contra Mundum,* ed. Kendall, Nellie D. New Rochelle, NY: Arlington House, 1971.

Lamprecht, Sterling P., *The Moral and Political Philosophy of John Locke.* New York: Columbia University Press, 1918.

Laski, Harold Joseph, *Authority in the Modern State,* New Haven: Yale University Press, 1919, 3rd printing, 1927.

———, *Liberty in the Modern State.* New York and London: Harper & Bros., 1930.

———, "England Confronts a New World," in Schmalhausen, Samuel D., ed., *Recovery through Revolution.* New York: Covici-Friede-Publishers, 1933.

———, *Democracy in Crisis.* Chapel Hill: University of North Carolina Press, 1933.

———, "The *Areopagitica* of Milton after 300 Years," in Ould, Hermon, ed., *Freedom of Expression:* A Symposium ... to commemorate the tercentenary of the publication of Milton's *Areopagitica.* Port Washington, New York, and London: Kennikat Press, 1970; first published 1944.

Levy, Leonard W., *Legacy of Suppression: Freedom of Speech and Press in Early American History.* Cambridge, MA: Belknap Press of Harvard University Press, 1960.

———, *Jefferson and Civil Liberties: the Darker Side.* Cambridge, MA: Belknap Press of Harvard University Press, 1963.

Leyden, W. von, "John Locke and Natural Law," *Philosophy,* 21 (1956), reprinted in Schochet, Gordon J., ed., *Life, Liberty and Property: Essays on Locke's Political Ideas.* Belmont, CA: Wadsworth Publishing Co., 1971.

Lippmann, Walter, *The Public Philosophy.* New York: Mentor Books, 1956.

Locke, John, *The Works of John Locke.* A New Edition, Corrected. 10 vols. London: Thomas Tegg; et al., 1823. Reprinted by Scientia Verlag Aalen, Germany, 1963.

McCloskey, H. J., *John Stuart Mill: A Critical Study.* London: Macmillan, 1971.

McLachlan, H., *The Religious Opinions of Milton, Locke and Newton.* New York: Russell & Russell, 1941, reissued 1972.

McShea, Robert J., *The Political Philosophy of Spinoza.* New York and London: Columbia University Press, 1968.

Martin, Kingsley, *Harold Laski.* New York: Viking Press, 1953.

Matthews, the Very Rev. W. R., "The Philosophical Basis of Toleration," in Ould,

Hermon, ed., *Freedom of Expression*. Port Washington, New York, and London: Kennikat Press, 1970.

Maxey, Chester C., *Political Philosophies*. Rev. ed. New York: Macmillan, 1948.

Mayoux, Jean-Jacques, "Un classique de la liberté: l'Aréopagitique de John Milton," *Critique*, 13 (1947), 195–207.

Meiklejohn, Alexander, *Political Freedom: The Constitutional Powers of the People*. New York: Harper & Bros., 1960.

Mill, James, *Essays on Government, Jurisprudence, Liberty of the Press, and Law of Nations*. Written for the Supplement to the Encyclopedia Britannica (1825). New York: Augustus M. Kelley, 1967.

Mill, John Stuart, *On Liberty*, ed. Currin V. Shields. Indianapolis and New York: The Library of Liberal Arts, Bobbs-Merrill Co., 1956.

———, *Autobiography*, ed. John Jacob Coss. New York: Columbia University Press, 1924.

Milton, John, *The Complete Prose Works of John Milton*, vol. II, ed. Ernest Sirluck. New Haven: Yale University Press; London: Oxford University Press, 1959.

Mugnier-Pollet, Lucien, *La philosophie politique de Spinoza*. Paris: J. Vrin, 1976.

Pope, Alexander Upham, "Alexander Meiklejohn," *American Scholar*, 34 (1965), 641–645.

Prude, J., "Portrait of a Civil Libertarian: The Faith and Fear of Zechariah Chafee, Jr.," *Journal of American History*, 60 (1973), 633–656.

Ragan, F. D., "Justice Oliver Wendell Holmes, Jr., Zechariah Chafee, Jr., and the Clear and Present Danger Test for Free Speech: the First Year, 1919," *Journal of American History*, 58 (1971), 24–45.

Read, Herbert, *A Coat of Many Colours*. New York: Horizon Press, 1956.

Rees, J. C., "A Re-reading of Mill *On Liberty*," *Political Studies*, 8 (1960), 113–129.

The Report of the Commission on Obscenity and Pornography. New York: Random House, 1970.

Rice, Warner G., "A Note on *Areopagitica*," *Journal of English and Germanic Philology*, 40 (1941), 474–481.

Robson, John M., "J. S. Mill's Theory of Poetry," *University of Toronto Quarterly*, 39 (1960), reprinted in Schneewind, J. B., ed., *Mill* (London: Macmillan, 1969).

———, *The Improvement of Mankind: The Social and Political Thought of John Stuart Mill*. London: Routledge and Kegan Paul, 1968.

Rosen, Stanley, "Benedict Spinoza," in Strauss, Leo, & Cropsey, Joseph, eds., *History of Political Philosophy*. 2nd ed. Chicago: Rand McNally, 1972.

Sabine, George, "The Two Democratic Traditions," *Philosophical Review*, 61 (1952), 451–474.

St. John-Stevas, Norman, *Walter Bagehot*. Bloomington: Indiana University Press, 1959.

Sandoz, Ellis, "Civil Theology of Liberal Democracy: Locke and His Predecessors," *Journal of Politics*, 34 (1972), 2–36.

Sisson, C. H., *The Case of Walter Bagehot*. London: Faber & Faber, 1972.

Soltau, R. H., "Professor Laski and Political Science," *Political Quarterly*, 21 (1950), 301–310.

Spinoza, Benedict de, *The Political Works of Benedict de Spinoza*, trans. and ed. by

A. G. Wernham. Oxford: Clarendon Press, 1958.

Stephen, James Fitzjames, *Liberty, Equality, Fraternity,* ed. with an introduction and notes by R. J. White. Cambridge: Cambridge University Press, 1967. First published 1873.

Strauss, Leo, *Natural Right and History.* Chicago and London: University of Chicago Press, 1953.

Thomas, Donald, *A Long Time Burning: The History of Literary Censorship in England.* New York and Washington: Frederick A. Praeger, 1969.

Troeltsch, Ernst, *The Social Teaching of the Christian Churches,* vol. II. New York: Macmillan, 1931.

Unger, Roberto Mangabeira, *Knowledge and Politics.* New York: Free Press, 1975.

Wittreich, Joseph A., Jr., "Milton's *Areopagitica:* Its Isocratic and Ironic Contexts," in Simmonds, James D., ed., *Milton Studies,* 4. Pittsburgh: University of Pittsburgh Press, 1972.

Wolfe, Don Marion, *Milton in the Puritan Revolution.* New York: Thomas Nelson & Sons, 1941.

Wolin, Sheldon S., *Politics and Vision.* Boston and Toronto: Little, Brown and Co., 1960.

Woodhouse, A. S. P., "Milton, Puritanism and Liberty," *University of Toronto Quarterly,* 4 (1935), 483–513.

Woods, Thomas, *Poetry and Philosophy: A Study in the Thought of John Stuart Mill.* London: Hutchinson, 1961.

Wortman, Tunis, *A Treatise Concerning Political Enquiry and the Liberty of the Press.* New-York, 1800; reprinted New York: Da Capo Press, 1970.

Zerby, L., "Normative, Descriptive and Ideological Elements in the Writings of Laski," *Philosophy of Science,* 12 (1945), 134–145.

Index

Hitler, Adolph, 120, 121
Hobbes, Thomas, 55
Holmes, Oliver Wendell, Jr., vi, 4, 12, 26,
    124, 125, 131, 141, 148, 149
Holthon, F. L. Van, 97, 98
Hughes, Charles Evans, 3, 10
Humboldt, Wilhelm Von, 92, 100
International Brotherhood of Electrical Workers v.
    Labor Board, 4
Jackson, R. H., 3, 4, 29, 37, 135
Jefferson, Thomas, vi, 72, 80, 81, 85, 86,
    107, 133
Jesus Christ, 63, 64, 65
St. John-Stevas, Norman, 105
Jonson, 51
de Jouvenel, Bertrand, 143
Kendall, Wilmore, 41, 42, 44, 87, 89, 135
Knight, Frank, 133
Kovacs v. Cooper, 25
Lamprecht, Sterling, 70
Laski, Harold Joseph, vi, 101, 111–120, 121,
    122, 123, 124, 125, 144, 145
Lawrence, D. H., 118
Levy, Leonard, vi, 43, 44, 54, 80, 126
Lincoln, Abraham, i, ii
Lippmann, Walter, 39, 40, 101
Locke, John, vi, 42, 54, 55, 56, 57, 58, 59,
    60, 61, 62, 63, 64, 65, 66, 67, 68, 69,
    70, 71, 79, 108, 144
Lombardi, Vincent T., 133
Lovelace, Linda, iii
Madison, James, vi
Mailer, Norman, 151
Marquis de-Sade, 50, 146
Marshall, Thurgood, v, 17, 19, 20, 21, 22,
    24, 27, 28
Martin, Kingsley, 111, 112
Mathews, W. R., 44, 45, 53
Mayoux, Jean-Jacques, 50
McCloskey, H. J., 92
McLaclan, H., 63
McShea, Robert, 73
Meiklejohn, Alexander, vi, 124, 135–142,
    144, 148
Meyer, Edith L., vii
Mill, John Stuart, vi, vii, 42, 83, 84, 87, 88,
    89, 90, 91, 92, 93, 94, 95, 96, 97, 98,
    99, 100, 101, 107, 109, 111, 118, 119,
    123, 126, 132, 133, 144, 146, 149
Miller v. California, 35
Milton, John, vi, vii, 41, 42, 43, 44, 45, 46,

47, 48, 49, 50, 51, 52, 53, 65, 66, 132,
    133, 144
Moliere, 151
Princess Monique, 37
More, Alexander, 51
Muquier-Pollet, Lucien, 76, 79
Murphy, Frank, 11
New York Times v. Sullivan, 3, 11
Nichols, Mike, iii
Nixon, Richard M., 18, 19
Paine, Thomas, 80, 81, 86
Papish v. University of Missouri, 39
Plato, vi, 42, 50
Plautus, 51
Pope Pius xii, 119
Pound, Roscoe, 125
Powell, Lewis, 21, 28, 152
Priestley, Joseph, 81
Proast, Jonas, 66
Prude, J., 125, 126, 130
Queen Victoria, 101
Read, Herbert, 50
Redup v. New York, 34
Reems, Harry, iii
Rees, J. D., 99
Rehnquist, William, 22, 26, 135
Rembar, Charles, iii
Roberts, O. J., 11
Robson, John M., 90
Roosevelt, Franklin D., 111
Rosenfeld v. New Jersey, 39
Roth v. U. S., 11, 18, 20, 31, 34
Rousseau, J. J., 89
Sabine, George, 65
Sandoz, Ellis, 55
Schenck v. U. S., 1, 12, 125
Selden, John, 46
Shakespeare, William, 51, 151
Shaw, George Bernard, 119
Prince Sihanouk, 37
Soltau, R. H., 112
Spinoza, vi, 42, 62, 72, 73, 74, 75, 76, 77, 78,
    79
Stalin, Joseph, 151
Stammler, 114
Stevens, John Paul, 21, 27, 28, 29
Stewart, Potter, 17, 22, 26, 27, 28, 29, 37, 39
Strauss, Leo, 55
Swift, Jonathan, 146
Talese, Gay, iii
Thomas, Donald, 51, 146, 147